THE SACRED MONSTER OF THOMISM

Other Titles of Interest from St. Augustine's Press and Dumb Ox Books

Thomas Aquinas, *Disputed Questions on Virtue*

Thomas Aquinas, *Commentary on Aristotle's De Anima*

Thomas Aquinas, *Commentary on Aristotle's Metaphysics*

Thomas Aquinas, *Commentary on Aristotle's Nicomachean Ethics*

Thomas Aquinas, *Commentary on Aristotle's Physics*

Thomas Aquinas, *Commentary on Aristotle's Posterior Analytics*

John of St. Thomas, *Introduction to the Summa Theologiae of Thomas Aquinas*. Translated by Ralph McInerny

Francisco Suarez, *On Creation, Conservation, & Concurrence: Metaphysical Disputations 20–22*

Francisco Suarez, *The Metaphysical Demonstration for the Existence of God: Metaphysical Disputations 28–29*

William of Ockham, *Ockham's Theory of Terms: Part I of the Summa Logicae*

William of Ockham, *Ockham's Theory of Terms: Part II of the Summa Logicae*

Roger Bacon, *Roger Bacon's Philosophy of Nature*. Translation of *De multiplicatione specierum and De speculis comburentibus*

Aristotle, *Aristotle – On Poetics*, translated by Seth Benardete and Michael Davis

Joseph Owens, C.SS.R., *Aristotle's Gradations of Being in* Metaphysics *E–Z*

Plato, *The Symposium of Plato: The Shelley Translation*, translated by Percy Bysshe Shelley, edited by David K. O'Connor

Leszek Kolakowski, *Religion: If There Is No God . . . On God, the Devil, Sin, and Other Worries of the So-Called Philosophy of Religion*

Zbigniew Janowski, *Augustinian-Cartesian Index*

Josef Pieper, *Scholasticism: Personalities and Problems*

Josef Pieper, *The Silence of St. Thomas*

Jacques Maritain, *Natural Law: Reflections on Theory and Practice*

Gabriel Marcel, *The Mystery of Being* (in two volumes)

Yves R. Simon, *The Great Dialogue of Nature and Space*

THE SACRED MONSTER OF THOMISM

An Introduction to the Life and Legacy of Réginald Garrigou-Lagrange, O.P.

Richard Peddicord, O.P.

St. Augustine's Press
South Bend, Indiana

Manufactured in the United States of America.

1 2 3 4 5 6 20 19 18 17 16 15

Library of Congress Data in Cataloging Data
Peddicord, Richard, 1958–
The sacred monster of Thomism: an introduction to the life and legacy of Reginald Garrigou-Lagrange / Richard Peddicord.
p. cm.
Includes bibliographical references and index.
ISBN 1-58731-752-4 (clothbound: alk. paper)
1. Garrigou-Lagrange, Réginald, 1877–1964.
2. Dominicans – Biography. 3. Theologians – Biography. I. Title.
BX4705.G2495P43 2004
230'.2'092 – dc22 2004011955

Paperback edition: 978-1-58731-764-4

∞ *The paper used in this publication meets the minimum requirements of the International Organisation for Standardization (ISO) – Paper for documents – Requirements for permanence – ISO 9706: 1994.*

St. Augustine's Press
www.staugustine.net

Dedicated to the memory of my mother
Shirley Anne (Legault) Peddicord

Contents

Abbreviations

CCC	*Catechism of the Catholic Church* (2nd ed., 1997)
CE	*Catholic Encyclopedia* (1913 ed.)
DBF	*Dictionnaire de biographie francaise* (Paris: Letouzey et Ané, 1980)
Denz.	Henry Denzinger, *Enchiridion Symbolorum*, trans. Roy J. Deferrari [*The Sources of Catholic Dogma*] (St. Louis: B. Herder, 1957)
DS	*Dictionnaire de spiritualité* (Paris: Beauchesne, 1937 ff.)
DT	*Dictionnaire de théologie* (Paris: Letouzey et Ané, 1903 ff.)
FZPT	*Freiburger Zeitschrift für Philosophie und Theologie*
GS	Second Vatican Council, *Gaudium et spes*
LG	Second Vatican Council, *Lumen gentium*
NCE	*New Catholic Encyclopedia* (1967 ed.)
RSPT	*Revue des sciences philosophiques et théologiques*

RT	*Revue thomiste*
ST	St. Thomas Aquinas, *Summa theologiae* (1266–1273)
VS	*La vie spirituelle*

Preface

This is not the book that I initially set out to write. I had proposed to the Faculty Development Committee of Aquinas Institute of Theology a plan to study the work of M.-Michel Labourdette (1908–1991) – the eminent Dominican moral theologian from the Toulouse *studium*. Labourdette's moral theology was reported to be greatly influenced by Thomistic spirituality. I had planned to see what could be profitably "retrieved" from Labourdette's approach for contemporary Catholic moral theology.

Further research revealed that Labourdette, directed in his doctoral studies by Réginald Garrigou-Lagrange, was greatly dependent upon his master. He had spent his career reflecting upon the theological and spiritual principles that ought to inform Catholic moral theology – principles that were substantially those of Garrigou-Lagrange and the "Strict-Observance" Thomists. Garrigou became more interesting to me than Labourdette!

It is not that he was an unknown quantity. I had used *Reality: A Synthesis of Thomistic Thought* in my teaching of a course entitled "The Use of Philosophy in Theology." It was a godsend for introducing the metaphysics of St. Thomas to first-year graduate students. I had at least heard of his masterpiece in spirituality, *The Three Ages of the Interior Life*. I knew, too, that Garrigou was a controversial figure in Dominican circles. The generation of friars ahead of me in the Order – those who came to theological consciousness at the time of Vatican II and in the decade or so before the Council – had little good to say about him. The generation ahead of them – those formed in the 1940s and earlier – took him as an icon of Dominican life and ministry. For this group of friars, Garrigou was the epitome of fidelity to the Dominican ideal; for the others his approach to philosophy and theology was hopelessly out of date. There was not a little unease about Garrigou's fundamental stance as a theologian and there were questions about the role he may have played in the placing of strictures on the work of fellow Dominicans Yves Congar and M.-Dominique Chenu.

The fact that there was no book-length introduction to Garrigou-Lagrange and his legacy led me to put off a study of Labourdette and to work at filling that lacuna. I hope that this present work will help to introduce Garrigou to contemporary students of theology and lead them to consider what his life's project might mean for our time.

I would like to express my gratitude to the following Dominican friars whose conversation both sparked my interest in Garrigou and whose encouragement helped to see this work to fruition: Benedict Ashley, Michael Mascari, Ralph Powell (R.I.P.), and Benedict Viviano.

1. Introduction

I find that you are attributing to Père Garrigou sentiments and actions that, to my knowledge, never existed. . . . Truly, dear brother, you are being unjust. Paul Philippe, o.p., to Yves Congar, o.p., 20 May 1946.[1]

Réginald Garrigou-Lagrange was the most prominent Dominican Neo-Thomist theologian of the first half of the twentieth century. He was professor of dogmatic and spiritual theology at the Pontifical University of St. Thomas Aquinas in Rome – the Angelicum – from 1909 until 1959. The printed record of his written works runs to over fifty pages.[2] He was involved in one way or another with most of the controversies of the pre-Vatican II Church.

In spite of his prominence there are few works on the life and thought of Garrigou-Lagrange. What accounts for this lacuna? One significant factor concerns the date of Garrigou's death. He died early in 1964 – a year before the end of the Second Vatican Council. Those most in a position to comment on his life and legacy found themselves occu-

1 Paul Philippe, O.P. to Yves Congar, O.P., 20 May 1946, in Yves Congar, *Journal d'un théologien, 1946–1956*, ed. Etienne Fouilloux (Paris: Cerf, 2000), 116, n. 256. [*Je trouve en effet, que vous prêtez au P. Garrigou des sentiments et des actes, qui, à ma connaissance n'ont jamais existé. . . . Vraiment, cher vieux frère, vous êtes injuste.*]

2 See: B. Zorcolo, "Bibliografia del P. Garrigou-Lagrange," *Angelicum* 42 (1965): 200–250.

pied in the deliberations of the various commissions of the Council. After the close of the Council, these same thinkers faced the Herculean task of explaining its teachings and implementing its mandates. Any thought of commenting on the life and work of Garrigou-Lagrange was sidelined.

Also, as a result of the Council, Catholic theology openly embraced pluralism: the hegemony of Neo-Thomism quickly became a thing of the past. Theologians like Henri de Lubac, Jean Daniélou, Yves Congar, and M.-Dominique Chenu, under suspicion of heterodoxy in the preconciliar Church, rose to prominence. Garrigou-Lagrange, who had opposed dimensions of their thought, became identified with the *ancien régime*. His fidelity to the Thomistic tradition in theology was no longer lauded; it signaled rigidity and intransigence.

For many, Garrigou-Lagrange symbolizes a theological ethos that was utterly discredited by the Second Vatican Council. François Mauriac, the influential litterateur, expressed his disdain for Garrigou-Lagrange, calling him "that sacred monster (*monstre sacré*) of Thomism."[3] By and large, Mauriac's sentiment has held the day: Garrigou-Lagrange has been effectively identified with theological rigidity and ecclesiastical repression.

All of this notwithstanding, in this work Garrigou-Lagrange will be approached from a hermeneutic of appreciation: we will struggle to understand his thought and values, his sympathies and antipathies. In the end, we will argue that Garrigou's vilification ought to be judged an unjust exaggeration. Moreover, since Thomism continues to have a role to play in contemporary Catholic theology, we will identify aspects of Garrigou's thought that are ripe for retrieval.

This work is an introduction to the life and thought of Réginald Garrigou-Lagrange. The word "introduction"

3 François Mauriac in *Le Figaro* (26 May 1966), cited by Bernard E. Doering, *Jacques Maritain and the French Catholic Intellectuals* (Notre Dame, Ind.: University of Notre Dame Press, 1983), 95.

should be emphasized: Garrigou lived a long life – just shy of eighty-seven years – and he wrote twenty-eight books and over 600 articles. He was a significant figure in the pontificates of Popes Benedict XV (1914–1922), Pius XI (1922–1939) and Pius XII (1939–1958). He disputed with a host of philosophers and theologians during his long career. The man, the theologian, and the ecclesiastic: each of these warrants much more than what we will be undertaking here. However, something will be said about all three: all the while recognizing that it will not be exhaustive and hoping that it will lead others to continue the reflection.

Faced with such a daunting *opus* the good news is that Garrigou's thought was remarkably consistent. There is not much sense in speaking of the "early Garrigou" or the "late Garrigou." In this regard, he was not unlike his master, St. Thomas Aquinas. Brian Davies, in his *The Thought of Thomas Aquinas*, says of St. Thomas: "He was a man of many thoughts, but he always had a single vision, albeit one presented with varied nuances and with different degrees of attention to detail. On that count he is relatively easy to expound."[4] Garrigou, similarly possessed of a single vision, is as easy to expound as St. Thomas: recognizing with Davies that "easy" is a relative term.

The first part of this work is primarily biographical and historical. We begin with a biographical sketch of Réginald Garrigou-Lagrange. The foundation for this will be the articles written by his friends and colleagues shortly after his death, as well as a number of articles in theological and philosophical encyclopedias and dictionaries. These works provide the basic chronology of Garrigou's life and the general context of his life's work.

Secondly, we discuss the single most important factor in Garrigou's life: his affiliation with the Order of Preachers.

4 Brian Davies, *The Thought of Thomas Aquinas* (New York: Oxford University Press, 1992), viii.

To this end, we undertake a study of the Dominican Order and its renewal in the nineteenth century, as well as its reinvigoration as a result of Pope Leo XIII's call for a revival of the thought of St. Thomas Aquinas. Themes present in these historical developments will help to explain the stance that Garrigou maintained to the end of his life.

One of the practices in the *studia* of the Dominican Order in Garrigou's day (and up to the 1960s) was the scholastic disputation: a philosophical or theological debate modeled on the example set by the medieval universities. This practice, understood as a method for arriving at the truth, is an important hermeneutical tool for understanding the mindset of Garrigou-Lagrange. In light of it, we examine his philosophical disputations with Henri Bergson and Maurice Blondel in Chapter 4; we examine his political and ecclesiastical disputations with Jacques Maritain and M.-Dominique Chenu in Chapter 5.

This leads to the second part of the work: an introduction to Garrigou's Thomism (Chapter 6), his understanding of theology (Chapter 7), and his spirituality (Chapter 8). Guided primarily by Pope John Paul II's teaching in *Fides et ratio*, we conclude with an evaluation of Garrigou's importance for Catholic theology in the unfolding of the third Christian millennium.

2. Garrigou-Lagrange: A Biographical Sketch[1]

The mystery of the Incarnation teaches us . . . that the human personality develops in the measure that the soul, elevating itself above the merely sensible world, places itself in closer dependence on what constitutes the true life of the spirit. That means closer dependence on truth and grace, and, in the ultimate analysis, on God. Réginald Garrigou-Lagrange, *The Last Writings*

Gontran-Marie Garrigou-Lagrange was born in Auch, France on February 21, 1877. Auch, the capital of the

1 The following works were consulted in constructing this biographical sketch: Hugh Bredin, "Garrigou-Lagrange, Réginald," in *Biographical Dictionary of Twentieth Century Philosophers*, 1996 ed.; Editors, "Le Père Garrigou-Lagrange, 1877–1964," *VS* 44 (1964): 360–61; P. M. Emonet, "Un maître prestigieux," *Angelicum* 42 (1965): 195–99; M.-Rosaire Gagnebet, "L'œuvre du P. Garrigou-Lagrange: itinéraire intellectuel et spirituel vers Dieu," *Angelicum* 42 (1965): 7–31; M.-Benoît Lavaud, "Le Père Garrigou-Lagrange: *In memoriam*," *RT* 64 (1964): 181–99; M.-Benoît Lavaud, "Garrigou-Lagrange (Réginald)," in *DS*; Ralph McInerny, "Garrigou-Lagrange, Réginald (1887 [*sic*]–1964)," in *Routledge Encyclopedia of Philosophy*, 1998 ed.; Jean-Hervé Nicolas, "*In Memoriam*: Le Père Garrigou-Lagrange," *FZPT* 11 (1964): 390–95; R. M. Pizzorni, "Garrigou-Lagrange, Réginald," in *NCE*, 1967 ed.; H. Tribout de Morembert, "Réginald Garrigou-Lagrange," in *DBF*.

département of Gers, is a quiet city in southwest France, approximately one hundred kilometers due west of Toulouse. It has been the site of an episcopal see since the fifth century; during Garrigou's childhood, it was reestablished as an archdiocese – undoing, as it were, one of the ravages of the French Revolution.[2] To this day, Auch is remembered as the home of the real d'Artagnan – Charles de Batz – and it is known for its cathedral of Ste-Marie "whose Renaissance windows . . . [are] said to be the most beautiful in France."[3]

At the time of Garrigou's birth, France's decidedly anticlerical Third Republic was beginning its eighth year. The humiliation of the country's defeat in the Franco-Prussian War was still a feature of national consciousness. France was a study in extremes, particularly as regards the questions of religious affiliation and models of Church-State relationships. It is safe to say that a Frenchman's attitude toward Catholicism, for instance, served to determine a whole set of socio-political commitments.

As a witness to the extremes in French society, Owen Chadwick recounts the following vignette from France's celebration of the centenary of Voltaire's death in 1878:

> By an unfortunate coincidence the day of the commemoration was Ascension Day. For weeks beforehand Bishop Dupanloup of Orléans filled his newspaper *Défense* with extracts of impiety, and unsuccessfully tried to persuade the minister to prosecute Victor Hugo for printing other extracts. . . . In the Gaiety theatre Victor Hugo made a speech on Voltaire's *smile*, while an open-air assembly of 6000 stood round a ten-foot-high statue of Voltaire draped in red and lowered their flags in processional salute to the tune of revolutionary music. "No inconsiderable portion" of the French people, commented an English observer sadly,

2 Georges Goyau, "Auch," *CE*. He notes that before the Revolution the archbishopric of Auch had ten suffragan sees.

3 Ibid.

"exalted the memory of the most inveterate enemy of Christianity and its founder."[4]

Chadwick concludes: "Those were the days of the fiercest politics in the French Third Republic."[5] However, as our narrative unfolds, we will see that the fiercest *policies* of the Third Republic would not see the light of day until just after the turn of the century.

Gontran Garrigou-Lagrange was born into a family that was solidly bourgeois and Catholic, although his childhood was not particularly marked by the piety associated with late nineteenth-century Catholicism. His father, François Garrigou-Lagrange, was a civil servant in Auch. His mother, Clémence Lasserre, belonged to the same family that produced Henri Lasserre (1828–1900), whose history of Lourdes was one of the most popular books of the nineteenth century.[6] Claims to minor nobility were found in the person of Garrigou's maternal grandmother, who was a member of the David de Lastour family.[7]

4 Owen Chadwick, *The Secularization of the European Mind in the 19th Century* (New York: Cambridge University Press, 1990), 157.

5 Ibid.

6 The twenty-sixth [*sic*] edition of Lasserre's *Notre-Dame de Lourdes* (Montréal: J. B. Rolland & Fils, 1871) was published with a congratulatory note to the author by Pope Pius IX. An English edition (*Our Lady of Lourdes*) was published by New York's D. & J. Sadlier Company in 1870.

7 See: Gagnebet, "L'œuvre du P. G.-L.," 8. In speaking of Garrigou's family ties, it is necessary to underscore that he was *not* the nephew of Marie-Joseph Lagrange, O.P. Matthew Hoehn [*Catholic Authors: Contemporary Biographical Sketches, 1930–1947* (Newark, N.J.: St. Mary's Abbey, 1948), 258] appears to be the instigator of this misinformation; he wrote: "He is the nephew of the famous Father Lagrange, who was the founder of the Biblical School of Jerusalem. . . ." James M. Connolly [*The Voices of France: A Survey of Contemporary Theology in France* (New York: Macmillan, 1961), 24] also got his facts wrong: "Père Garrigou-Lagrange was born in 1877 at Auch Gerst [*sic*] in France, the nephew of the celebrated Scripture scholar, Père Lagrange." This erroneous connection is further perpetuated by the publicity for the reprints of Garrigou's books by TAN Books.

The member of Garrigou's family who would most enthrall his imagination was his grandfather's brother, Maurice-Marie-Matthieu Garrigou (1766–1852).[8] The older Garrigou had been a canon of the diocese of Toulouse. During the French Revolution and its aftermath he carried out his priestly ministry under perilous conditions.[9] In 1802 he became attached to the Basilica of Saint-Sernin in Toulouse – where the relics of St. Thomas Aquinas had been transported at the time of the Revolution.[10] He was the founder of a religious congregation of women – the Institut de Notre-Dame de la Compassion – and his reputation for sanctity was well known. A segment of his spiritual writings was eventually published in the *Revue d'ascétique et de mystique*.[11] The process for his beatification officially began in 1966.[12] M.-Rosaire Gagnebet recounts that Garrigou used to frequently find inspiration in the writings of his illustrious granduncle.[13]

After his primary schooling in Auch, Gontran Garrigou-Lagrange studied at secondary schools in Roche-sur-Yon and Nantes. This was followed by a year of philosophical studies at Tarbes.[14] Having discerned a vocation in

8 Gagnebet, "L'œuvre du P. G.-L.," 8. See: T. de Morembert, "Garrigou, Maurice-Marie-Matthieu," in *DBF*. A biography was written by Claude Tournier, *Le chanoine Maurice Garrigou, fondateur de l'Institut de Notre-Dame de la Compassion* (Toulouse, 1945).

9 See: Gagnebet, "L'œuvre du P. G.-L.," 8. [Cf.: *Au péril de sa vie, il avait exercé le ministère durant la Révolution et, après la tourmente, il s'en fut vivre près de la Basilique Saint-Sernin où l'on avait alors transporté les reliques de s. Thomas d'Aquin.*]

10 St. Thomas's relics are now enshrined in the Church of the Jacobins in Toulouse. This church was the first to be built by the Order of Preachers. It is now in the hands of the French government.

11 Maurice-Marie-Matthieu Garrigou, "Considérations sur la vie intérieure d'une âme religieuse," *Revue d'ascétique et de mystique* 18 (1937): 124–40.

12 On 14 March 1966 the necessary initial paperwork was filed with the Congregation for Causes. See: Morembert, art. cit.

13 Gagnebet, "L'œuvre du P. G.-L.," 8. [Cf.: *Le P. Garrigou lisait sans cesse les instructions de ce saint prêtre à ses filles sur la vie intérieure et sur la compassion du Christ à l'imitation de la Vierge.*]

14 Gagnebet recounts the following concerning Garrigou's year at

medicine, the young Garrigou-Lagrange began studies at the University of Bordeaux in 1896. While at Bordeaux he experienced a profound religious awakening, occasioned, as it were, by his reading Ernest Hello's *L'Homme: la vie – la science – l'art.*[15] Years later, he would recount the general parameters of this experience to his Dominican confrere M.-Rosaire Gagnebet:

> I was able to glimpse how the doctrine of the Catholic Church is the absolute Truth concerning God and his intimate life and concerning the human person, his origin and his supernatural destiny. I saw in a wink of an eye that it was not a truth relative to our time and place but an absolute truth that will not change but will become more and more apparent up to the time when we see God face to face. A ray of light shone before my eyes and made clear the words of the Lord: "The heavens and the earth will pass away, but my words will not pass away." I understood that this truth must bear fruit like the grain of wheat in good soil. . .[16]

Tarbes: *Sa classe de philosophie au Lycée de Tarbes fut son triomphe. . . . En 1950, un de ses anciens condisciples de Tarbes, neveu du Maréchal Foch, apporte au P. Garrigou une dissertation du jeune Gontran, qu'il a fait copier dans le cahier d'honneur du Lycée. Elle est consacrée au problème de la douleur. Le jeune lycéen insiste sur les avantages intellectuels, moraux et artistiques de la souffrance. Mais il passe sous silence sa signification religieuse.* ["L'œuvre du P. Garrigou-Lagrange," 9.]

15 Ernest Hello (1828–1885) was a French philosopher and essayist. Influenced by Lacordaire and instructed in theology by Bishop Baudry, he became a champion of Catholic orthodoxy. His first book, *Renan, l'Allemagne et l'athéisme* was a refutation of Ernest Renan's attack on Christianity. "*L'Homme* is looked upon by his critics as his chief work. It is a collection of essays arranged under the three heads, life, science, art, and united by the Catholic standpoint of their author and their bearing upon the different departments of human activity." [Susan Tracy Otten, "Hello, Ernest," in *CE*.] *L'Homme* was reprinted in 1919 by Perrin et compagnie with a preface by Garrigou's cousin Henri Lasserre (written for an earlier edition).

16 Gagnebet, "L'œuvre du P. Garrigou-Lagrange," 9–10. [*J'ai entrevu que la doctrine de l'Eglise Catholique était la Vérité absolue sur Dieu, sa vie intime, sur l'homme, son origine et sa destinée surnaturelle. J'ai vu comme un clin d'œil que c'était là non une*

This episode, which he would refer to later in life as his "conversion,"[17] led the young Garrigou to consider the religious life and priesthood. He investigated a few religious orders, spending time with the Trappists of Echourniac and the Carthusians of Vauclair, before settling on the Order of Preachers.[18] He entered the novitiate of the Paris province at Amiens in the fall of 1897.[19] He received the Dominican habit on 10 October 1897 along with the religious name Réginald.[20]

The novitiate was an extended trial period. The novice and the community entered into a mutual discernment process: he would live the life of a Dominican friar – focused on prayer and study – and together with the community he would get a sense whether Dominican life was right for him. To help in this process of discernment, the novitiate was under the care of a master of novices – a friar known for his personal maturity and spiritual insight. Père Constant served as novice master in Garrigou's day. He is remembered as an austere friar, but "one who greatly loved the Order and knew how to lead others to love it."[21]

vérité relative à l'état actuel de nos connaissances, mais une vérité absolue qui ne passera pas, mais apparaîtra de plus en plus dans son rayonnement jusqu'à ce que nous voyons Dieu facie ad faciem. *Un rayon lumineux faisait resplendir à mes yeux les paroles du Seigneur : 'Le ciel et la terre passeront, mais mes paroles ne passeront pas.' J'ai compris que cette vérité doit fructifier comme le grain de froment dans une bonne terre. . .*]

17 Ibid., 9.

18 See: Lavaud, "Le Père Garrigou-Lagrange," 183.

19 One notes that Martin-Stanislaus Gillet, Master of the Order from 1929 to1946, was a member of Garrigou's novitiate class.

20 His patron was Blessed Réginald of Orléans (1183?–1220), one of the first members recruited by St. Dominic for the Order of Preachers. He had been a professor at the University of Paris before entering the Order; he became a zealous preacher as a Dominican and was responsible for literally hundreds of the early vocations to the Order. See: Mary Jean Dorcy, *St. Dominic's Family* (Dubuque, Ia.: Priory Press, 1964), 12–14.

21 Lavaud, "Le Père Garrigou-Lagrange," 183. [Cf.: *Il eut pour maître des novices le P. Constant, religieux austère, aimant beaucoup et sachant faire aimer l'Ordre . . .*]

Friar Réginald professed his vows as a Dominican on 30 April 1900; according to the vow formula, he promised obedience to God, to Blessed Mary, to Blessed Dominic, and to the Master of the Order and his successors, until death.[22]

After the novitiate, Garrigou was assigned to the Paris province's *studium* in Flavigny for studies in preparation for ordination to the priesthood. A significant amount of this preparation entailed the assiduous study of St. Thomas' *Summa theologiae* under the guidance of the redoubtable Ambroise Gardeil, O.P. We will have occasion to comment on Garrigou's indebtedness to Gardeil as our narrative unfolds; for now it suffices to note that Gardeil's Thomism found its fulfillment in the career of Garrigou-Lagrange.[23]

Garrigou was ordained to the priesthood on 28 September 1902. He began complementary philosophical studies at the Sorbonne in 1904. By virtue of his performance in the *studium*, his superiors recognized that he was destined for the intellectual apostolate of the Order; Gardeil's plan as Regent of Studies was to have Garrigou-Lagrange join the philosophy faculty of the province's house of studies.

At the Sorbonne, Garrigou attended lectures by the likes of Emile Durkheim, Gabriel Séailles, and Lucien Lévy-Bruhl; he heard Henri Bergson at the Collège de France. Later in life, he would point out that he had been present at a lecture where Alfred Loisy rehearsed his trademark theme: "Jesus preached the Kingdom of God, and it was the Church that came."[24] It was at the Sorbonne

22 Until the 1917 Code of Canon Law, the friars took solemn vows immediately following the novitiate. Contemporary practice mandates a period of at least three years of "simple" vows before solemn vows.

23 For a glimpse at the early relationship between Garrigou and Gardeil, see "Lettres de jeunesse au P. Ambroise Gardeil," *Angelicum* 42 (1965): 137 ff.

24 Gagnebet, "L'œuvre du P. Garrigou-Lagrange," 11. [*Jésus a prêché le royaume et c'est l'Eglise qui est venue.*] Loisy, ordained priest in

that Garrigou met a young Bergsonian – destined to become one of the most eminent Thomists of the twentieth century – Jacques Maritain. As we will see, Garrigou and Maritain developed a fruitful colleagueship during the 1920s and 1930s.

In 1905, Garrigou returned to the house of studies and began teaching the history of philosophy, with special emphasis on Leibniz and Spinoza.[25]

The *studium* had moved from Flavigny to Gand in Belgium and then to the village of Le Saulchoir (also in Belgium) because of the anticlerical laws of the administration of Emile Combes.[26] The name of the latter village would, for all intents and purposes, become the name of the school: it would be known as "Le Saulchoir" even after it was allowed to return to France.

As things worked out, Garrigou taught philosophy at Le Saulchoir for just one year. In 1906, Etienne Hugueny's health failed, and he was forced to give up teaching. As a result, Garrigou was called to accede to the chair of dogmatic theology at Le Saulchoir. This unexpected turn of events would prove to be utterly decisive for the shape of his life. He had envisaged a life devoted to the study of philosophy; his superiors trusted that his gifts would be put to better use in theology. With this change, Garrigou began what his former student, Benoît Lavaud, calls his *approfondissement* of the works of St. Thomas and the key figures of the Thomist school "which he would follow the rest of his life and which would make him an eminent master of this same school."[27]

1879, was excommunicated in 1908 for refusing to accept St. Pius X's *Pascendi dominis gregis*.

25 Lavaud, "Le Père Garrigou-Lagrange,"184.

26 In Chapter 5 we will discuss the anticlerical policies of the Third French Republic.

27 Lavaud, "Le Père Garrigou-Lagrange,"184. [*Il commença donc, comme professeur, cet approfondissement des œuvres de saint Thomas et des maîtres de l'école thomiste qu'il devait poursuivre*

Garrigou had his first article published just before his appointment to Le Saulchoir.[28] It appeared in the *Revue thomiste* and would be the first of a myriad of contributions to that journal.

While at Le Saulchoir, along with his teaching duties, Garrigou was occupied with the writing of his first major work, *Le sens commun, la philosophie de l'être et les formules dogmatiques*.[29] This work was an important critique of the thought of Henri Bergson's disciple, Edouard Le Roy. Le Roy had attempted to interpret the dogmas of the Church with a Bergsonian hermeneutic; Bergson's evolutionism led Le Roy to downplay the Church's emphasis on radical dogmatic continuity throughout history.[30]

The publication of *Le sens commun* caught the attention of many – including the Master of the Order, Hyacinthe Cormier.[31] Père Cormier, intent on strengthening the Order's Roman university – the "Collegio Angelico," or

toute sa vie, et qui fit de lui, à son tour, un maître éminent de cette école.]

28 Réginald Garrigou-Lagrange, "La vie scientifique. Note sur la preuve de Dieu par les degrés des êtres chez saint Thomas," *Revue thomiste* 12 (1904): 363–81.

29 (Paris: Beauchesne, 1909). *Le sens commun* went into four French editions; it has not been translated into English. Its precursor was an article Garrigou submitted to the *Revue thomiste* that was published with the same name in volume 16 (1908): 259–300; 566–616.

30 Garrigou's critique did not deter Le Roy from interpreting the doctrine of God from a Bergsonian perspective in his *Le problème de Dieu* (Paris: L'Artisan du livre, 1930). See Garrigou's review of this work in *RT* 35 (1930): 262–72.

31 Hyacinthe Cormier (1832–1916), first provincial of the reestablished province of Toulouse, was elected the seventy-sixth Master of the Order of Preachers in 1904. "Father Cormier wrote incessantly, mostly devotional works or instructions for novices. . . . He wrote biographies of many eminent Dominicans, including Blessed Raymond of Capua and Father Jandel. His pen helped to make permanent the work done by Father Lacordaire and his companions in reestablishing the Order in France and in the world. . . . He had a universal reputation for the soundness of his spiritual direction." [Dorcy, *St. Dominic's Family*, 570.] Hyacinthe Cormier was beatified by Pope John Paul II on 20 November 1994.

"Angelicum" – assigned Garrigou to teach there in 1909. He was to continue teaching dogmatic theology, with attention to the course *De revelatione* – "on Revelation."

During his first year at the Angelicum, Garrigou encountered a figure who, after St. Thomas and Ambroise Gardeil, would have the most impact on his theological project. That figure was the eminent Spanish Dominican mystical theologian, Juan González Arintero. Lavaud writes that even though Arintero would only remain in Rome for Garrigou's first year, their profound discussions would be "decisive for the definitive orientation of Garrigou's thought and the positions which he would defend for the rest of his life."[32] Arintero, author of the influential *La Evolucíon mística*, brought Garrigou to see that the full development of the Christian life cannot but be of the mystical order. All Christians are called to contemplation and personal holiness. God does not reserve this to a select minority, say, to priests and religious, as the popular conception of the day held. As we will see in Chapter 9, Garrigou's contributions in the field of spirituality have much to do with his fruitful association with Juan Arintero.[33]

Garrigou was occupied with his course on Revelation for eight years. It would eventually be published in Latin as *De Revelatione per Ecclesiam catholicam proposita*.[34]

Before long, he had had occasion to teach all the major treatises of St. Thomas's *Summa theologiae*. Also during this period he published his major contribution to the

32 Lavaud, "Le Père Garrigou-Lagrange,"184. [*La première année de son séjour à Rome, le P. G.-L. connut, entre autres collègues, le P. Juan Arintero, qui ne devait rester qu'un an à l'Angelicum ; mais cette année suffit à des entretiens fructueux et décisifs pour l'orientation définitive du dominicain français vers les positions qu'il défendra toujours.*]

33 In particular, Arintero's love for St. John of the Cross coincided with an appreciation that Garrigou had acquired through his reading of Ernest Hello. [See: Lavaud, "Le Père Garrigou-Lagrange," 183.]

34 (Rome and Paris: Ferrari-Gabala, 1918). *De Revelatione*, like *Le*

philosophical study of God: *Dieu: son existence et sa nature. Solution thomiste des antinomies agnostiques.*[35] R. M. Pizzorini calls this Garrigou's most important philosophical work;[36] Jean-Hervé Nicolas concurs and says that in *Dieu: son existence et sa nature* Garrigou made a lasting contribution.[37]

The First World War did not interrupt Garrigou's teaching at the Angelicum. Whereas other Dominicans served as chaplains during the war, Garrigou, who was thirty-seven years old at its outbreak, recognized that he was not suited for such service. Lavaud reveals the judgment of Garrigou's superiors on this point when he writes: "It was better that Père Garrigou-Lagrange continue teaching than to go into the trenches. Moreover, he did not have a disposition for life in the military or for life as a soldier and the *castrorum pericula* frightened him even from afar."[38]

Immediately after the First World War, Garrigou entered into an important collaboration with his Dominican confrere Vincent Bernadot in the creation of the journal *La vie spirituelle*. He offered significant encouragement to Bernadot's vision of a journal under Dominican auspices that would be devoted to reflection on the spiritual life. Over the years he contributed a plethora of articles to *La vie spirituelle* – starting with three articles on ascetical and mystical theology in the journal's first volume.[39]

35 Two volumes, (Paris: Beauchesne, 1914). This would go into eleven editions. It was published in English as *God: His Existence and His Nature. A Thomistic Solution of Certain Agnostic Antinomies*, 2 vols., trans. Bede Rose (St. Louis: B. Herder, 1934 and 1936). Its precursor was Garrigou's article, "Dieu," in the *Dictionnaire apologétique de la foi catholique* (1911).

36 R. M. Pizzorini, "Garrigou-Lagrange, Réginald." in *NCE*.

37 Jean-Hervé Nicolas, *"In Memoriam," Freiburger Zeitschrift für Philosophie und Theologie* 11 (1964): 393.

38 Lavaud, "Le Père Garrigou-Lagrange,"186. [*Il valait mieux que le P. G.-L. continuât d'enseigner que d'aller au tranchées. Il n'avait d'ailleurs aucune disposition pour la vie militaire et guerrière, et les* castrorum pericula *l'épouvantaient même de loin.*]

39 Cf. "La théologie ascétique et mystique ou la doctrine spirituelle," *Vie spirituelle* 1 (1919): 7–19; "L'ascétique et la mystique. Leur dis-

Garrigou's teaching at the Angelicum was marked by a remarkable regularity and stability. For decades he taught three courses: fundamental theology, the metaphysics of Aristotle, and spiritual theology. His course on spirituality would most account for his international recognition and add luster to the Angelicum's standing among the other Roman universities.

In 1917 the Angelicum established – with the encouragement and support of Pope Benedict XV – the first chair of ascetical-mystical theology in the Church's history.[40] Garrigou-Lagrange was from the beginning its intended recipient. He held this honor until the end of 1959. The major work of the chair of spirituality was to give a public lecture every Saturday afternoon while the Angelicum was in session. Garrigou's lectures attracted people from all parts; they would become one of the unofficial tourist sites on the itineraries of theologically minded visitors to Rome. The lecture material for this course would eventually be published in Garrigou's two monumental works of Catholic spirituality: *Perfection chrétienne et contemplation* and the now classic *Les trois âges de la vie intérieure*.[41] P. M. Emonet, O.P., a student at the Angelicum during the early 1940s, speaks of Garrigou's spirituality course in the following terms:

> The course on spirituality had this in particular for us who lived at the Angelicum: it meant that we would see new faces. There were students from the Gregorian University or other Roman seminaries attracted by the reputation of the professor. We also saw at times even old priests, who came, no doubt, to look for teachings that would help in directing souls . . . . Garrigou would focus on his preferred

tinction et l'unité de la doctrine spirituelle," *Vie spirituelle* 1 (1919): 145–65; "La mystique et les doctrines fondamentales de saint Thomas," *Vie spirituelle* 1 (1919): 216–28.

40 Gagnebet, "L'œuvre du P. Garrigou-Lagrange," 13.

41 Emonet, "Un maître prestigieux,"195.

> themes: the great purifications that open the way to infused contemplation or the call of souls to contemplation.[42]

Garrigou taught his course on metaphysics each Thursday morning. The lectures were based on St. Thomas's commentary on Aristotle's metaphysics. Emonet gives us a first-hand account of these lectures:

> In this course, we felt that he was at home. It was perhaps during this hour that he knew his most strongly felt joys. He loved passionately the thought of Aristotle. At times, to translate his enthusiasm, he would say to us with his inimitable mimicry: 'I could teach Aristotle for three hundred years and never grow tired.' And I willingly believed him![43]

Garrigou's course of fundamental theology was usually given in the Angelicum's *aula magna* – the auditorium which would allow for the largest assembly possible. Not surprisingly, St. Thomas's *Summa theologiae* was its inspiration. Emonet remarks that what most struck him about this course was the power of Garrigou's synthesis. "He excelled in putting in relief the arrangement of the articles into a question or the questions into a treatise."[44]

42 Ibid., 195. [*Le cours de mystique avait ceci de particulier pour nous qui habitions l'Angelicum, c'est qu'on y voyait des visages nouveaux. C'étaient des étudiants de la Grégorienne ou d'autres séminaires romains attirés par la réputation du professeur. On remarquait même parfois des prêtres âgés, qui venaient sans doute chercher des enseignements pour la conduite des âmes. . . . Il s'arrêtaient volontiers sur ses thèmes préférés : les grandes purifications qui ouvrent le chemin de la contemplation infuse ou l'appel des âmes à la contemplation.*]

43 Ibid., 196. [*Dans ce cours, on le sentait chez lui. C'est peut-être durant cette heure qu'il connaissait ses joies les plus fortes. Il aimait avec passion la pensée d'Aristote. Parfois, pour traduire son enthousiasme, il nous disait avec sa mimique inimitable: 'Je pourrais enseigner Aristote pendant trois cents ans, sans ressentir de fatigue.' Et je le crois volontiers!*]

44 Ibid., 197. [*Ce qui me frappait dans ce cours, c'était la puissance de synthèse. Il excellait à mettre en relief l'agencement des articles dans*

By all accounts, Garrigou-Lagrange was an engaging professor. Lavaud says that that one could not help but be struck by his mastery of his subject.[45] Gagnebet writes that Garrigou's courses were known for their drama; his lectures were never monologues.[46] Garrigou knew wonderfully well how to pose problems, to present the state of the question, to show the connections between ideas, to highlight the problems in reasoning – particularly the errors in an author's choice of first principles.[47] During his early years at the Angelicum, he had the reputation of being a passionate lecturer – vehement in his principles and armed to do battle with his intellectual adversaries.[48] As he aged, as one might expect, his stance became more serene. Lavaud gives the following testimony:

> Père Garrigou-Lagrange had long been a vigorous polemicist, but with the passing of the years he calmed down greatly, without losing his reasoned attachment to his chosen positions nor his opposition to the eclecticism that dulls the sharp edges of thought. He also kept his sense of the errors of rationalism, agnosticism, modernism, neo-modernism, and others, while growing progressively in serenity. He communicated the delight and the love of the truth that he lived.[49]

une question, ou des questions dans un traité.] Lavaud, "Le Père Garrigou-Lagrange," 187, for his part, remarks that what most struck him about Garrigou's course of theology was the vast perspectives that he uncovered and the connections he had between the ideas of the masters of speculation and the great spiritual masters. [*En théologie, ce qui me frappa le plus, c'étaient les vastes perspectives qu'il découvrait, les rapprochements qu'il opérait entre les vues des maîtres de la spéculation et celles des grands spirituels.*]

45 Lavaud, "Le Père Garrigou-Lagrange,"187. [*On ne pouvait pas n'être pas frappé de sa maîtrise!*]

46 Gagnebet, "L'œuvre du Père Garrigou-Lagrange," 13. [*Ses cours ne sont pas des monologues parlés, ce sont des drames joués.*]

47 Lavaud, "Le Père Garrigou-Lagrange,"187, remarks that one of Garrigou's favorite sayings of St. Thomas, one that he quoted often, was *parvus error in principe, maximus in fine*.

48 Emonet, "Un maître prestigieux,"195. The received wisdom is that Garrigou loved to rage at dead philosophers and living Jesuits!

49 Lavaud, "Le Père Garrigou-Lagrange,"188. *[Le P. G.-L. a été*

For his part, Emonet gives the following testimony: "I knew a Père Garrigou who had become wise, filled with gentleness and serenity. Now and then, some sudden outburst would allow, nevertheless, the ardor of yesteryear to be witnessed."[50]

Emonet also remarks that Garrigou had a gift for comedy and that rarely would a class period go by without at least a moment or two of hilarity. In this, Garrigou "was aided by . . . his small eyes filled with mischief and laughter, a body in constant motion, a head practically completely bald, a face able to mime horror, anger, irony, indignation, and wonder."[51] The serenity which marked the end of his life, says Emonet, came from the grace he was given to live profoundly the three wisdoms of which the *Summa theologiae* speaks: the wisdom of metaphysics, of theology, and of mysticism. It was no coincidence that these three wisdoms formed the basis of his long teaching ministry: "It responded to a profound need within him. This synthesis made him live."[52]

Another aspect of Garrigou's tenure at the Angelicum, of course, was the direction he gave to myriads of doctoral candidates. Under his tutelage, men like M.-Dominique Chenu, O.P., Benoît Lavaud, O.P., M.-Michel Labourdette,

longtemps un polémiste vigoureux, mais avec les années il s'apaisa beaucoup, sans rien perdre de son attachement raisonné aux positions choisies ni de son opposition à l'éclectisme qui efface les arêtes vives de la pensée. Il garda toujours aussi vif le sens des erreurs rationalistes, agnostiques, modernistes, néomodernistes et autres, mais gagna progressivement en sérénité. Il communiquait le goût et l'amour de la vérité dont il vivait.]

50 Emonet, "Un maître prestigieux,"195. [*J'ai connu un Père Garrigou assagi, imprégné de douceur et de sérénité. Parfois quelques saillies laissaient deviner pourtant la fougue d'antan.*]

51 Ibid., 197. [*Il était aidé . . . de petits yeux pleins de malice, rieurs, mobiles extrêmement, la tête presque complètement dégarnie, un visage pouvant mimer l'horreur, la colère, l'ironie, l'indignation, l'émerveillement.*]

52 Ibid., [*Cela répondait chez lui à un besoin profond. Cette synthèse le faisait vivre.*]

O.P., Louis-Bertrand Gillon, O.P., and Karol Wojtyla – the future John Paul II – were to receive the doctorate in theology. We will have occasion to speak more of the significance of some of these relationships as Garrigou's story unfolds.

The period between the two world wars was an extremely productive one for Garrigou-Lagrange. His teaching at the Angelicum continued with no significant interruptions, as did his preaching of retreats and his lecturing during the summer months. His international reputation as a master of Catholic spirituality brought him requests for conferences from across Europe and North America.[53] Garrigou authored the following books during this period: *Perfection chrétienne et contemplation selon S. Thomas d'Aquin et S. Jean de la Croix*[54]; *L'amour de Dieu et la croix de Jésus;*[55] *La providence et la confiance en Dieu. Fidélité et abandon;*[56] *Le réalisme du principe de finalité;*[57] *Les trois conversions et les trois voies;*[58] *Le Sauveur et son amour pour nous;*[59] *Le sens du mystère et le clair-obscur intellectuel. Nature et surnaturel;*[60] *La prédestination des saints et la grâce. Doctrine de S. Thomas comparée aux*

53 Matthew Hoehn reports that Garrigou's only appearance in the United States "was on October 13, 1939 when he delivered the Jubilee Theological Lecture at the Catholic University of America before a capacity audience of theologians . . ." [*Catholic Authors*, 259–60.]

54 (Var: Saint-Maximin, 1923); English translation: *Christian Perfection and Contemplation according to St. Thomas Aquinas and St. John of the Cross*, trans. M. Timothea Doyle (St. Louis: B. Herder, 1937).

55 (Paris: Cerf, 1929); English translation: *The Love of God and the Cross of Jesus*, 2 vols., trans. Sr. Marie of Maryknoll (St. Louis: B. Herder, 1948–1951).

56 (Paris: Desclée de Brouwer, 1932); English translation: *Providence*, trans. Bede Rose (St. Louis: B. Herder, 1937).

57 (Paris: Desclée de Brouwer, 1932).

58 (Paris: Cerf, 1933).

59 (Paris: Cerf, 1933); English translation: *Our Savior and His Love for Us*, trans. A. Bouchard (St. Louis: B. Herder, 1951).

60 (Paris: Desclée de Brouwer, 1934).

autres systèmes théologiques;[61] *De Deo Uno. Commentarium in primam partem S. Thomae;*[62] *Les trois ages de la vie intérieure prélude de celle du ciel. Traité de théologie ascétique et mystique.*[63]

Unlike the First World War, the Second World War did interfere with Garrigou's teaching. When the "intervention of Italy was imminent, he returned to France with his French confreres on the order of the Master General, Fr. Gillet, who himself had moved provisionally to Switzerland."[64] He was not able to return to Rome until October of 1941. During this absence from the Angelicum, he gave classes in dogma in the Dominican *studium* at Coublevie.[65]

During his years at the Angelicum, Garrigou was consulted numerous times by the Holy Office on doctrinal matters. In Roman parlance, he was a "qualificator" – one who qualified as a theological authority. Garrigou served in this capacity from the pontificate of Benedict XV through that of John XXIII.

In 1955 he was named a "consultor" for the Holy Office and for the Congregation for Religious. Now, rather than being an auxiliary to decision-making, Garrigou became an active participant in the work of the Roman curia. Every Monday morning the chauffeur of the Holy Office made the rounds of the Roman universities, picking up the consul-

61 (Paris: Desclée de Brouwer, 1936); English translation: *Predestination*, trans. Bede Rose (St. Louis : B. Herder, 1939).

62 (Paris: Desclée de Brouwer, 1938); English translation: *The One God : A Commentary on the First Part of St. Thomas' Theological Summa*, trans. Bede Rose (St. Louis: B. Herder, 1943).

63 (Paris: Cerf, 1938); English translation: *The Three Ages of the Interior Life*, 2 vols., trans. M. Timothea Doyle (St. Louis: B. Herder, 1947–1948).

64 Lavaud, "Le Père Garrigou-Lagrange," 186. [*Durant la seconde guerre mondiale, quand l'intervention de l'Italie fut imminente, il rentra en France avec ses confrères français sur l'ordre du maître général, le P. Gillet qui, lui, se rendit et séjourna provisoirement en Suisse.*]

65 Ibid.

tors: Garrigou from the Angelicum, the rector of the Lateran, several Jesuits from the Gregorianum.[66] Two or three hours later, he would drive them back to their residences. Lavaud writes that as the years went on, Garrigou appeared more and more exhausted with this schedule. Yet, because the Master of the Order had told him that it was an honor for the whole Order that he served in this way, Garrigou was reluctant to ask for a lighter workload.[67]

By the fall of 1959, Garrigou's energy had greatly dissipated. He was eighty-two years old and had been teaching at the Angelicum for fifty years. It was clear that the time had come for him to retire from active ministry. In 1960 he moved to the Priory of Santa Sabina in Rome – the headquarters of the Dominican Order and home of the Master of the Order. Due to his condition, he was unable to accede to Pope John XXIII's request that he join the theological commission's preparatory work for the Second Vatican Council.[68] Little by little, Garrigou lost his faculties; it became necessary for him to be transferred to the hospital of the Fraternité Sacerdotale Canadienne on Rome's via Camilluccia. He died there on February 15, 1964 – the feast of the fourteenth-century Dominican Rhineland mystic, Blessed Henry Suso. The day before his death he had received the last sacraments. His funeral was celebrated on 17 February 1964 in the Church of SS. Dominic and Sixtus, the College Church of the Dominicans at the Angelicum. In a public statement, Pope Paul VI lauded

66 Garrigou marveled at how well he was able to work with the Jesuits who were also consultors. He used to remark: *Comme c'est curieux, moi qui ai jadis rompu tant de lances avec les Pères de la Compagnie, je ne pensais que je finirais mes jours en si bons termes avec eux*. [See: Lavaud, "Le Père Garrigou-Lagrange," 198.]

67 Lavaud, "Le Père Garrigou-Lagrange," 197–98. [*Le maître général lui avait dit que ç'avait été de la part du Saint-Père un honneur pour l'Ordre de le nommer consulteur, et de cet honneur il craignait de paraître faire peu de cas. C'était là un scrupule.*]

68 The Editors, "Le Père Garrigou-Lagrange," 361.

Garrigou-Lagrange as "a faithful servant of the Church and of the Holy See."[69]

Benoît Lavaud's words provide a segue into the next chapter's discussion of Garrigou the Dominican friar:

> He leaves us in parting, along with his monumental written oeuvre, an admirable example of religious life and of fidelity to his vocation, to work and to the love of the truth, to apostolic zeal, docility to the Church, to abandon to the will of the Lord whom he served for so long and who just called him to Himself: *Euge, serve bone . . .*[70]

In the next chapter we will examine the contours of Garrigou-Lagrange's life as a Dominican friar and the issues associated with his sixty-seven-year affiliation with the Order of Preachers.

69 Quoted in Gagnebet, "L'œuvre du P. Garrigou-Lagrange," 31. [*un fidèle serviteur de l'Eglise et du Saint-Siège*] [The full text of Pope Paul's statement can be found in *Analecta* 72 (1964): 420: *Nous apprenons avec une vive peine la mort du vénéré Père Réginald Garrigou-Lagrange, et c'est avec une profonde émotion et une grande gratitude qu'en évoquant la mémoire de cet illustre théologien Nous élevons Notre prière vers Dieu pour le repos de l'âme de ce fidèle serviteur de l'Eglise et du Saint-Siège et adressons en gage des divines grâces à sa Famille religieuse éprouvée Notre paternelle Bénédiction Apostolique.*]

70 Lavaud, "Le Père Garrigou-Lagrange,"199. [*Il nous laisse en partant, avec son œuvre écrite monumentale, un admirable exemple de vie religieuse et de fidélité à la vocation, de travail et d'amour de la vérité, de zèle apostolique, de docilité à l'Eglise, d'abandon à la volonté du Seigneur qu'il servait depuis si longtemps et qui vient de l'appeler à Lui :* Euge, serve bone. . . .]

3. Garrigou-Lagrange: Dominican Friar

As a fearless athelete, Dominic sedulously pursued the paths of justice (Ps. 22:3) and the way of the Saints. And not leaving the tabernacle of the Lord even for a moment, he did not abandon his role as teacher and minister in the militant church. Subjecting his flesh to his spirit and his sensitivity to reason, he became one and the same spirit with God (1 Cor. 6:17), and completely devoted his attention to seeking Him through the excess of his mind (Ps. 30:23). Moreover, in the eagerness of his companions, he never departed from love for his neighbor. When he destroyed the pleasures of the flesh and illuminated the stony minds of the impious, the whole sect of the heretics trembled and the whole Church of the faithful rejoiced. Pope Gregory IX, "The Bull of Canonization of St. Dominic" (1234)

Of all the distinctive marks that one could adduce about Garrigou-Lagrange, the most significant and the most determinative is the fact that he was a Dominican friar. Profession in the Order of Preachers set the stage for all that would follow: his philosophical and theological formation under the direction of Ambroise Gardeil, his education at the Sorbonne, his teaching career at Le Saulchoir and the Angelicum, his international reputation as a Catholic theologian. At the same time, not only did Garrigou live the Dominican life, he also became a leading commentator on the meaning of Dominican spirituality. In this chapter we will begin with a brief introduction to the history of the Order of Preachers; this will provide a sense of the ethos of the Order Garrigou-Lagrange joined. We will then focus attention on his life as a Dominican friar and, in reference to his article, "Le caractère et les principes de la spiritualité dominicaine,"[1] we will analyze the impact of Dominican spirituality on his life.

St. Dominic and the Order of Preachers

Dominic de Guzman (1170–1221)[2] began his ecclesiastical career as a canon regular in the cathedral chapter of Osma, Spain. He was inspired to found an order of preaching friars after an encounter with the Albigensians in Languedoc while on a preaching mission with his bishop, Diego. The Albigensians, or Cathars, were a group of medieval gnostics intent on living lives pleasing to God, yet their intellectual and spiritual formation in the Christian faith had been radically skewed by the Manichean heresy. They were strict dualists: their programmatic belief was that all of material reality is evil. Albigensian society was two-tiered. On the one hand, there were the "Perfect," those who were leading lives of great asceticism, avoiding as much as possible corruption from the material order. On

1 *VS* 4 (1921): 365–84.

2 See: Guy Bedouelle, *Saint Dominic: The Grace of the Word*, trans. Mary Thomas Noble (San Francisco: Ignatius, 1987); Bede Jarrett, *Life of St. Dominic* (Washington, D.C.: Dominicana Publications, n.d.); Simon Tugwell, *The Way of the Preacher* (Springfield, Ill.: Templegate, 1979); M.-Humbert Vicaire, *Saint Dominic and His Times*, trans. Kathleen Pond (Green Bay, Wisc.: Alt Publishing Co., n.d.) – first published by Les Editions du Cerf, 1957 under the title *Histoire de saint Dominique*.

the other hand, there were the "believers," those who accepted Manicheanism but whose praxis had not yet arrived at perfection. M.-Humbert Vicaire explains:

> Two contradictory principles explained the radical opposition of the world with good. 'Two Gods,' said the Albigensian Catharists . . . the God of good was the God of the Gospel; the other was the God of the Old Testament. Souls were angels fallen into matter, i.e., under the domination of the God of evil. . . . The extreme austerity of the 'Perfect' was a preparation for their liberation which was effected by death. The imperfect liberation of the 'believers' required fresh incarnations upon this earth, a metempsychosis which might go so far as a return into the body of an animal.[3]

The belief that all matter is evil because it is the work of an evil God was absolutely irreconcilable with the Christian doctrine of the Incarnation (and hence the Redemption) and the sacramental principle that informs Catholic life and practice. St. Dominic, deeply moved by his encounter in Languedoc, was filled with zeal to win the Albigensians back to Christ. He envisioned an Order devoted to the Word of God – an Order that would be especially committed to preaching the gospel, reconciling sinners, and converting heretics. Such an Order would thereby both support and invigorate Christ's Body, the Church. Confirming this vision, Pope Honorius III, in one of the earliest bulls addressed to the Order, spoke of the genius, spirit, and purpose of the Order of Preachers in the following way:

> God who continually makes his Church fruitful in new children, wishing to bring our times into conformity with earlier days and spread the Catholic faith, has inspired you to embrace a life of poverty and regular discipline and to devote yourselves to preaching the Word of God and proclaiming the name of our Lord Jesus Christ throughout the world.[4]

3 Vicaire, *Saint Dominic and His Times*, 51–52.

4 Cited by William A. Hinnebusch, *The Dominicans: A Short History* (Staten Island, N.Y.: Alba House, 1975), 10.

Its official confirmation on 22 December 1216 by Pope Honorius III consecrated the Order of Preachers to the intellectual presentation of the Catholic faith. The Pope, in a second bull of 21 January 1217, addressed the friars of the Order as "Christ's unconquered athletes, armed with the shield of faith and the helmet of salvation. Fearing not those who can kill the body, you valiantly thrust the word of God which is keener than any two-edged sword, against the foes of the faith."[5] It was clear to all that the task of preaching demanded a commitment to assiduous study of the faith, and in the early years of the thirteenth century that meant primarily the Scriptures and the Fathers of the Church.

Dominican hagiography marvels at the report that St. Dominic "spoke only to God or about God."[6] He was *vir evangelicus*, a man of the Gospel, one who was on fire with the desire to make Christ better known and better loved. The following is a sampling of the testimony offered at his canonization process by those who knew him best:

> *Testimony of Brother Amizo of Milan (8 August 1233)*: He . . . said that [Dominic] was persistent in prayer, by day and by night. . . . He was very fervent in prayer and in preaching, and, because he was zealous for souls, he encouraged his brethren most insistently to be the same.[7]

> *Testimony of Brother Buonviso (9 August 1233):* The witness said that when he was a novice and had no skill in preaching, because he had not yet studied

5 Cited in Ibid., 9.

6 The earliest use of this expression in reference to the praxis of St. Dominic seems to come from "The Canonization Process of St. Dominic" (1233). [In Simon Tugwell, ed., *Early Dominicans: Selected Writings* (New York: Paulist, 1982), 66–85.] There are several instances like Brother Ventura of Verona's testimony (6 August 1233): ". . . on a journey or wherever he was, (Dominic) wanted to be always preaching or talking or arguing about God, either in person or through his companions" (66).

7 "The Canonization Process of St. Dominic," 71.

> scripture, the holy father told him to go to Piacenza to preach. He excused himself, but he spoke so charmingly that he induced him to go, saying that the Lord would be with him and would put words in his mouth. God did in fact give him such grace in his preaching that many people were converted and three entered the Order.8
>
> *Testimony of Brother John of Spain (10 August 1233)*:
> He [Dominic] was zealous for souls and used to send his brethren out to preach, bidding them look to the salvation of others. He had such confidence in God's goodness that he even sent unlearned men out to preach, saying to them, 'Do not be afraid; the Lord will be with you and will put power in your mouths.' And it turned out as he said.[9]
>
> *Testimony of Brother Rudolph of Faenza (11 August 1233)*:
> I never saw a man whose service of God pleased me more than did that of blessed Dominic. He longed for the salvation of all men, including Christians and Saracens, and especially the Cumans, to whom he wanted to go.[10]

St. Dominic's one desire for his Order was that it be useful to the salvation of souls. This theme is sounded over and over again in the earliest documents of the Order. And, it has acted as a perennial challenge throughout the Dominican Order's history. The "Fundamental Constitution" of the Friar Preachers puts it this way:

> . . . the Order of Friars Preachers founded by St. Dominic "is known from the beginning to have been instituted especially for preaching and the salvation of souls." Our brethren, therefore, according to the command of the founder "must conduct themselves honorably and religiously as men who want to obtain their

8 Ibid., 73.
9 Ibid., 73–74.
10 Ibid., 77.

salvation and the salvation of others, following in the footsteps of the Savior as evangelical men speaking among themselves or their neighbors either with God or about God."[11]

The history of the Order of Preachers has been told admirably well in a number of places.[12] What is most important for our present narrative is a discussion of the reestablishment of the Order in France in the mid-nineteenth century.

Henri Lacordaire and the Reestablishment of the Order of France

The French Revolution and its aftermath wreaked havoc on most of the traditional structures of Western European civilization. A significant target for revolutionary zeal was the Church and her religious orders. By 1815, the year that marks the end of France's hegemony in Europe, the Dominican Order was but a shadow of its former self.[13] The radically enfeebled state of the Order of Preachers led John Henry Newman in 1846 to ask "Whether it is not a great

11 "Fundamental Constitution of the Order of Friars Preachers," in *Book of Constitutions and Ordinations of the Order of Friars Preachers* (Rome: General Curia of the Order of Friars Preachers, 1984), 3. The two quotations in this passage are taken from the primitive constitutions of the Order.

12 The best history of the Order of Preachers (from its foundation to 1500) in English remains William A. Hinnebusch, *The History of the Order of Preachers*, 2 vols. (Staten Island, N.Y.: Alba House, 1966 and 1973). See also Benedict M. Ashley, *The Dominicans* (Collegeville, Minn.: Liturgical Press, 1990) and Mary Jean Dorcy, *Saint Dominic's Family: Lives and Legends* (Dubuque, Ia.: Priory Press, 1964).

13 At the outbreak of the French Revolution, the Order had "52 provinces, many congregations and monasteries, and about 20,000 members." (Hinnebusch, *The Dominicans*, 151.) By 1844, there were only 4562 Dominican friars in the entire world. (See: Hubert Jedin and John Dolan, eds., *History of the Church*, vol. 8, *The Church in the Age of Liberalism*, by Roger Aubert, et al., trans. Peter Becker (New York: Crossroad, 1981), 11, n. 15.

idea extinct?"[14] There were only a few priories in Spain, Portugal, the Russian Empire, and Italy, a handful of English friars in exile in Belgium, and a fledgling foundation in the boondocks of Kentucky.

Hinnebusch calls this Kentucky foundation under the leadership of Edward Dominic Fenwick, O.P. (the first American-born Dominican friar) the first event in the nineteenth century that "gave the Order hope for a better future."[15] The second such event was "the reception of the habit by Henri Lacordaire, the noted preacher of Notre Dame."[16] Lacordaire, writes Hinnebusch,

> . . . enjoyed a European reputation as a fearless and independent thinker, a powerful preacher, and a prominent ecclesiastic. After completing his novitiate at Viterbo, he returned to France in 1840 and was soon joined by other Frenchmen, also newly professed in Italy. Determined to restore the Order to France, Lacordaire resumed his preaching at Notre Dame, attracting many vocations. He opened a novitiate and several priories before the 1840s ended and was appointed first provincial when France again became a province on September 15, 1850.[17]

Under Lacordaire's guidance and by dint of his perseverance, the Order of Preachers was reestablished in France; this foundation would be instrumental in the intellectual and spiritual renaissance that the Order knew in the last part of the nineteenth century. A period of great expansion ensued – one that eventuated, in France, in the creation of two other provinces with the full panoply of required structures: novitiates, *studia*, priories, provincialates.

Lacordaire, much like St. Dominic, envisioned a profound *engagement* between God's Word and the needs of

14 Cited by Hinnebusch, *The Dominicans*, 155.
15 Ibid., 154.
16 Ibid., 155.
17 Ibid.

the men and women of his time. He was convinced that the ills of nineteenth-century France could be traced to un-Christian philosophies which had usurped the Truth. The best way for the Dominican friar to respond to this situation was to bring the Word of God to birth in his own life and in the lives of others.

In his essay, "Profile of Father Lacordaire," Yves Congar notes that Lacordaire, who can rightly be called the second founder of the Order of Preachers, was also one of the great restorers of the priesthood in nineteenth-century France.[18] In this, one should keep in mind that in the early days of the nineteenth century

> Catholicism in France was laughed at. . . . Priests were discredited and despised. Under the Empire they had been made servants of the State; during the Restoration they became badly compromised with a government that aimed at imposing religious behavior by legal edicts. . . . [Later] a pitiful popularity was granted them, not as priests, but as good fellows, socially useful, preservers of the peace of village life.[19]

After Lacordaire, writes Congar,

> A priest no longer appeared as a man engaged in a curious, inoffensive and somewhat futile occupation . . . but as a minister of a word, of a demand, a promise and a hope which God utters for the world.[20]

The history of the Dominican Order from 1789 through the mid-nineteenth century was "one of almost continuous crisis."[21] But by the time of the death of Vincent Jandel, O.P., Master of the Order, in 1872, "the Order had faced the worst series of crises in its history and come dangerously close to extinction, but had survived and was looking hope-

18 Yves Congar, "Profile of Father Lacordaire," *Faith and Spiritual Life* (New York: Herder and Herder, 1968), 98.

19 Ibid., 98.

20 Ibid., 98–99.

21 Hinnebusch, *The Dominicans*, 162.

fully into the future."[22] The charismatic gifts of Henri Lacordaire and his zeal for the Order's traditional ministries of preaching and teaching helped immensely in assuring the Order's future.

When Gontran Garrigou-Lagrange entered the Order of Preachers, Lacordaire, who had died in 1861, was still a part of the living memory of the older friars. His vision of providing support to the Church through well-reasoned preaching was not a pious platitude from the distant past: it was a lived reality. The Order had undergone an amazing growth: it would have been difficult for the young Garrigou and his confreres to imagine the days when it had all but faced extinction.

Leo XIII and the revival of Thomism

Apart from the charismatic inspiration of Henri Lacordaire, the other historical factor that accounted for a nineteenth-century Dominican renaissance was Pope Leo XIII's clarion call for the Church's reappropriation of the philosophy and theology of St. Thomas Aquinas. Since St. Thomas had been a Dominican friar, and since the light of the Order's Thomistic tradition of philosophy and theology had not been completely extinguished, the Order gained a new prestige with Leo's call for a revival. Rather than being viewed as an exotic holdover from the Middle Ages, the Order of Preachers found itself in the vanguard of a "new" movement in the Church. This aspect of *nova et vetera* attracted many recruits to the Order's ranks. Lacordaire's vision received a wonderfully gratuitous approbation.

Leo XIII believed that reviving the doctrine of St. Thomas would reinvigorate the intellectual life of the Church. As Gerald McCool remarks, "Leo was convinced that, once it had been revived, the wisdom of St. Thomas could provide nineteenth-century Catholics with the

22 Ibid., 163.

philosophical resources needed to integrate modern science and culture into a coherent whole under the light of their Christian faith."[23] Catholic theology had reached a nadir in the early decades of the nineteenth century. The structures of the Church's intellectual life had been decimated by the revolutions of 1789, 1830, and 1848. What is more, the work that had been done in dialogue with the emerging philosophies did not bode well for a new theological synthesis.[24]

Leo issued *Aeterni Patris* on the feast of St. Dominic, 4 August 1879.[25] Writing to the bishops of the Church, Leo said:

> While, therefore, we hold that every word of wisdom, every useful thing by whomsoever discovered or planned, ought to be received with a willing and grateful mind, we exhort you, venerable brethren, in all earnestness to restore the golden wisdom of St. Thomas, and to spread it far and wide for the defense and beauty of the Catholic faith, for the good of society, and for the advantage of all the sciences. . . . Let carefully selected teachers endeavor to implant the doctrine of Thomas Aquinas in the minds of students, and set forth clearly his solidity and excellence over others. Let the academies already founded or to be founded by you illustrate and defend this doctrine, and use it for the refutation of prevailing errors. But, lest the false for the true, or the corrupt for the pure be drunk in, be watchful that the doctrine of Thomas be drawn from his own fountains, or at least from

23 Gerald McCool, *The Neo-Thomists* (Milwaukee: Marquette University Press, 1994), 1.

24 See, for instance, Alec R. Vidler, *The Church in an Age of Revolution: 1789 to the Present Day* (New York: Penguin Books, 1990), especially chapter 2, "Theological Reconstruction in Germany," and chapter 6, "Liberal Catholicism and Ultramontanism in France." See also: Aidan Nichols, *Catholic Thought since the Enlightenment: A Survey* (Pretoria: University of South Africa Press, 1998).

25 The liturgical renewal following the Second Vatican Council transferred the feast of St. Dominic to August 8.

> those rivulets which, derived from the very fount, have thus far flowed, according to the established agreement of learned men, pure and clear; be careful to guard the minds of youth from those which are said to flow thence, but in reality are gathered from strange and unwholesome streams.[26]

One would be hard-pressed to find a clearer statement on the priority of St. Thomas. Moreover, it is remarkable that the Pope chose to single-out a particular school of thought within Thomism – the school of interpretation that is in historical continuity with St. Thomas himself. Who but the Dominicans could claim to possess such continuity?

Leo added that St. Thomas's pride of place comes from the fact that "he most venerated the ancient doctors of the Church, [and] in a certain way seems to have inherited the intellect of all."[27] Leo continues:

> The doctrines of those illustrious men, like the scattered members of a body, Thomas collected together and cemented, distributed in wonderful order, and so increased with important additions that he is rightly esteemed the special bulwark and glory of Catholic faith.[28]

The importance of Leo XIII's Thomistic revival for the shape of Catholic theology up to the Second Vatican Council and for the fortunes of individual theologians cannot be overemphasized. In this regard, Leo was most intent, says Gerald McCool, on preserving the distinction between philosophy and theology – between reason and faith – a distinction that was often blurred in modern philosophy. "By preserving that distinction, scholastic philosophy could mount strong philosophical arguments for the

26 Leo XIII, *Aeterni Patris* (New York: Daughters of St. Paul, n.d.), p. 21.

27 Ibid., p. 14. The Pope is citing Cardinal Cajetan.

28 Ibid.

credibility of revelation without compromising the transcendence of Christianity's revealed mysteries."[29]

There were two great enemies of the distinction that Leo wished to preserve: Immanuel Kant (1724–1804) and Friedrich Schleiermacher (1768–1834).[30] For both of these thinkers, "speculative reason could have no knowledge either of God or of the extramental world of 'things in themselves.'"[31] Philosophical demonstrations of the existence of God or revealed truths guaranteed by the Gospels' account of miracles were judged untrustworthy and taken to be irresponsible foundations for one's act of faith. "The religious sentiment of a wholly immanent human consciousness then became the sole source of faith and the only norm of Christian revelation."[32] For those influenced by Kant and Schleiermacher, the concept of historical revelation could be summarily dismissed. The human person's interior life of consciousness and its intellectual and moral development does not call for knowledge of such external facts. "Even if Christ had lived, and if the alleged witnesses of Revelation had told the truth, these were just external facts of history. They were no different from thousands of other singular facts which ancient historians could verify."[33] As we shall see, these are ideas that Garrigou would spend his Dominican life countering.

Neo-Thomism

Gerald McCool identifies Leo XIII's publication of *Aeterni Patris* as the beginning of the "Third Scholasticism" – the

29 McCool, *The Neo-Thomists*, 34.

30 Vidler remarks that Schleiermacher's work "came to bear the same relation to subsequent liberal Protestant theology as the *Summa* of St. Thomas does to Thomism or as Calvin's *Institutes* do to Reformed theology." See: "Theological Reconstruction in Germany," *The Church in an Age of Revolution*, 26.

31 McCool, *The Neo-Thomists*, 46.

32 Ibid.

33 Ibid.

third historical moment of the appropriation of the teaching of the medieval schoolmen and in particular of the doctrine of St. Thomas Aquinas. The First Scholasticism was contemporaneous with the Angelic Doctor and St. Bonaventure and the other medievals. It was dealt a mortal blow by William of Ockham and his nominalism. The Second Scholasticism was born in the sixteenth century in response both to the Protestant Revolt and the discovery of the New World. The documents of the Council of Trent and the works associated with the Dominicans at Salamanca are the high points of the Second Scholasticism. Its demise was assured by the French Revolution, Napoleon's wars, and the radical decline of Catholic institutions of higher learning. The Third Scholasticism lasted up to the Second Vatican Council and was responsible for the school of thought known as Neo-Thomism. Réginald Garrigou-Lagrange, as we have noted, was the epitome of the Neo-Thomist project.[34]

Brian Davies says that "Neo-Thomists are writers who stand within a tradition of thinking traceable for various reasons to that of Aquinas."[35] For the Dominican Neo-Thomists of the twentieth century, the commentaries on the works of St. Thomas by men like John of St. Thomas, Bañez, and Cardinal Cajetan were taken with the utmost seriousness: they were significant monuments in the *tradition vivante*. All in all, it is safe to say that in Garrigou's day being a Dominican and certainly being a Dominican theologian meant that one was a follower – in one way or another – of St. Thomas.[36]

34 It bears highlighting that Gerald McCool identifies no less than five distinct periods of neo-scholasticism in the twentieth century. See his "Twentieth-Century Scholasticism," *The Journal of Religion* (supplement) 58 (1978): 198 ff.; see the discussion of this in Thomas F. O'Meara, *Thomas Aquinas Theologian* (Notre Dame, Ind.: University of Notre Dame Press, 1997), 174 ff.

35 Brian Davies, preface to McCool, *The Neo-Thomists*, v.

36 From the end of the thirteenth century the Constitutions of the Dominican Order had mandated the study of St. Thomas for the

In a later chapter we will discuss the particulars of the Thomism of Garrigou-Lagrange. Now, we will focus our attention on Garrigou's article on the character and the principles of Dominican spirituality. We will see that he masterfully synthesized two fundamental foci of the Order: the evangelical impulse of St. Dominic and the intellectual achievement of St. Thomas.

Dominican Spirituality

The first thing that strikes one about Dominican spirituality, says Garrigou, is the multiplicity of elements that comprise it. Prayer, ministry, study, and community life are the four pillars of Dominican life. At first glance the various principles that undergird these pillars do not seem to be easily reconciled. This sense is most pronounced when one recognizes that the Dominican is called to be a contemplative-in-action: "While certain Orders are dedicated exclusively to the contemplative life and others to the active life, Dominican spirituality desires to unite these two."[37]

In this regard, it would seem that contemplation, which is of the mystical order and presupposes silence and solitude, would be impeded by a life of study and active ministry. Concurrently, it would appear that one's apostolic endeavors would be somewhat half-hearted if one is forever seeking quiet and explicit times for prayer. Garrigou

friars. The present *Book of Constitutions and Ordinations of the Order of Friars Preachers* has this to say: "The best teacher and model in fulfilling this duty (i.e., of assiduous study) is St. Thomas, whose teaching the Church commends in a unique way and the Order receives as a patrimony which exercises an enriching influence on the intellectual life of the brethren and confers on the Order a special character. Consequently, the brethren should develop a genuine familiarity with his writings and thought, and, according to the needs of the time and with legitimate freedom, they should renew and enrich his teaching with the continually fresh riches of sacred and human wisdom." [III, a. I, n. 84]

37 Réginald Garrigou-Lagrange, "Le caractère et les principes de la spiritualité dominicaine," *VS* 4 (1921): 367.

asks, "How can these elements so opposed in appearance be reconciled in one and the same ideal? What is the dominant character which unites them?"[38]

Garrigou begins his answer by recalling the most elemental principle of St. Thomas's theology of grace: "grace does not destroy nature but perfects it."[39] God's grace elevates human nature, making it to be what God intended it to be. In deference to this basic theological understanding, Dominican spirituality "does not suppress anything that can truly lead to one's perfect sanctification and to that of one's neighbor."[40] Therefore it "does not hesitate to affirm principles which appear to be contrary, as long as each one for its part appears to be absolutely certain."[41]

This spirit of openness in Dominican spirituality comes from its dedication to truth. The ultimate object of Dominican "apostolic contemplation"[42] is "*Veritas*: the divine truth and the universal irradiation of the Light of life."[43] Garrigou reminds his readers that the motto of the Order of Preachers is *contemplari et contemplata aliis tradere*: contemplate and to give to others the fruit of one's contemplation.[44]

The contemplation undertaken by the Dominican is not ultimately an end in itself. It is directed toward being of service to one's neighbor. Dominican contemplation finds its perfection in the preaching of the Gospel and an impor-

38 Ibid.

39 Ibid., 365. [*La grâce ne détruit pas la nature mais la perfectionne.*]

40 Ibid., 368. [*(la spiritualité dominicaine) s'attache à ne rien supprimer de ce qui peut vraiment concourir à notre parfaite sanctification et à celle du prochain.*]

41 Ibid. [*Elle n'hésite pas à affirmer des principes en apparence contraires, pourvu que chacun pris à part paraisse absolument certain.*]

42 Ibid.

43 Ibid. [*Veritas*: *la Vérité divine et l'irradiation universelle de la lumière de la vie.*"]

44 Ibid. Rather than literally translating the Latin, Garrigou offers the following gloss: . . . *contempler et livrer aux autres sa contemplation pour les sauver.*

tant part of this preaching is done through the Order's intellectual apostolate. Garrigou provides the following distinction:

> Contemplation is not ordered to apostolic activity as a means is subordinated to an end . . . ; but it produces it as an eminent and superabundant cause. The culminating point of the life of an apostle is the hour of union with God in prayer. From this divine union he must descend toward others, his soul filled with charity and the light of life, in order to speak to them of God and to turn them toward God.[45]

Garrigou grounds his conception directly on the example of St. Dominic. The Order's founder was "a great contemplative who used to spend habitually his nights in prayer, giving himself over to a heroic penitence, and who preached during the day, 'knowing only how to speak to God or about God.'"[46] To give added weight to his argument, Garrigou quotes from St. Catherine of Siena's *Dialogue*. In the following passage, God the Father speaks to Catherine concerning St. Dominic:

> Your father Dominic, my beloved son, desired that his brothers not have any other thought except my honor and the salvation of souls, by the light of learning. It is this light that he wanted to make the object of his Order . . . in order to root out the errors of his time. His

45 Garrigou-Lagrange, "Le caractère . . . ," 382–83. [*Le contemplation n'est pas ordonné à l'action apostolique, comme un moyen subordonné à une fin . . . ; mais elle la produit comme une cause éminente et surabondante. Le point culminant de la vie de l'apôtre, c'est l'heure d'union à Dieu dans l'oraison. De cette union divine il doit descendre vers les hommes, l'âme pleine de charité et de lumière de vie, pour leur parler de Dieu et les tourner vers Lui.*] One notes that St. Thomas held that a religious order that includes both contemplation and apostolic activity is more excellent than one that is focused on one or the other. See: *Summa theologiae*, IIa-IIae, q. 188, a. 6.

46 Ibid., 369. [*. . . ce grand contemplatif qui passait habituellement ses nuits en prière, en se livrant à une pénitence héroïque, et qui prêchait le jour, "ne sachant parler qu'à Dieu ou de Dieu."*]

> charge was that of the Word, my only Son. . . . He was himself a light that I gave to the world through Mary. . . .[47]

Garrigou comments that "to those souls who thirst especially for Truth, God proposes as a guide St. Dominic and the great lights of his Order: immutable Truth, infinitely superior to the fluctuations of opinion; Truth superior also to liberty which it regulates, that it preserves from error and crime."[48]

Garrigou emphasizes three principles that animate Dominican spirituality. First, this spirituality "counsels the full development of human nature under grace, but without the least bit of naturalism, because it considers this development from the point of view of wisdom, in its first cause and its final end, and sees in it an accomplishment of grace."[49]

Second, once it has been shown "that which the most gifted and inspired of human natures can do, Dominican spirituality adds that all of that is absolutely nothing in comparison with the supernatural life, the infinite elevation of which stands out all the more."[50] At the same time,

47 See: Ibid., 370. The translation of St. Catherine's *Dialogue* ("Treatise on Obedience," chapter 5) used here is that of Suzanne Noffke (New York: Paulist, 1980).

48 Ibid., 370–71. [*Aux âmes qui surtout ont soif de Vérité, Dieu propose comme guide saint Dominique et les grandes lumières de son Ordre: Vérité immuable, infiniment supérieure aux fluctuations de l'opinion; Vérité supérieure aussi à la liberté qu'elle règle, qu'elle preserve de l'égarement et du crime.*]

49 Ibid., 372–73. [. . . *cette spiritualité conseille le plein développement de la nature sous la grâce, mais sans le moindre naturalisme, car elle considère ce développement du point de vue de la sagesse, dans sa cause première et sa fin dernière, et voit en lui un fruit de la grâce.*]

50 Ibid., 373. [. . . *ce que peut la nature la mieux douée et la plus géniale, elle ajoute que tout cela n'est absolument rien en comparaison de la vie surnaturelle, dont l'élévation infinie ressort par là bien davantage.*]

Dominican spirituality allows one to see "the sublime harmony of these two orders infinitely distant one from the other."[51]

Finally, from this "higher" point of view, Dominican spirituality "insists upon the efficaciousness of grace and the passivity of the creature; consequently, it considers the mystical life as the normal crowning of asceticism and it wishes that apostolic action be derived from the fullness of contemplation."[52]

Garrigou sees in these three principles the fundaments of Dominican life and practice. They were part and parcel of St. Dominic's "grace of founding," yet would not be clearly articulated until St. Thomas and St. Catherine of Siena. One notes how central God's grace is in this schema. Grace perfects human nature; grace elevates the human to the supernatural; grace is efficacious and leads to mystical union with the Godhead. Two passages from the Pauline epistles are utterly programmatic for Garrigou: Philippians 2: 13 [". . . for it is God who is at work in you, enabling you both to will and to work for his good pleasure."] and 1 Corinthians 4: 7 ["What do you have that you have not received?"][53]

Garrigou concludes his article with the following word of encouragement:

> This contemplative and apostolic life is not impossible: the saints and the blesseds of the Order of St. Dominic and many other religious families have lived it. By the

51 Ibid. [. . . *l'harmonie sublime de ces deux ordres infiniment distants l'un de l'autre.*]

52 Ibid. [. . . *elle insiste sur l'efficacité de la grâce, sur la passivité de la créature; elle considère par suite la vie mystique, comme le couronnement normal de l'ascèse et veut que l'action apostolique dérive de la plénitude de la contemplation.*]

53 Ibid., 378. [*C'est Dieu qui opère en nous le vouloir et le faire, selon son bon plaisir (Phil. 2: 13); Qu'as-tu que tu ne l'aies reçu? (1 Cor. 4: 7).*] [English translation from the *New Revised Standard Version* (1989).]

power of divine grace we can and must live it. Let the Patriarch of Preachers obtain for us this grace; let us ask him for it with this prayer which characterizes so well the mission that he received and which he protects: O Light of the Church, Doctor of truth, rose of patience, ivory of chastity, freely you poured forth the waters of wisdom: Preacher of grace, unite us to the blessed."[54]

Friar Réginald

Réginald Garrigou-Lagrange professed his vows in the Order of Preachers in 1900. He lived the life of a Dominican friar for 64 years – striving to incarnate in his own life the ideals proposed by the example of the saints of the Order. Let us now examine the testimony of his Dominican brothers concerning his living of Dominican life.

Shortly after Garrigou's death, his confrere M.-Benoît Lavaud, professor of moral theology at the University of Fribourg, published an article in the *Revue thomiste* in his memory.[55] What is perhaps most striking in Lavaud's presentation is the fundamental austerity of Garrigou's life and his constant striving after Christian perfection. Garrigou found that the study of theology and a life devoted to teaching and scholarship demanded of him a rigorous discipline, a single-minded devotion.

Garrigou was an exemplary religious. His superiors

54 Ibid., 384. [*Cette vie contemplative et apostolique n'est pas impossible, les saints et les bienheureux de l'Ordre de Saint-Dominique et de plusieurs autres familles religieuses l'ont vécue. Par la force de la grâce divine nous pouvons et devons la vivre. Daigne le Patriarche des Prêcheurs nous obtenir cette grâce; demandons-la-lui par cette prière qui caractérise si bien la mission qu'il a reçue et qu'il conserve*: O lumen Ecclesiae, doctor veritatis, rosa patientiae, ebur castitatis, aquam sapientiae propinasti gratis: Praedictor gratiae, nos junge beatis.]

55 M.-Benoît Lavaud, "Le Père Garrigou-Lagrange: *In Memoriam*," *Revue thomiste* 64 (1964): 181–99.

never had reason to question his obedience and always appreciated his unwavering embrace of the regular life: his presence in choir at the appointed hours for common prayer and his presence at all the other communal exercises were constants in his living Dominican life. Lavaud lists the following characteristics that marked the religious life of Garrigou-Lagrange: He never accepted an invitation to eat in a restaurant if he was in a city that had a Dominican priory. He did not take advantage of the dispensations that the Dominican constitutions allowed for lectors in theology. He recited the Rosary every day, and in his later years, with his eyesight failing, it became his constant prayer. He was of an extreme sobriety and reserve as regards food and drink: he took only a small breakfast and he never ate between meals. He never smoked, viewing the use of tobacco as incompatible with religious poverty.[56] Except for the many books on his shelves, Garrigou's cell at the Angelicum was the most Spartan. It lacked all ornamentation whatsoever; his bed was nothing but a "pallet and the mattress was so thin that it was practically an empty sack."[57]

The following anecdote emphasizes the austerity that marked Garrigou's life:

> One year, not without great need, we put running water in the cells [i.e., at the Angelicum]; in others the walls and the ceilings were painted, nothing that was too much. He asked that nothing be touched in his room: "May they wait until my departure or my death." As it turned out, they did not renovate his cell until he left for the clinic and from which he was never able to return.[58]

56 Ibid. Lavaud remarks: *Il pratiqua toujours une très stricte pauvreté et l'usage du tabac lui paraissait peu compatible avec la pauvreté religieuse.*

57 Ibid., 196. [. . . *un grabat et le matelas si peu épais que c'était presque un sac vide.*]

58 Ibid., 195. [*Une année, ce n'était pas sans besoin, on mit l'eau courante dans les cellules; une autre, on repeignit les murs et le plafond, ce qui n'était pas de trop non plus. Il demanda en grâce*

One might be tempted to think that Garrigou, living an austere religious life in the heart of Rome and involved in such a prolific theological project, would be rather removed from the concerns of the "real" world. However, his "other-worldliness" did not keep him from carrying out a direct, hands-on ministry to the poor of the city of Rome. It was not unusual for him to meet the downtrodden in one of the parlors in the priory at the Angelicum. His Dominican brothers would often "see him shaken by the troubles which were shared with him in confidence in the parlor."[59] In his room there was a box with the inscription, *Pour mes pauvres* (i.e., "For my poor"). Garrigou would seek donations from those who visited him and then make the rounds of the city giving alms to the poor.[60] "He had a rare degree of understanding and a constant concern for the poor."[61]

On top of this, Garrigou was a much-sought-after spiritual director. His reputation at the Angelicum and his many writings on spirituality meant that he had a large clientele throughout the years of his priestly ministry. He was, says Rosaire Gagnebet, "always compassionate to the trials of souls."[62]

In the next section, we will focus our attention on a most significant aspect of Garrigou's formation as a Dominican theologian: the *disputatio*. This formation accounts for any

qu'on ne touchât rien chez lui: 'Qu'on attende mon départ ou ma mort.' De fait, on ne rafraîchit sa cellule que lorsqu'il fut parti pour la clinique et qu'il ne devait plus rentrer.]

59 Ibid., 196. [. . . *le voyait bouleversé par les détresses dont il recevait la confiance au parloir*.]

60 See: Gagnebet, "L'œuvre du P. Garrigou-Lagrange," 30: *Pour subvenir à leurs nécessités le P. Garrigou se faisait quémandeur près de tous, mêmes des ministres, des rois, des Présidents de la République et des Papes eux-mêmes.*

61 Lavaud, "Le Père Garrigou-Lagrange," 196. [*Il avait à un rare degré l'intelligence et le souci constant des pauvres.*]

62 Gagnebet, "L'œuvre du P. Garrigou-Lagrange," 30. [. . . *toujours compatissant aux épreuves des âmes*.]

number of misunderstandings concerning the intentionality that underlies the work of Réginald Garrigou-Lagrange.

Disputatio

Study is an essential element of Dominican spirituality. From the very beginning, St. Dominic had recognized that the intellectual preparation of his friars was supremely critical if his Order was to be indeed 'an Order of Preachers.' An ignorant preacher is nothing but "a noisy gong, a clanging cymbal" (1 Cor. 13: 1). And so St. Dominic sent his brethren to the universities of Europe to engage the Gospel with secular learning and the issues of urban life.

In 1995, Timothy Radcliffe, eighty-sixth Master of the Order of Preachers (1992–2001), addressed a letter to the entire Order entitled "The Wellspring of Hope: Study and the Annunciation of the Good News."[63] Fr. Radcliffe explained his rationale in the following manner:

> The conviction which I explore in this letter to the Order is that a life of study is one of the ways in which we may grow in the love which "bears all things, believes all things, hopes all things, endures all things." (1Cor. 13: 7).[64]

Study, essentially an act of hope, expresses "our confidence that there is meaning to our lives and the sufferings of our people."[65]

Fr. Radcliffe was aware of how odd an emphasis on study may be for many of his contemporaries. He opines:

> In part it is because we are marked by a culture which has lost confidence that study is a worthwhile activity and which doubts that debate can bring us to the truth for which we long. If our century has been so marked

63 Timothy Radcliffe, "The Wellspring of Hope: Study and the Annunciation of the Good News," *Sing a New Song: The Christian Vocation* (Springfield, Ill.: Templegate, 1999): 54–81.

64 Ibid., 54.

65 Ibid., 55.

> by violence it is surely partly because it has lost confidence in our ability to attain the truth together.[66]

The Master of the Order, as one might expect, was quick to single out for attention the example of St. Thomas. It is clear that St. Thomas "was the man of questions, who learnt to take every question seriously, however foolish it might appear."[67] St. Thomas's entire theological project was predicated upon seeking out as many questions as possible and wrestling with the disparate answers given to them down through the ages. This led him to become the master of the fine distinction.

St. Thomas's respect for the questions and reverence for the truth highlights a fundamental claim of Dominican spirituality – a claim that has a rather audacious ring to it: "when we argue and reason we honor our Creator and Redeemer who gave us minds with which to think and draw near to him."[68] So firmly does Fr. Radcliffe hold to this principle that he could say to the Synod of Bishops gathered in 1994 to discuss religious life: "Debates and arguments are the signs of a Church which is always being renewed by the Spirit. A perfect unanimity would be a sign of the immobility of death."[69]

The importance of this struggle to understand cannot be overstated. Speaking to his brothers and sisters in the Order, Fr. Radcliffe warned:

> We can never build community unless we dare to argue with each other. I must stress, as so often, the importance of debate, argument, the struggle to understand.[70]

66 Ibid., 60.

67 Ibid., 61.

68 Ibid., 61.

69 Timothy Radcliffe, "Dialogue and Communion," address to the Episcopal Synod on Religious Life, Rome, November 1994, in *Sing a New Song*, 249.

70 Radcliffe, "The Wellspring of Hope," 71.

This theme of the relationship between argument and community is at the heart of another of Fr. Radcliffe's letters, "Truth and Conflict: Rebuild Human Communities."[71] Here, he begins by focusing attention on George Steiner's *Real Presences: Is There Anything in What We Say?*[72] Steiner holds that it is the "break of the covenant between word and world which constitutes one of the few genuine revolutions of spirit in Western history and which defines modernity itself."[73] Radcliffe points out that the Dominican tradition is committed to an *adaequatio* between word and world; it is in opposition to the separation that appears as the very ethos of modernity. The Dominican tradition holds that study is "the cultivation of humanity's natural inclination to the truth;"[74] and with the eyes of faith it sees in the Incarnation of the Word the perfect expression of this *adaequatio*.

> This inclination to truth that we need to cultivate is not just a human desire to know many things, but a natural desire to reach out to those who are different, to break the tight hold of our egocentricity. It wakens us from the illusion that we are the centre of the world. Whether we are studying the ending of Mark's gospel or the sexual habits of a rare snail, our eyes are being opened to see what is other. Study is ecstatic.[75]

Garrigou-Lagrange was steeped in this Dominican way of viewing debate and argument and disagreement. For him they were not things to be scrupulously avoided; they were not vicious habits to be overcome. Rather, they were to be embraced as the only way to arrive at the truth. An

71 Timothy Radcliffe, "Truth and Conflict: Rebuild Human Communities," in *Sing a New Song*, 233–47.

72 (Chicago: University of Chicago Press, 1989).

73 George Steiner, *Real Presences* in Ibid., 235.

74 Radcliffe, "Truth and Conflict," 244, quoting from the Constitutions of the Friars of the Order of Preachers.

75 Ibid., 244.

intellectual struggle underlies every arrival at the truth: it is hard work; it is agonistic. A fulsome embrace of argument may alienate those not formed in this tradition; the non-Dominican might even interpret it as a form of belligerence. Nonetheless, following his master, St. Thomas, Garrigou embraced the *disputatio* in order to serve the truth.

M.-Dominique Chenu situates the *disputatio* in the progressive development of a scholastic methodology in the Middle Ages:

> The "style" of the Scholastics in its development as well as in its modes of expression can be reduced, as if to its simple elements, to three procedures. These followed progressively one upon the other and typify, moreover, both their historical genesis and their progress in technique. First came the *lectio* [reading]; from the reading was developed the *quaestio* [question], the *disputatio* [disputation]; and in *summas*, the "article," somewhat as the residue of the disputed question, became the literary component.[76]

Chenu explains that in the European universities

> Things so developed that apart from the *lectio* . . . special exercises were held during which one of the masters submitted, in the presence of the school body, some question of current interest to be discussed with his fellow masters. Objections were raised, points discussed, retorts flung back, with the debate finally come to an end with the master in charge giving his own conclusion or "determination" on the question. Picture the renewal in liveliness in sessions of this sort and what they did for competition in research! They produced the "disputed question."[77]

76 M.-Dominique Chenu, *Toward Understanding St. Thomas*, trans. A.-M. Landry and D. Hughes (Chicago: Henry Regnery, 1964), 80.

77 Ibid., 89. Chenu notes that before the thirteenth century there had been plenty of theological 'disputes' between masters of theology. However, in the earlier period they "were not yet part of an academic order of things set up in an organized university and with a definite apparatus and regularity" (89, n. 18).

It bears noting that St. Thomas, during his tenure at the University of Paris, led a disputation at least once a month.[78] Some 63 of these disputations are extant, having been redacted after the fact. Chenu comments:

> The redaction of these elaborations, however objective and serene it may be in general, has preserved for us, in the objections and answers copiously enveloping the master's determination, those elements that were placed in opposition to one another in those dialogues. To treat such texts as if they were the results of classroom exercises would be to render them stale.[79]

Jean-Pierre Torrell offers us the following description of a day of teaching for St. Thomas at the University of Paris and in what that day would ultimately culminate:

> In the first hour of the day, Thomas gave his lecture; after that came the lecture of his bachelor; in the afternoon, both gathered with their students to "dispute" on a chosen theme. The three hours of this active pedagogy not being sufficient to exhaust the subject, they continued, article after article; eventually certain articles that were very short could be regrouped into a single session and, conversely, a longer or more delicate subject could be broken down into several sessions. The result (objections, responses, and magisterial determinations) was gathered together later into a final version, with a view to publication within the ultimate unity of the question.[80]

Argumentation, disputation, and active discussion of controversial positions formed the backbone of scholastic

78 Ibid., 281.

79 Ibid., 284. Jean-Pierre Torrell reminds us that we ought to distinguish "between the dispute itself and its conversion into writing; the latter, not being subject to the time limits of the actual discussion, could become the object of a more extensive elaboration and of a fullness of development that the oral exchange never permitted." [*Saint Thomas Aquinas*, vol. 1, "The Person and His Work," trans. Robert Royal (Washington, D.C.: Catholic University of America Press, 1996), 61.]

80 Torrell, *Saint Thomas Aquinas*, 62.

life in the Middle Ages. These fundamental activities of the intellectual life were preserved – with varying degrees of success – in the *studia* of the Dominican Order.[81]

Garrigou-Lagrange lived and breathed and gloried in this ethos. One might even be tempted to say that he was an embodiment of it. He strove for insight; he worked hard at clarity of expression. He was not afraid to dispute the facts and to argue about varying approximations of the truth. Indeed, there is a *disputatio* of one kind or another at the heart of every one of his books – whether it be with the critics of St. Thomas's "Five Ways" in *Dieu: son existence et sa nature* or with Edouard Le Roy's Bergsonian conception of dogma in *Le sens commun* or with both the Quietists and Jesuits in *La Providence et la confiance en Dieu*.[82] In all of this, as a Dominican friar it was the truth – the truth of Jesus Christ – the Way, the Truth and the Life – that Garrigou desired to serve. He recognized no other loyalty.

It is easy to take potshots at such a figure: the charge of "fanaticism" or "mean-spiritedness" might readily come to mind. It may be a tempting to direct our sympathy toward those who lost the *disputatio* and to view them as having been victimized by Garrigou-Lagrange. However, a Dominican perspective counsels that such a temptation

81 This is not to imply that this was the only *locus* for their preservation. "Scholastic disputations" were features of seminary life throughout the Catholic world. For instance, Pope Pius XI, in his encyclical on St. Thomas Aquinas, *Studiorum ducem* (1923), mandated the following: "In addition, a disputation shall be held in seminaries and other institutions for the education of priests on some point of philosophy or other important branch of learning in honor of the Angelic Doctor. And that the festival of St. Thomas may be kept in the future in a manner worthy of the patron of all Catholic schools, We order it to be kept as a holiday and celebrated not only with a High Mass, but also, at any rate in seminaries and among religious communities, by the holding of a disputation as aforesaid" (n. 33).

82 There is some truth in the oft-repeated line that Garrigou's favorite sparring partners were dead philosophers and live Jesuits!

ought to be resisted. Arguments and disagreements are not intrinsic evils: they are necessary tools for more meaningful appropriations of the truth.

Those who knew Garrigou speak of his single-minded pursuit of the truth. He did not cultivate a personal *animus* against anyone. Nor did he practice character assassination or attempt to vilify his discussion partners. One looks in vain for an *ad hominem* argument in Garrigou's numerous publications.

None of this, however, was enough to keep people from attributing bad faith and malice to him. It appears that the majority of those with whom he disputed took his critiques personally. Let the example of Henri de Lubac suffice to illustrate this point.

As we will see in a later chapter, Garrigou had been disputing with the ideas of de Lubac and his Jesuit confreres Teilhard de Chardin, Henri Bouillard, Yves de Montcheuil, and Jean Daniélou since the beginning of the 1940s. De Lubac would eventually include a number of references to Garrigou-Lagrange in his memoir, *At the Service of the Church*.[83] Here are a few examples:

De Lubac says that "a violent campaign" was unleashed against Jean Daniélou's "Les orientations présentes de la pensée religieuse;"[84] Garrigou is mentioned in conjunction with this "violence."[85]

In a journal entry for 9 October 1946, de Lubac writes: "Father Garrigou is reportedly doing everything he can to disturb the conscience of the Pope in private conversations."[86]

De Lubac's journal entry for 3 January 1947 reports: "M. Augros, who is returning from Rome, saw Father

83 Henri de Lubac, *At the Service of the Church*, trans. Anne Elizabeth Englund (San Francisco: Ignatius, 1993). It was originally published as *Mémoire sur l'occasion de mes écrits* (Namur, Belgium: Culture et Vérité, 1989).

84 *Etudes* 249 (1946): 5–21.

85 De Lubac, *At the Service of the Church*, 242.

86 Ibid., 252.

Garrigou there, who was in a violent furor 'against Fourvière and especially against Father de Lubac.'"[87]

Shortly after this, de Lubac speaks of "a new attack" by Garrigou "against Father Bouillard."[88]

A final example follows this same train of thought. In a letter addressed to an assistant to the Jesuit Superior General (2 January 1947), de Lubac speaks of "attacks" by Garrigou "aimed at Father Bouillard, Father de Montcheuil and a teaching on original sin."[89] He alerts his superior to a "systematic offensive on the part of Father G.-L., who seeks to provoke scandal everywhere and who is succeeding to a certain degree."[90] He concludes by claiming that the Jesuits need to work "to stop the kind of dictatorship that Father G.-L. is trying to exercise in the Church."[91]

Garrigou-Lagrange was intent on supporting the teaching of the Church and remaining faithful to the Dominican school's interpretation of St. Thomas. On any number of occasions he believed that the positions of certain of his contemporaries were heterodox. In these matters, he adduced reasons and argued his case; to repeat: his arguments were not based on attacking the person who held the problematic positions. Indeed, most of the time, Garrigou had never even met his interlocutors. Of course, this is not to say that Garrigou was always right: he was not infallible. But this *is* to say that it is lamentable for de Lubac and others to move the discourse to the rhetoric of "violence," "attack," and "dictatorship" when it comes to what Garrigou actually had to say.

87 Ibid., 256. Fourvière was the Jesuit house of studies in the south of France.

88 Ibid., 265.

89 Ibid., 275. De Lubac does not have a name to correspond with the "teaching on original sin" but he notes parenthetically that he thinks that Garrigou is out to get Henri Rondet, S.J.

90 Ibid.

91 Ibid., 276.

This chapter's discussion of Garrigou's use of the *disputatio* has been limited to brief examples in the realm of theology. In the next chapter, it will be expanded with examples in philosophy. We will discuss the philosophical disputations that were of long-standing duration in Garrigou-Lagrange's career: his arguments with the philosophies of Henri Bergson and Maurice Blondel.

4. Garrigou-Lagrange: Disputing with Bergson and Blondel

> *For a soul consecrated to God it is a duty, an indispensable obligation, to nourish in itself zeal for the glory of God and the salvation of souls. Always it is a question, fundamentally, of the same zeal, of the flame of the one and same love.* Réginald Garrigou-Lagrange, *The Last Writings*

In the last chapter, we saw that the scholastic disputation provided Garrigou-Lagrange with a model and a method for arriving at the truth. Indeed, the disputation ought to be seen as the heuristic key for understanding Garrigou's fundamental style in philosophy and theology. In this chapter we will focus our attention on two of his favorite disputation partners – the philosophers Henri Bergson and Maurice Blondel – and their disciples in the world of theology. Garrigou's writings in Thomistic philosophy as well as his works in theology were most often directed against the positions of one or both of these thinkers. In light of this, we will begin by undertaking an introductory discussion of the thought of Bergson and Blondel. We will then move to outline the contours of Garrigou's disputes with their thought in light of the

Modernist crisis in early-twentieth-century Catholicism. In Chapter 6 we will reflect on Garrigou's own appropriation of Thomistic philosophy in a more systematic manner.

Henri Bergson (1859–1941)

The young Friar Réginald first encountered Henri Bergson while studying at the Sorbonne. Bergson had been lecturing at the prestigious Collège de France since before the turn of the century;[1] as part of his plan of studies, Garrigou attended Bergson's lectures.

Bergson, "the man who reintroduced the spiritual life in the world,"[2] is remembered for his five major works: *Données immédiates de la conscience* (his 1889 thesis), *L'idée de lieu chez Aristote* (his "secondary thesis"), *Matière et mémoire* (1896), *L'évolution créatrice* (1907), and *Les deux sources de la morale et de la religion* (1932).[3] These works assured Bergson the following honors: He was inducted into the *Académie des sciences morales et politiques* in 1901, he became a member of the *Académie française* in 1914, and he was awarded the Nobel Prize for literature in 1927.[4]

1 Leszek Kolakowski writes: "Bergson's lectures in the Collège de France were weekly social events attended by a good many of the Parisian elite. . . ." [*Bergson* (New York: Oxford University Press, 1985; South Bend, Ind.: St. Augustine's Press, 2001), 1.]

2 Charles Péguy, cited by André Devaux, "Bergson, Henri," *Dictionnaire des philosophes* (Paris: Presses Universitaires de France, 1984), page. [. . . *l'homme qui a réintroduit la vie spirituelle dans le monde*.]

3 Ibid. For the standard edition of Bergson's works, see: Henri Bergson, *Œuvres* (Paris: Presses Universitaires de France, 1970). The following English translations are readily available: *Creative Evolution*, trans. Arthur Mitchell (New York: Modern Library, 1944); *The Two Sources of Morality and Religion*, trans. R. Ashley Audra and Cloudesley Brereton (London: Macmillan, 1935); *Matter and Memory*, trans. Nancy Margaret Paul and W. Scott Palmer (New York: Macmillan, 1911).

4 Ibid.

Although Bergson's philosophical work defies easy categorization, the following discussion helps to characterize his thought:

> (F)or Bergson, reality was the vital thrust of the *élan vital* through the varied levels and forms of being. . . . Science and the positivism which had made science its model were not in touch with the vital process of reality. For reality could not be grasped through the abstract concepts of the discursive intelligence. Reality was reached through the intuition of the metaphysician, a form of knowledge more akin to instinct in some respects than to intelligence.[5]

Bergson's philosophy was an intuitionism allied with a process conception of metaphysics. Like most twentieth-century philosophers, he was ultimately concerned with epistemology. His overarching goal was to show that "the concepts of the discursive intellect had no hold on being."[6] According to Bergson, the discursive intellect operates by breaking up "reality's undivided flow into static 'pieces' thereby transforming the *élan vital* into static, divisible space."[7] In this, "the fluidity of process was frozen into a plurality of static, quantified 'things.'"[8] Consequently, Bergson held that the human person was out of touch with the very life-force permeating the universe if he or she failed to appreciate the priority of *becoming* over *being*. It is true that the human intellect gives the impression that it is being that is most important, but it is the dynamic process of becoming which underlies all that is of value in human experience.

Bergson's intuitionism, with its scathing critique of the work of the intellect, "was extremely attractive to a younger generation weary of arid positivism and its hostility to metaphysics."[9] Bergson carved out space for freedom,

5 McCool, *The Neo-Thomists*, 51.
6 Ibid.
7 Ibid.
8 Ibid.
9 Ibid., 50–51.

novelty, and all-importantly, the spiritual dimension of human existence. In this he provided an antidote to the despair many felt as a result of the determinism espoused by positivism.[10] McCool summarizes Bergson's significance:

> Relativizing the intelligence by exposing its purely practical function, Bergsonian epistemology submitted conceptual knowledge to rigorous criticism and restored the intelligence to its proper – and secondary – place in the scale of knowledge. Philosophy had been opened once again to a world of freedom and self-development, a world of moral action in which, as many young Catholics thought, a free and personal God could reveal Himself. The timeless determinism of both positivism and rationalism had been overcome.[11]

Henri Bergson was not a Catholic, and he steered clear of the theological controversies of his day.[12] However, "Bergsonianism – usually as presented by imprudent disciples – turned out to be a source of serious problems for Catholic theology as became evident in the heat of the Modernist controversy."[13]

In this regard, the work of Bergson's disciple, Edouard Le Roy, raised the most questions in Garrigou's mind. Garrigou's *Le sens commun: la philosophie de l'être et les formules dogmatiques* was directed toward the refutation of the positions of Le Roy. The general lines of Garrigou's critique can be found in the following questions:

> . . . if concepts were valid only in the ongoing process of conscious action, and, if, as Bergson claimed, they

10 Cf. "Maritain never forgot that it was to Bergson that he owed his liberation from the despair to which the meaninglessness of a positivist universe had driven him." [Ibid., 52]

11 Ibid., 52.

12 However, in 1937 "Bergson wrote his last will, in which he says that he would receive baptism in the Catholic Church were it not for the growth of anti-Semitism: he wants to remain among the persecuted." [Kolakowski, *Bergson*, viii.]

13 Ibid., 53.

> were of no more than practical value, what became of the speculative value the Church assigned to her conceptually formulated dogmas? Were they no more than relative symbols whose value was to be determined by the practical needs of a religious experience grasped through non-conceptual intuition? Were dogmas then mutable like the concepts through which they were framed, and should they be constantly revised to adjust to changing religious experience of the God found in consciousness and to the changing needs of the individual or the whole ecclesial community?[14]

Bergson published his most important work, *L'évolution créatrice*, in 1907.[15] Garrigou, who at that time was still teaching at Le Saulchoir, was enlisted by the *Revue des sciences philosophiques et théologiques* to review it.[16] As one might expect, Garrigou was at pains to demonstrate the priority of being over becoming. His review set the two positions in the following juxtaposition:

> The question is to know if there is *more* in movement than in that which is stable. Every conceptualist will say no; because, from the point of view of the understanding that brings every idea and every judgment to being, that which is stable is for him that which *is*, as opposed to that which is becoming and is not yet. . . . On the contrary, the nominalist will say: there is *more* in the movement; because, from the point of view of the senses, that which is stable is simply that *which is at rest*, and with rest and stoppages one never makes any movement.[17]

14 Ibid.

15 (Paris: F. Alcan, 1907).

16 Réginald Garrigou-Lagrange, "Bulletin d'histoire de la philosophie," *Revue des sciences philosophiques et théologiques* [*RSPT*] 1 (1907): 732–40, at 735–38. The *RSPT*, founded in 1907 and still in publication, is a work of the Dominican province of France (Paris).

17 Ibid., 736. [*La question est de savoir s'il y a* plus *dans le mouvement que dans l'immobile. Tout conceptualiste dira non; parce que, placé au point de vue de l'intelligence qui ramène toute idée et tout jugement à l'être, l'immobile pour lui c'est ce qui* est, *par opposition à ce qui devient et n'est pas encore. . . . Le nominaliste dira au contraire: il y a* plus *dans le mouvement; parce que, placé au point de vue des*

The key to this dilemma, argued Garrigou, is to ask the question whether or not the intelligence as a faculty of the human person is superior or inferior to sense or conscience. Or, "if philosophy consists in seeking the intelligible under the sensible, or as is said, 'the sensible under the false intelligible which covers and masks it.'"[18]

Simply put, to choose the latter and thus side with Bergson would be to deny that there is anything unique about the human person. Without an appreciation of the work of the intellect, there is nothing to separate humanity from the rest of the animal world. As Garrigou asks: "In what would man be differentiated from the animal? And how would one explain judgment and the soul of judgment, the verb 'to be'?"[19]

Garrigou concluded his review by evoking the most fundamental principle of Thomism – a principle to which we will return in Chapter 6 – the principle of noncontradiction, or, stated positively, the principle of identity.[20] He writes:

sens, l'immobile pour lui c'est seulement ce qui est en repos, *et qu'avec du repos et des arrêts on ne fera jamais du mouvement.*]

18 Ibid., 736–37. [. . . *si la philosophie consiste à chercher l'intelligible sous le sensible, ou comme on l'a dit, 'le sensible sous l'intelligible mensonger qui le recouvre et qui le masque.'*]

19 Ibid., 737. [*En quoi l'homme diffère-t-il alors de l'animal? Et comment expliquer le jugement et l'âme du jugement, le verbe 'être'?*] One notes that according to both Plato and Aristotle the object of the intellect was being; for Bergson the object of the intellect was *la matière et plus spécialement les solides où notre action trouve son point d'appui et notre industrie ses instruments de travail.* [Bergson, *L'évolution créatrice*, 1; cited in Ibid., 737.] In this position, according to the Thomists, "Bergson disgraces human nature and falls prey to the Manichean error; our contact with spiritual reality becomes anti-natural and anti-intellectual because it is void of concepts" [Kolakowski, *Bergson*, 95, explaining, in particular, the position of Jacques Maritain.]

20 In its most elemental form, this principle says that "A is A; A is not B." According to Garrigou, this principle is the fundamental law of thought and of reality itself.

> Mr. Bergson, by his own admission, is today exactly on the other side of the principle of identity, which is, he will recognize, the natural metaphysic of human intelligence. He is led to say that the last word of modern philosophy consists in affirming that the fundamental reality is *becoming*. Well, that returns one to say, as Hegel recognized, that *the intimate nature of things is a realized contradiction*. To deny the principle of identity as the fundamental law of the real, is to affirm that contradiction is at the very heart of the real. *To suppress pure Act, which is to being as A is to A, to suppress divine transcendence, is to put absurdity at the root of everything.*[21]

For Garrigou, this meant that the philosophy of Henri Bergson must be opposed. His faith told him that reality is not absurd; his reason confirmed what was revealed by his faith. The thought of Bergson, so welcomed by many at the end of the nineteenth century as providing a safe harbor for the spirit in a world dominated by positivism, simply could not provide the philosophical underpinnings to uphold the fullness of Christian faith.[22]

21 Ibid., 738. [*M. Bergson, de son propre aveu, est aujourd'hui exactement à l'opposé de cette philosophie de l'identité, qui est, il le reconnaît, la métaphysique de l'intelligence humaine. Il est ainsi amené à dire que le dernier mot de la philosophie moderne consiste à affirmer que* la réalité fondamentale est devenir. *Or cela revient à dire, comme l'a reconnu Hégel, que* la nature intime des choses est une contradiction réalisée. *Nier le principe d'identité comme loi fondamentale du réel, c'est affirmer que la contradiction est au sein même du réel.* Supprimer l'Acte pur, qui est à l'être comme A est A, supprimer la transcendance divine, c'est mettre l'absurdité à la racine de tout.]

22 This judgment is now all but incontestable; *pace* Antonin-D. Sertillanges [*Henri Bergson et le catholicisme* (Paris: Flammarion, 1941)], Kolakowski writes: "When we look at Bergson's position – or rather lack of position – in today's intellectual life, we find it hard to imagine that some decades ago he was not just a famous thinker and writer; in the eyes of Europe's educated public he was clearly *the* philosopher, the intellectual spokesman *par excellence* of the era. . . . Not much of this glamour has remained. . . . Bergson has survived only as a dead classic. Even in France interest in his work is only residual" (*Bergson*, 1–2).

Maurice Blondel (1861–1949)

Maurice Blondel is remembered for his philosophy of action that saw its debut in his 1893 work *L'Action*.[23] Blondel's fundamental claim is that "philosophy must take its impetus from action rather than pure thought. . . . One must turn from abstract thought to actual experience in all its fullness and richness."[24] At the same time, "action" cannot be reduced to the "idea of action." For Blondel, "the fatal error of the 'intellectualists' was their failure to see that, unless abstract concepts and 'ideas' were restored to their proper context in the dynamic action of the concrete subject and integrated in the light of it, reason could not find the truth."[25] Because of this, Blondel held that "the concrete will, striving beyond all conceptual objects, and not the conceptual intellect, was the primary faculty of truth and being."[26]

The question of truth and its definition was an important part of Blondel's philosophy. For the Thomist school of thought, truth was defined as *adaequatio rei et intellectus* – the conformity of the mind with reality. Thomism held that reality is intelligible; through one's intellect one is able to be in touch with the really real. Falsehood, therefore, is a judgment of the intellect that fails to conform to the way things really are. Blondel, emphasizing action and inter-subjectivity, devised what the Thomists considered to be a pragmatic definition of truth. "In place of the . . . definition of truth as the adequation of intellect and reality,"

23 Maurice Blondel, *L'Action: essai d'une critique de la vie et d'une science de la pratique* [1893], second edition (Paris: Presses Universitaires de France, 1950); English translation: *Action: Essay on a Critique of Life and a Science of Practice*, trans. Oliva Blanchette (Notre Dame, Ind.: University of Notre Dame Press, 1984).

24 John Macquarrie, "Blondel, Maurice," in *The Encyclopedia of Philosophy* (1967 ed.).

25 McCool, *The Neo-Thomists*, 49.

26 Ibid.

he held that truth must be defined as "the adequation of intellect and life."[27]

Blondel's philosophical program was on a collision course with Thomism. Its fundamental propositions stood in sharp contrast to the metaphysics of St. Thomas. What accounts for Blondel's philosophical project?

The first thing to note is that Maurice Blondel was a practicing Catholic; his contribution to philosophy was fundamentally an apologetic for Christian faith. The problem is that his attempt at apologetics was influenced greatly by the theological writings of Friedrich Schleiermacher – and led to the validation of an intrinsic apologetic over an extrinsic apologetic.

The distinction between intrinsic and extrinsic apologetics is an important one; it is one that Blondel emphasized in his *Lettre sur les exigences de la pensée contemporaine en matière d'apologétique.*[28] McCool explains:

> The *Lettre* distinguished between an 'extrinsic apologetics' built upon external justification of the authenticity of Christian Revelation through signs, miracles, and the historically verified credibility of its witnesses and an 'intrinsic apologetics' directed toward man's inner desires and exigencies.[29]

Blondel was convinced that only an intrinsic apologetic could speak to his contemporaries. The symbols of Christian faith and the various doctrines of Christianity must be grounded in the human person and be shown to be elemental expressions of the longings of the human heart:

> Objective justifications of Christianity based on strictly intellectual arguments would have little effect. For

27 Réginald Garrigou-Lagrange, *Reality: A Synthesis of Thomistic Thought*, trans. Patrick Cummins (St. Louis: B. Herder, 1950), 381, citing Maurice Blondel, "Point de départ de la recherche philosophique," *Annales de philosophie chrétienne* (15 June 1906), 235.

28 Blondel's *Lettre* was published in *Annales de philosophie chrétienne* in 1896.

29 McCool, *The Neo-Thomists*, 49.

> the contemporary difficulties with Christian Revelation did not concern its reasonableness but rather its relevance to human life.[30]

It was Friedrich Schleiermacher who had first come to this conclusion with significant clarity. Granting Immanuel Kant's conclusion that "speculative reason could have no knowledge either of God or of the extramental world of 'things in themselves,'"[31] Schleiermacher was led to establish Christian faith solely on "the religious sentiment of a wholly immanent human consciousness."[32] In such a grounding of Christian faith, the will takes precedence over the intellect, sentiment over cognition, praxis over theory.

Blondel was in agreement with Schleiermacher: the only foundation for a philosophical defense of Christian faith is human consciousness itself. The following quotation provides the rationale which motivated Blondel's lifelong work:

> Remaining strictly within the immanence of consciousness, a scientifically rigorous reflection on its dynamic movement must be able to show that the inner development of human consciousness, directed by its own universal laws, cannot achieve that inner perfection which the idealists claim to be its goal without a humble recognition of a personal God who transcends human consciousness and a corresponding openness to the revelation of His inner life which that personal God can make, should He freely choose to do so. In that case, the *possibility* of historical supernatural Revelation is *necessarily* demanded by the exigencies of consciousness' own immanent fulfillment.[33]

It was an ingenious solution to a vexing question. Blondel was able to find a place for the God of Christian

30 Ibid., 50.
31 Ibid., 46.
32 Ibid.
33 Ibid., 48.

revelation under the hostile conditions of a Kantian world-view and its *a priori* agnosticism. Logical consistency would mean that Christian faith could no longer be dismissed as unreasonable or morally irresponsible. The *fin de siècle* philosophers would have to admit that the grounds for any level of confidence in life – like the hope implicit in human consciousness – calls for the acknowledgement of a personal God.

Of course, that is not what happened. The academics addressed by Blondel's intrinsic apologetics did not turn from their hostility to Christianity and embrace baptism and the demands of Christian discipleship. Blondel's program was directed toward such an objective but its effect was negligible. Rather, his work had primarily an intramural effect, influencing, as it were, a younger generation of theologians to attempt to ground Catholic faith upon philosophical idealism.[34]

As should be clear, Blondel was "no supporter of the 'Back to Aquinas' movement"[35] so strongly advocated by Pope Leo XIII and reiterated by subsequent pontiffs. "In his opinion the Christian thinker, concerned with the development of philosophy of religion, should not attempt to go back but rather to enter into the development of modern philosophy and to go beyond it from within."[36] Fr. Copleston explains:

> In Blondel's opinion it was only by means of this approach that a philosophy of religion could be developed which would mean something to modern man. For God to become a reality for him and not simply an object of thought or of speculation, man must rediscover God from within, not indeed as an object which can be found by introspection but by coming to see

34 Macquarrie, *art. cit.*

35 Frederick Copleston, *A History of Philosophy*, volume 9: "Maine de Biran to Sartre," part II: "Bergson to Sartre" (Garden City, N.Y.: Doubleday, 1974), 19.

36 Ibid.

> that the Transcendent is the goal of his thought and will.[37]

The difficulty is at least two-fold. First, Christian faith, as enunciated in the primitive kerygma up to the most recent papal encyclical, has always been predicated upon assertions pertaining to extramental realities: the God-man, Jesus of Nazareth, "was made flesh of the Holy Spirit and the Virgin Mary, and became man, and was crucified for us under Pontius Pilate, and suffered and was buried, and rose again on the third day . . . and ascended into the heavens . . . and cometh again with glory to judge the living and the dead. . ."[38] Blondel's method of immanence is dangerously close to "a doctrine of immanence, asserting that nothing exists outside human consciousness or that the statement that anything so exists is devoid of meaning."[39]

Secondly, Blondel's thought raises questions concerning the traditional distinction between the natural and the supernatural. If the desire for God, for example, is found naturally in human consciousness and if by one's appropriate use of the will one strives for God, questions are raised about grace and the utter gratuity of God's revelation of himself. As Jean Lacroix explains: "On the one hand, it is necessary that reason summon faith without alienating its own autonomy and, on the other hand, the supernatural must be necessary without ceasing to be gratuitous."[40] In this same vein, Fr. Copleston writes: "Catholic critics . . . understood Blondel as claiming that

37 Ibid.

38 "The Nicene Creed" or "Nicaeno-Constantinopolitan Creed" (read and approved at Chalcedon, A.D. 451), in Henry Bettenson, ed., *Documents of the Christian Church* (New York: Oxford University Press, 1963), 36–37.

39 Copleston, "Bergson to Sartre," 20.

40 Jean Lacroix, "Blondel, Maurice," in *Dictionnaire des philosophes*, 334. [*Il faut d'une part que la raison appele la foi sans aliéner sa propre autonomie et que, d'autre part, le surnaturel soit obligatoire sans cesser d'être gratuit.*]

supernatural revelation and life were not gratuitous but necessary, fulfilling, that is to say, a demand in the nature of man, a demand which man's creator had to satisfy."[41]

The following quotation from John Macquarrie provides a good summary of Blondel's thought and will help to account for certain difficulties in reconciling his work with traditional Catholic notions of grace, original sin, and the very freedom of God:

> God is immanent within man, in the sense that human action is already directed beyond the phenomenal order. To will all that we do will is already to have the action of God within us. Yet this quest for realization would be a frustrating one were it not that God in turn moves toward us in his transcendence, and human action is supported and supplemented by divine grace.[42]

The Modernist Crisis

The one event that most affects the present narrative, that shifted the fortunes of the Catholic disciples of Henri Bergson and Maurice Blondel, and that provided the lion's share of the inspiration for Garrigou-Lagrange's work was Pope St. Pius X's publication of *Pascendi dominici gregis* in 1907. In this section, we will discuss the crisis within Catholicism occasioned by this encyclical and its condemnation of what it termed "Modernism." Our study will be far from exhaustive: we will restrict our examination to the theological propositions that were determined to belong under the umbrella of Modernism.

Catholic theology had been fairly well insulated from the critical movements at work in Western Europe during

41 Copleston, "Bergson to Sartre," 24. Copleston agrees that there are statements in Blondel's *œuvres* which provide for the *justesse* of this interpretation; there are also those which affirm "that man should accept and surrender himself to the Transcendent" (Ibid.).

42 Macquarrie, *art. cit.*

the nineteenth-century. Catholicism had developed a fortress mentality vis-à-vis the intellectual currents beyond her aegis: the French Revolution and the Revolutions of 1830 and 1848 were not interested in dialogue with the Church's intellectual heritage and the chairs of philosophy and theology once under the Church's patronage during the *ancien régime* became things of the past.

By the end of the nineteenth century, Catholic theological circles began to be touched by the higher criticism at work particularly in Germany. It is safe to say that the one's reaction to the conclusions reached by men like Reimarus, Wellhausen, and Renan went a long way toward determining if one were a Modernist or not. This is to say that Modernism was often more a theological attitude than a clearly articulated set of doctrines.

Fr. Copleston provides a helpful example in his discussion of Alfred Loisy who, with Lucien Laberthonnière, was the leading proponent of Modernism in France. Loisy held that Catholic theology needed to be recast in light of contemporary historical and biblical studies. At first glance, this appears rather innocuous; after all it is a truism that in the Catholic conception of things, theology is "faith seeking understanding." However, what Loisy judged to be the conclusions of contemporary studies was utterly problematic:

> For instance, Loisy believed that Jesus as the Son of God was the creation of Christian faith reflecting on and transforming the man Jesus of Nazareth. This transformation involved also a deformation inasmuch as, for example, it involved attributing to the man Jesus miraculous actions the acceptance of which as historical events was ruled out by modern thought and knowledge. The task of historical criticism was to rediscover the historical figure hidden beneath the veils which faith had woven about it. In brief, Loisy maintained in effect that the historian of Christianity

> must approach his subject as he would approach any other historical theme, and that this approach demanded a purely naturalistic account of Christ himself and of the origins and rise of the Christian Church.[43]

Many have commented that Modernism is a rather haphazard way of speaking about a complex phenomenon that involved many players. Bernard M. G. Reardon, for instance, offers the insight that "Modernism, like Liberalism, connotes an attitude of mind which is not necessarily tied to a single inheritance of faith and practice."[44] However, one need not go so far as to accept Loisy's judgment that "there are as many Modernisms as there are Modernists."[45] There is a rather stable set of propositions that run through the work of men like Loisy, Laberthonnière, George Tyrell, Baron von Hügel, and Ernesto Buonaiuti. Reardon explains: "Modernism could fairly be defined as the attempt to synthesize the basic truths of religion and the methods and assumptions of modern thought, using the latter as necessary and proper criteria."[46]

Pascendi was the most controversial encyclical of the pontificate of St. Pius X. It is a passionate defense of Catholic doctrine and an equally passionate denunciation of Modernism. It begins with the following recognition:

> It must . . . be confessed that these latter days have witnessed a notable increase in the number of the enemies of the Cross of Christ, who, by acts entirely new and full of deceit, are striving to destroy the vital energy of the Church, and as far as in them lies, utterly subvert the very Kingdom of Christ. Wherefore We

43 Copleston, "Bergson to Sartre," 39–40.

44 Bernard M. G. Reardon, ed. with an introduction, *Roman Catholic Modernism* (Stanford, Calif.: Stanford University Press, 1970), 9.

45 Alfred Loisy, *Mémoires pour servir à l'histoire religieuse du notre temps* (1930–31), in Reardon, *Roman Catholic Modernism*, 10. [. . . *il y a autant de modernismes que de modernistes.*]

46 Reardon, *Roman Catholic Modernism*, 9.

> may no longer keep silence, lest We should seem to fail in Our most sacred duty, and lest the kindness that, in the hope of wiser counsels, We have hitherto shown them, should be set down to lack of diligence in the discharge of Our office.[47]

The Pope was cognizant of the difficulties associated with coming to a clear-cut definition of Modernism. "It is," he wrote, "one of the cleverest devices of the Modernists to present their doctrines without order and systematic arrangement, in a scattered and disjointed manner, so as to make it appear as if their minds were in doubt or hesitation, whereas in reality they are quite fixed and steadfast."[48] The object of *Pascendi*, then, was to bring to light by way of systematic exposition, the errors of Modernism. This would be a monumental undertaking because

> . . . the Modernist sustains and includes within himself a manifold personality; he is a philosopher, a believer, a theologian, an historian, a critic, an apologist, a reformer. These roles must be clearly distinguished one from another by all who would accurately understand their system and thoroughly grasp the principles and the outcome of their doctrines.[49]

For our purposes, we will concentrate on the encyclical's critique and condemnation of the philosophical and theological positions of the Modernists.

St. Pius identified the philosophical foundation of Modernism with a variety of agnosticism. The reason for this is that the Modernists held that "human reason is confined entirely within the field of phenomena, that is to say, to things that appear, and in the manner in which they appear: it has neither the right nor the power to overstep these limits."[50] The Catholic tradition holds for a much more robust understanding of the powers of human reason.

47 St. Pius X, *Pascendi dominici gregis* (1907), n. 1.
48 Ibid., n. 4.
49 Ibid., n. 5.
50 Ibid., n. 6.

Through reason, the human person can even come to the knowledge of God's existence; the truths of the faith, while suprarational, are not irrational; nor are they incapable of rational explanation. A denial of these propositions contravenes the First Vatican Council's teaching that the one true God can be "known with certainty by the natural light of human reason by means of the things that are made."[51]

The doctrine of the Modernists was also directly allied with what St. Pius called "religious immanence."[52] This doctrine is summarized in the following quotation:

> Religion, whether natural or supernatural, must, like every other fact, admit of some explanation. But when natural theology has been destroyed, and the road to revelation closed by the rejection of the arguments of credibility, and all external revelation absolutely denied, it is clear that this explanation will be sought in vain outside of man himself. It must, therefore, be looked for in man; and since religion is a form of life, the explanation must certainly be found in the life of man. . . .[53] It is thus that the religious sense, which through the agency of vital immanence emerges from the lurking places of the subconsciousness, is the germ of all religion, and the explanation of everything that has been or ever will be in any religion.[54]

In response to this teaching, St. Pius warned that "nothing assuredly could be more utterly destructive of the whole supernatural order."[55] Concurrently, he accepted the fittingness of the following condemnation from Vatican I: "If anyone says that man cannot be raised by God to a knowledge and perfection which surpasses nature, but that he can and should, by his own efforts and by a

51 First Vatican Council, *De Revelatione*, can. 1, cited in *Pascendi*, n. 6.

52 *Pascendi*, n. 7.

53 Ibid.

54 Ibid., n. 10.

55 Ibid.

constant development, attain finally to the possession of all truth and good, let him be anathema."[56]

When it came to theology, St. Pius was most concerned with the explicit relativizing of dogma by the Modernists. He offered the following explanation of the procedure employed by the Modernists:

> To ascertain the nature of dogma, we must first find the relation which exists between the religious formulas and the religious sense. This will be readily perceived by anyone who holds that these formulas have no other purpose than to furnish the believer with a means of giving to himself an account of his faith. These formulas therefore stand midway between the believer and his faith; in their relation to the faith they are the inadequate expression of its object, and are usually called symbols; in their relation to the believer they are mere instruments. Hence it is quite impossible to maintain that they absolutely contain the truth: for, in so far as they are symbols, they are the images of truth, and so must be adapted to the religious sense in its relation to man; and as instruments, they are vehicles of truth, and must therefore in their turn be adapted to man in his relation to the religious sense. . . . Consequently, the formulas which we call dogma must be subject to these vicissitudes, and are, therefore, liable to change.[57]

The Pope's judgment on this teaching could not have been clearer: "Here we have an immense structure of sophisms which ruin and wreck all religion."[58] Indeed, later in *Pascendi* he will render his now-famous judgment: "Modernism is the synthesis of all heresies."[59]

Faced with such a problematical set of philosophical and theological issues, St. Pius charged the bishops of the

56 First Vatican Council, *De Revelatione*, can. 3, cited in *Pascendi*, n. 10.

57 *Pascendi*, n. 12.

58 Ibid.

59 Ibid., n. 39.

Catholic world and the major superiors of the religious orders to vigilance over their seminaries, scholasticates, and *studia*. In particular, he ordained that "scholastic philosophy be made the basis of the sacred sciences."[60] To this he added the injunction,

> And let it be clearly understood above all things that when We prescribe scholastic philosophy We understand chiefly that which the Angelic Doctor has bequeathed to us, and We, therefore, declare that all the ordinances of Our predecessor on this subject continue fully in force, and, as far as may be necessary, We do decree anew, and confirm, and order that they shall be strictly observed by all.[61]

The publication of *Pascendi* coincided with the appearance of the first volume of the *Revue des sciences philosophiques et théologiques (RSPT)* – the philosophical and theological journal of the Dominicans at Le Saulchoir. In its maiden volume, the editors of the *RSPT* concurred with the Pope's judgment that the "pseudo-philosophy which they (the Modernists) have made the principle and the criterion of scientific research is destructive of all true science."[62] They added that if the Pope's order is to bear fruit, "what is needed from us is more than material obedience with which one executes an order, more than a purely passive submission of the spirit. A personal, extended effort and direct commerce with the thought of the Master and his authorized commentators will be indispensable."[63]

60 Ibid., n. 45.

61 Ibid.

62 The Editors, "L'encyclique *Pascendi dominici gregis*," Revue des sciences philosophiques et théologiques 1 (1907): 648. [. . . *pseudo-philosophie dont on a fait le principe et le critérium de la recherche scientifique est destructive de toute science véritable.*]

63 Ibid. The "Master" here is none other than St. Thomas Aquinas. [. . . *il y faudra de notre part plus que l'obéissance matérielle avec laquelle on exécute une consigne, plus même qu'une soumission purement passive de l'esprit. Un effort personnel et prolongé, un commerce direct avec la pensée du Maître et ses Commentateurs autorisés sont indispensables.*]

We note that Garrigou was teaching at Le Saulchoir when *Pascendi* was published; coincidentally, he had two articles published in the first volume of *RSPT*.[64] From what we know, Garrigou was in full accord with the judgment of the *RSPT*'s editors concerning the condemnation of Modernism. It is clear that he took to heart St. Pius's admonition to be grounded in the doctrine of St. Thomas; Garrigou's life would become nothing less than 'a personal, extended effort' to assimilate the teachings of the Angelic Doctor. M.-Rosaire Gagnebet writes:

> If the mystery of God is accessible to our understanding in an imperfect, but true, fashion, through the formulae of faith, it is possible for the human person, by his reason guided by faith, to obtain an analogical understanding of these very fruitful mysteries, according to the expression of the First Vatican Council. This is the goal toward which the theology of Father Garrigou was directed and toward which he consecrated all of the strength of his spirit.[65]

Of course, in Garrigou-Lagrange's case there was no real novelty in this approach: "his theology was the theology of St. Thomas."[66] And like St. Thomas before him, Garrigou understood the task of the theologian to be "the penetration and exposition of the principal mysteries of our faith the contemplation of which will be our beatitude in heaven and the truths that God has revealed to us to guide us there."[67]

64 Viz., "Le Dieu fini du pragmatisme," 252–65 and "Intellectualisme et liberté chez saint Thomas," 649–73 [concluded in *RSPT* 2 (1908): 5–32].

65 Gagnebet, "L'oeuvre du P. Garrigou," 24. [*Si à travers les formules de foi accessibles à notre intelligence se manifeste à nous d'une façon imparfaite, mais réelle, le mystère de Dieu, il sera possible à l'homme, par son intelligence guidée par la foi, d'obtenir une intelligence analogique de ces mystères très fructueuse, selon l'expression du Concile Vatican I. C'est le but vers lequel tend la théologie auquel le P. Garrigou consacra toutes les forces de son esprit.*]

66 Ibid., 25. [*Sa théologie fut la théologie de S. Thomas.*]

67 Ibid., 24. [. . . *la pénetration et l'exposition des principaux mystères*

Garrigou *versus* the thought of Bergson and Blondel

The philosophies of Henri Bergson and Maurice Blondel and their use as a framework for Catholic theology appeared to Garrigou to be counter-indicated by not only the letter but also the spirit of *Pascendi*. In this section, we will isolate some representative instances where Garrigou directly engaged the thought of Bergson and Blondel.

As we have seen, Garrigou's connection with Bergson was of a long-standing nature. He viewed Bergson and the other philosophical luminaries of his day as being radically in need. Speaking to Garrigou's time at the Sorbonne, Gagnebet reveals: "All his life Father Garrigou remembered those great thinkers for whom, for the most part, the way to faith was blocked by a fallacious philosophy."[68] In repeated acts of audacity, Garrigou would send his own books to his former teachers – hoping, of course, to persuade them of the truth of Christ. Bergson was one who responded to Garrigou's unsolicited gifts:

> The philosopher of becoming, whom Garrigou did not treat with caution, wrote to him of his profound emotion on having read *La providence et la confiance en Dieu*. After *Le Sauveur et son amour pour nous*, he acknowledged to him that the problem posed by the last chapter – the necessity of belonging to the Church – could not be eluded.[69]

Blondel was not as gracious in finding himself on the receiving end of Garrigou's attention. Garrigou, who was

de notre foi dont la contemplation au ciel fera notre béatitude et des vérités que Dieu nous a révélées pour nous y conduire.]

68 Ibid., 11. [*Toute sa vie le P. Garrigou gardera le souvenir de ces grands esprits auxquels, pour la plupart, une philosophie fallacieuse a fermé le chemin de la foi.*]

69 Ibid., 11. [*Le philosophe du devenir, que le P. Garrigou n'a pas ménagé, lui écrit son émotion profonde à la lecture de* La providence et la confiance en Dieu. *Après* Le Sauveur et son amour pour nous, *il lui avoue que le problème posé par le dernier chapître sur la nécessaire ahésion à l'Eglise ne saurait être éludé.*]

always most concerned with the metaphysical deficiencies of contemporary philosophies, used every means at his disposal to get Blondel to abandon his definition of truth – *adaequatio realis vitae et mentis* – and to return to the Thomistic understanding – *adaequatio rei et intellectus.*

In a letter of 17 October 1946, Garrigou pleaded with Blondel to repudiate his definition of truth or risk what he judged to be "a very painful, or long, purgatory."[70] As we will see in Chapter 7, Garrigou had also written an article that same year in which he undertook a critique of Blondel's position.

Blondel, exasperated, addressed a letter to the editor of *Angelicum* (dated 12 March 1947). He claimed that his thought was being unjustly represented by Garrigou-Lagrange. Blondel's letter was published in volume 24 of the journal. The following passage is most germane to our narrative:

> When one reproaches me for not recognizing the absolute sufficiency of the definition of truth, *adaequatio rei et intellectus*, it is for me to protest against this completely insufficient reduction to the words *res* and *intellectus: res* . . . does not suffice to describe the highest realities, and "intellect" does not exhaust the knowledge of things and beings, nor the reality of the intimate operations of our conscience or of our obligations, or the profound truth of our supernatural destiny. There is therefore a deficiency in the doctrine to which one would like to reduce me.[71]

70 Réginald Garrigou-Lagrange to Maurice Blondel, 17 October 1946, in Etienne Fouilloux, *Une Eglise en quête de liberté: la pensée catholique française entre modernisme et Vatican II (1914–1962)* (Paris: Desclée de Brouwer, 1998), 31. [. . . *un très douloureux ou très long purgatoire*.]

71 Maurice Blondel to the Editor of *Angelicum*, 12 March 1947, in *Angelicum* 24 (1947): 211. [*Quand on me reproche de méconnaître la suffisance absolue de la définition de la vérité,* adaequatio rei et intellectus, *ce serait à moi de protester contre cette réduction aux mots* res *et* intellectus, *à la contenance tout à fait insuffisante:* res *en effet ne suffit pas à désigner les plus hautes réalités, et l'intellect n'épuise pas la science des choses et des êtres, ni la réalité des*

Garrigou was given the opportunity to respond to Blondel's letter in the same volume of *Angelicum*. His response is an unrepentant critique of the metaphysical deficiencies of Blondel's philosophy. It comprises three main points.

First, Garrigou returned to Blondel's definition of truth. He wrote: "Our critique concerns especially two words in the proposition that he wrote in 1906: 'to the abstract and chimerical *adaequatio speculativa rei et intellectus* should be substituted the right methodical research, *adaequatio realis mentis et vitae*.'"[72]

Garrigou asked Blondel to remove the word 'chimerical' and to replace 'should be substituted' with "is completed by." Why does he ask for these changes?

> Because affective knowledge by connaturality or sympathy completes well notional knowledge, but supposes its value by conformity with the real, and does not substitute for her, if one wishes to avoid the pragmatism toward which the philosophy of action is sliding.[73]

Blondel, founder of the philosophy of action, had been defining truth in reference to action since the publication of his dissertation in 1893. He was obstinate in his refusal to define truth in reference to being – 'the mind's conformity with reality.' In light of this refusal, Garrigou wrote:

opérations intimes de notre conscience ou de nos devoirs, ni la vérité profonde de notre destinée surnaturelle. Il y a donc carence dans une doctrine à laquelle on voudrait me réduire.]

72 Réginald Garrigou-Lagrange to Maurice Blondel, in *Angelicum* 24 (1947): 212. [*Notre critique portait surtout sur deux mots de la proposition qu'il a écrite en 1906: 'A l'abstraite et chimérique* adaequatio speculativa rei et intellectus *se substitue la recherche méthodique de droit, l'*adaequatio realis mentis et vitae.'"]

73 Ibid. [*Parce que la connaissance affective par connaturalité ou sympathie complète bien la connaissance notionnelle, mais suppose la valeur de celle-ci par conformité au réel, et ne se substitue pas à elle, si l'on veut éviter le pragmatisme vers lequel glisse la philosophie de l'action.*]

"One ends with an ethic (a philosophy of human action) that does not have a sufficient ontological foundation. But the good supposes being and truth; otherwise it is not certain what would be a true good."[74]

Secondly, Garrigou highlighted the insufficiency of Blondel's philosophical approach to the question of God's existence. He recognized that the philosophy of action attempts to safeguard the existence of God by way of a phenomenological analysis of the exigencies of action. The problem is that that "proof" for God's existence, like that of Kantianism, is grounded in subjectivity; it is not "objectively sufficient (that is to say by reason of the demonstrative strength of the proofs for the existence of God)."[75]

> This, we say, is not sufficient; by this route one ends at not being able to prove the *fact of Revelation* by the conclusive strength of miracles; one only gets to a certitude that is subjectively sufficient for the fact of Revelation and one arrives at a religious experience that is not distinguished well enough from that of false religion, where sentimentalism and the search for self takes it away from the true faith and the true love of God. The encyclical *Pascendi* noted this, in speaking of religious experience that is not sufficiently grounded in truth, by that which does not have the evident credibility of the truths of faith (see: *Denz.* 2081)."[76]

74 Ibid. [*On aboutit ainsi à une éthique (philosophie de l'agir humain) qui n'a pas de fondement ontologique suffisant. Or le bien suppose l'être et le vrai; autrement il n'est pas certain que ce soit un vrai bien.*]

75 Ibid., 213. [. . . *objectivement suffisante (c'est à dire de par la force démonstrative des preuves de l'existence de Dieu.)*]

76 Ibid., 213; cf. *Denz.*, n. 2081. [*Cela, disons-nous, ne suffit pas; par cette voie on aboutit à ne pouvoir pas prouver le* fait de la Révélation *par la force probant du miracle; on arrive alors seulement à une certitude* subjectivement *suffisante de ce fait de la Révélation et l'on parvient ainsi à une* expérience religieuse *qui ne se distingue plus assez de celle d'une fausse religion, où le sentimentalisme et la recherche de soi l'emportent sur la foi véritable et le véritable amour*

Garrigou also underlined the necessity of maintaining the immutability of the terms[77] that have entered into conciliar definitions. Much like Edouard Le Roy, Blondel "grounds our concepts on 'schemas which are always provisional,' the stability of which arises 'from the artifice of language.'"[78]

The climax of Garrigou's argument came in his assertion that, following St. Thomas, truth is found formally in the judgment. He asks: "Are judgments universally recognized as true, true by conformity to the real? And in the case of first principles, is not their evidence absolute in itself and by reason of the very nature of our intelligence? Is it not evident for every person that he cannot both be and not be at the same time?"[79]

Finally, Garrigou remarked that in examining a number of proposals for "rethinking" the doctrines of grace, original sin, transubstantiation, and the Real Presence, he finds the not-so-subtle influence of Maurice Blondel's philosophy of action. As one would expect, Garrigou found these proposals to be wanting: their emphasis on "conformity to human life according to the exigencies of action" all but vitiated the transcendental foundation upon which they truly rest. In a word, Garrigou held that Blondel's philosophy was dangerous to the foundations of Catholic theology; it was an attempt to establish the Church's theology on a subjective version of pragmatism.

de Dieu. L'Encyclique Pascendi *l'a noté en parlant de l'expérience religieuse qui n'est pas suffisamment fondée en vérité, par ce qu'il n'y a l'évidente crédibilité des vérités de foi.*]

77 He speaks of *l'immutabilité des notions*. See: Ibid.

78 Ibid. Garrigou is citing Blondel's *La Pensée*, I, 130. [. . . *ramène nos concepts à des 'schèmes toujours provisoires,' dont la stabilité provient 'de l'artifice du langage.'*]

79 Ibid. [*Est-ce que les jugements universellement reconnus comme vrai, sont* vrai *par conformité au réel? Et dans le cas des premiers principes, leur* évidence *est-elle* nécessitante, *par elle-même et à raison de la nature même de notre intelligence? N'est-il pas évident pour tout homme, qu'il ne peut en même temps exister et ne pas exister?*]

Conclusion

A number of commentators use the adjectives "rigid" and "intransigent" when speaking of the fundamental stance of Garrigou-Lagrange. And this has a certain *justesse*: he held tenaciously to the metaphysical principles of St. Thomas. However, "rigidity" and "intransigence" often carry a pejorative sense: they are taken to be synonymous with closed-mindedness, with an unwillingness to engage the positions of another. This chapter would have one ask if it is fair to ascribe intransigence to Garrigou and not to his interlocutors. Were Bergson and Blondel any less "rigid" or "intransigent" than Garrigou in holding tenaciously to their positions? Refusing to start one's philosophical reflections with being (*à la* Bergson) is not *ipso facto* a mark of openness to the truth. Likewise, one is not necessarily more open to the truth by virtue of accepting the first principles of Immanuel Kant over those of St. Thomas (*à la* Blondel).

In the next chapter, the theme of disputation continues. We will undertake a study of the politics of Garrigou-Lagrange by examining his historically contingent disputations with Jacques Maritain, and M.-Dominique Chenu. In Chapter 6 we will return to a more detailed discussion of the philosophical commitments of Garrigou-Lagrange.

5. The Politics of Garrigou-Lagrange: Relationships with Jacques Maritain and M.-Dominique Chenu

> *Here below, even the saints sometimes can be found disagreeing and inflexibly defending their own opposite points of view with the conviction that it is a question of the will of God. . . . In the midst of such difficulties . . . how can one practice fraternal charity? Two things are necessary: (1) to look upon one's neighbor with the eyes of faith, that is, to discover in him the supernatural being that we ought to love; and (2) to love him by bearing with him, making ourselves useful and asking God for the union of hearts.* Réginald Garrigou-Lagrange, *The Last Writings*

In the last chapter, we examined the parameters of Garrigou-Lagrange's disputations with the philosophies of Henri Bergson and Maurice Blondel. We saw that he was intent upon engaging the new developments in philosophy – particularly Bergson's vision of a process metaphysics and Blondel's pragmatic understanding of the nature of truth – with the thought of St. Thomas. In the end, Garrigou concluded that neither the philosophy of Bergson nor the philosophy of Blondel provided a foundation strong enough to bear the full weight of orthodox Christian faith.

In this chapter, the theme of disputation continues. Now, the question turns upon issues in the socio-political realm as well as issues of ecclesiastical discipline. To this end, we will examine various dimensions of Garrigou's relationships with Jacques Maritain and with his Dominican confrere, M.-Dominique Chenu. This undertaking will speak to Garrigou's judgments concerning the application of his philosophical and theological commitments in the contingent world of politics and human relationships.

Garrigou and Jacques Maritain (1882–1973)

Garrigou first encountered Jacques Maritain during their mutual studies in philosophy at the Sorbonne. The young Maritain, then an ardent disciple of Henri Bergson, attended the lectures of Gabriel Séailles,[1] as did Garrigou. Years later, Garrigou would remember a particular day when Maritain pronounced

> a critique of Kantian morality by arguments advanced against conceptual philosophy. He showed himself in favor of an ethic beyond laws, one that seeks to grasp the absolute: "It is a dance," he concluded, "which plays across the kinds of becoming without ever stopping at any one."[2]

While he made an impression on Garrigou, Maritain was not encountered again until after the publication of his first book, *La philosophie bergsonienne*.[3] Garrigou was

1 Gabriel Séailles (1855–1922) is best remembered for his *Essai sur le génie dans l'art* (Paris: F. Alcan, 1897); *La philosophie de Charles Renouvier: introduction à l'étude du néo-criticisme* (Paris: F. Alcan, 1905); and *Léonard de Vinci: l'artiste et le savant, 1452–1519. Essai de biographie psychologique* (Paris: Perrin, 1906).

2 Gagnebet, "L'œuvre du P. Garrigou," 11. [. . . *critique la morale kantienne par les raisons alléguées contre la philosophie du concept. Il se prononce pour une éthique qui, au-delà des lois, cherche à saisir l'absolu: 'C'est une danse, conclut-il, qui se joue à travers les formes du devenir sans jamais s'arrêter à aucune.'*]

3 English translation: *Bergsonian Philosophy and Thomism*, trans. Mabelle L. Andison (New York: Philosophical Library, 1955). This

amazed that not only had the former Bergsonian become a Thomist, he had also become a Catholic.[4] Gagnebet writes that "the Catholic faith made Jacques Maritain a Thomist before he ever opened the *Summa*."[5]

Maritain was named professor of the history of modern philosophy at Paris's Institut Catholique in June of 1914. His position in the academy brought him into conversation with the leading figures of French intellectual life;[6] his religious piety led him to form close relationships with priests and pious lay people.[7] Maritain, invigorated by the Thomistic revival at work in Catholicism, soon began contemplating how he might best add his talents to the movement.

Garrigou, teaching in Rome since 1909, was on the periphery of the day-to-day happenings in French Catholic circles. His numerous book reviews, however, demonstrate that he kept up with the developments in philosophy, theology, and spirituality.[8] Nonetheless, his energy was

is a translation of the second edition of Maritain's work. It bears noting that in the second edition Maritain added several footnotes which direct his readers to various works of Garrigou-Lagrange.

4 Jacques Maritain, his wife Raïssa, and Raïssa's sister Vera Oumansoff were baptized on 11 June 1906 in the Church of St-Jean-l'Evangéliste in Paris's Montmartre district.

5 Gagnebet, "L'oeuvre du P. Garrigou," 12. [*La foi catholique a fait de Jacques Maritain un thomiste avant même qu'il ait ouvert la* Somme.]

6 See especially: Bernard E. Doering, *Jacques Maritain and the French Catholic Intellectuals* (Notre Dame, Ind.: University of Notre Dame Press, 1983).

7 The Dominican Humbert Clérissac was Maritain's first spiritual director; L'abbé Charles Journet, later named cardinal, would be Maritain's life-long friend – as would the novelist Julien Green.

8 Between the years 1910 and 1920, Garrigou reviewed the following books: Ambroise Gardeil, *Le donné révélé et la théologie* and *La crédibilité et l'apologétique*; Georges Michelet, *Dieu et l'agnosticisme contemporain*; Clodius Piat, *De la croyance en Dieu*; Ambroise Poulpiquet, *L'object intégral de l'apologétique*; Pierre Rousselot, *Les yeux de la foi*; Joseph de Tonquédec, *Les yeux de la foi*; P. Piny, *La clef du pur amour* and *La présence de Dieu*; and Desiré card.

invested rather completely in his duties at the Angelicum. At the same time, Garrigou was far from an unknown quantity in those very same French Catholic circles: his writings and his position in Rome assured significant name recognition.

In 1919 Maritain began what would eventually become the Thomist Study Circles.[9] He envisioned a network of local groups devoted to the study of St. Thomas. These groups would be coordinated by a director and bound together by a constitution. There would be an annual gathering of the local groups that would include time for spiritual renewal through a preached retreat. The following excerpts from the Statutes of the Thomist Study Circles[10] give a sense of Maritain's intentions:

> God, in making St. Thomas Aquinas the common Doctor of the Church, gave him to us for leader and guide in the knowledge of truth. The doctrine of St. Thomas is the doctrine which the Church recommends beyond all others, and which she enjoins her masters to teach. (I)

> We believe that in order for his thought to live among men, a special assistance of the Holy Spirit is and will always be needed. In particular, in our epoch so full of errors . . . we believe that it is impossible for Thomism

Mercier, *La vie intérieure: appel aux âmes sacerdotales*. See: B. Zorcolo, "Bibliografia del P. Garrigou-Lagrange," *Angelicum* 42 (1965): 200–250.

9 Maritain explains in his *Notebooks*: "It was in 1919 (at the beginning of the term, in autumn) that there really began, at our house in Versailles (rue Baillet-Reviron), regular meetings of philosophical studies attended by – by first in very small numbers – some of our personal friends and some of my students from the Institut Catholique (where I had been named professor in June 1914). This had emerged quite naturally, without any preconceived plan, from the need to examine a little more closely, in free discussions, the doctrine of St. Thomas, and to bring it face to face with the problems of our time." [Jacques Maritain, *Notebooks*, trans. Joseph W. Evans (Albany, N.Y.: Magi Books, 1984), 133.]

10 The Statutes are found in Ibid., 290–97.

> to be maintained in its integrity and in its purity, without the special aid of the life of prayer. (II)
>
> The Thomist Study Circles . . . (are) open to persons who, living in the world, wish to work for the diffusion of Thomism or to draw their inspiration from it, while remaining strictly faithful to the doctrine of St. Thomas and to his thought, which lives in his great disciples, such as Cajetan, John of Saint Thomas, or the Salmanticenses.[11] (IV)

This last point put Maritain squarely in the camp of the Dominican Neo-Thomists – the camp identified with Garrigou-Lagrange. As we have seen, the Dominican Neo-Thomists were not interested in what one might call "the quest for the historical Thomas"; they held that Thomism was a living tradition – a tradition maintained and further energized by St. Thomas's great commentators. The proper interpretation of St. Thomas is found not through historical erudition but through knowledge of the living tradition of Thomism. Focusing too minutely on what historiography can tell us concerning what the "historical Thomas" did or not hold runs the risk of obscuring the fact that it is the truth of the various propositions that most matters – not the fact that they can be attributed with certainty to St. Thomas himself.

This commitment of Maritain meant that it was a foregone conclusion that the Order of Preachers would be enlisted to help with the Thomist Study Circles. The Dominicans were the prime exemplars of the living tradition of Thomism; within the Order the tradition of Cajetan, John of Saint Thomas, and Bañez had been kept alive.

Because of this, Garrigou-Lagrange became the Dominican priest desired by the Maritains as general director of the Thomist Study Circles. In his *Notebooks* Maritain recounts a visit with Garrigou in October of 1921 – the year that he and Raïssa decided to give greater

11 The Salmanticenses were the Carmelite commentators of St. Thomas located at the University of Salamanca.

formality to the structures of the Thomist Study Circles. He wrote:

> With his goodness and simplicity which were full of playfulness, this great theologian set about relieving me to push Raïssa's wheelchair along the roads (she was benefiting greatly from these outings which I had begun in September). It was during one of these walks, Monday the 10th of October, I believe, that she made bold to say to him, while thinking that she was asking the impossible (Father Garrigou taught at Rome, at the Collegium Angelicum, and he passed his vacation preaching retreats for contemplatives): "My Father, there is a great anguish and a great thirst among those who live in the world, it is necessary that they also hear you in France. If, thanks to the Thomist circles, we can bring together, as I believe, a sufficiently large number of friends to hear you, would you consent to come each year, during the vacation, to preach a retreat for them, like those you preach to the contemplatives, but for those who are intellectuals in the world?" – To our great surprise and our great joy, he replied *yes* immediately. The annual retreats of the Thomist circles were founded in principle.[12]

With the permission of his provincial and the blessing of the Master of the Order, Garrigou assumed the position of general director of the Thomist Study Circles. Statute VIII of the organization was made to read: "The general director of the Thomist Study Circles will always be a friar of the Order of St. Dominic [sic]. The first general director chosen by the Very Reverend Father Provincial of France and approved by the Most Reverend Father General, will be Father Garrigou-Lagrange, professor of theology at the Angelicum, Rome."[13] The next statute spelled out the role of the general director:

> The general director guides and supervises the studies of the diverse groups by keeping in touch with the director of studies; he also gives a general orientation

12 Maritain, *Notebooks*, 139–40.

13 Ibid., 294.

concerning the spiritual life, thanks above all to an annual retreat preached, theoretically, by him, according to the approval of the Ordinary of that place. It would be good to profit from the annual retreat by having, outside of the exercises of the retreat itself, a general meeting presided over by the general director, who could then give instructions concerning the studies and the intellectual work of the year.[14]

Garrigou-Lagrange preached all but one of the annual retreats of the Thomist Study Circles from their inception in 1922 until 1937.[15] The first retreat took place in Versailles; Maritain notes that there were approximately thirty retreatants. Among them were the following:

> Abbés Journet, Lallemant, Lavaud, Péponnet, Dondaine, Maquart, Richaud, Canon Rageth, Brother Bruno; Mlles Denis, Clément, Leuret, Moreau, Pimor, Ressinger, Mme Lequeux; Dr. Pichet, Henri Ghéon, Jean-Pierre Altermann, Henri Croville, Yves Congar (then a student at the Institut Catholique), Albert Camilleri, René Philipon; four or five less regular attendants, and the three of us.[16]

During the five-day experience (September 30 through October 4, 1922), Garrigou preached on the following themes: "the union of the intellectual life and of the spiritual life," "the ultimate End of human life," "the natural desire to see God," "the love of God for us and the redemptive act of Christ," "Mortification," "Humanity," and "Prayer."[17] Maritain's *Notebooks* refers to the last day of the retreat in these terms:

> [October 4, 1922] Closing of the retreat. Father Garrigou leaves for Paris, and from there for Vienna.

14 Ibid., 295. N.B.: Jacques Maritain held the position of director of studies for the Thomist Study Circles.

15 Garrigou was unable to preach the 1928 retreat. He enlisted Vincent Bernadot, O.P., to lead that year's retreat.

16 Maritain, *Notebooks*, 148. "The three of us" refers to Maritain, Raïssa, and Vera.

17 Ibid., 149.

> He is very happy, we likewise. The union of minds has been marvelous.[18]

As the list of retreatants revealed, the young Yves Congar – future Dominican theologian, *peritus* at Vatican II, and cardinal – was present for the first retreat of the Thomist Study Circles. Although his theological project would not run parallel to Garrigou's, Congar, interviewed many years later by Patrick Granfield, had this to say concerning the retreats he was able to attend:

> *Interviewer*: Did you know Garrigou-Lagrange very well?
>
> *Father Congar*: Oh yes. I belonged to a kind of intellectual fraternity, before I became a Dominican. It was a spiritual fraternity, a Thomist fraternity. In September every year, we had a retreat that was preached by Garrigou-Lagrange. He impressed me very much with his profound grasp of the spiritual life, but most of all by his strong sense of affirmation. As a young man, I admired his positive spirit.[19]

The same sentiments are found in the journal that Congar kept during a most difficult period of his theological career.[20] Speaking of Garrigou's presence and preaching, Congar, recalling his experience of more than twenty years past, wrote:

> He made a profound impression on me. Some of his sermons enthused me and overwhelmed me with their clarity, their rigor, their fullness, their purity of lines, their spirit of faith allied to an impressive intellectual rigor.[21]

18 Ibid.

19 Patrick Granfield, *Theologians at Work* (New York: Macmillan, 1967), 245.

20 Yves Congar, *Journal d'un théologien, 1946–1956*, ed. and presented by Etienne Fouilloux (Paris: Cerf, 2000).

21 Ibid., 36. [*Il fit pour moi une impression profonde. Certains de ses sermons m'enthousiasmèrent et me comblèrent par leur clarté, leur rigueur, leur ampleur, leur pureté de lignes, leur esprit de foi allié à une rigueur intellectuelle impressionnante.*]

For his part, Maritain had this to say about Garrigou's preaching:

> Father Garrigou-Lagrange gave as nourishment sermons which he would have preached to cloistered contemplatives and instructions which he would have delivered before his students at the Angelicum or his colleagues at the Academy of St. Thomas. And this nourishment was received by all with joy and with a real profit. All of which proves on the one hand that one should not underestimate the powers of natural intelligence superelevated by faith, and on the other hand that what souls thirst for above all is to enter into the paths of doctrinal truth and into those of an authentic spiritual experience, and in this way to be enabled to realize within themselves the unity required by life. *O Sapientia!*[22]

Through the 1920s and early 1930s, Garrigou and Maritain worked side by side in promoting the thought of St. Thomas and in attempting to bolster the intellectual and spiritual life of the Church. During this time, it seemed to them that the *Action Française* movement of Charles Maurras (1868–1952) would be an important socio-political support to their program.[23]

Charles Maurras and his *Action Française* movement – part political party, party literary vehicle for a cultural revolution – "provided the fundamental doctrines of the whole Extreme Right in France and of important nationalist and traditionalist groups in Belgium, Italy, Portugal, Spain, Romania, and Switzerland, as well as the theoreti-

22 Maritain, *Notebooks*, 155.

23 See especially: André Laudouze, *Dominicains français et Action Française (1899–1940): Maurras au couvent* (Paris: Editions Ouvrières, 1989) and Philippe Chenaux, *Entre Maurras et Maritain: Une génération intellectuelle catholique (1920–1930)* (Paris: Cerf, 1999). Eugen Weber's *Action Française: Royalism and Reaction in Twentieth-Century France* (Stanford, Calif.: Stanford University Press, 1962) remains the most complete picture of Maurras's organization.

cal background of the National Revolution of Vichy."[24] Its history between 1899 and 1944 is marked by one paradox after another:

> The fiercest champion of the Catholic party, it was condemned by the Pope; responsible for making royalism a fashionable cause, it was disowned by the princes it professed to serve; above all patriotic and anti-German, it came into its own when France reached her lowest point since Joan of Arc rode into Bourges, and gave unreserved support to a Head of State whose policy included collaboration with the German enemies of France.[25]

Action Française was born with the Dreyfus Affair. In Maurras's eyes, this complex of issues – which eventually culminated in Dreyfus's exoneration – witnessed to the "liberal and democratic misconceptions which the French Revolution had broadcast throughout the world."[26] Ultimately, the French Revolution "was responsible in his eyes for the decay and corruption of the moral and political fiber of every people it had touched."[27] Returning to traditional values was the only way to revive the greatness that once was France. And that greatness could not be revived under the conditions set by the Third Republic: the monarchy must be restored and the Catholic Church must regain its traditional place at the heart of French social life and culture.

Both Maritain and Garrigou-Lagrange were sympathetic to Maurras and *Action Française*. As for Maritain, it was at the instigation of Humbert Clérissac, O.P., his first guide in Catholicism, that he subscribed to Maurras's newspaper, *Action Française*. The zeal of the convert and the desire to be obedient in all things accounts for much of his

24 Weber, *Action Française*, vii.
25 Ibid.
26 Ibid., 13.
27 Ibid.

initial sympathy.[28] Garrigou, one might surmise, was enticed not least by the fact that *Action Française* "denounced relentlessly the influence of Bergson, and the anti-intellectualism of Blondel or Laberthonnière."[29] In any event, the following quotation, which summarizes Maritain's stance, holds equally well for Garrigou:

> He tried to keep . . . [his] association completely apolitical. He considered the association not so much membership in a political party as a kind of rallying of friends and kindred spirits to defend common philosophical causes and to attack common philosophical enemies.[30]

It is beyond the scope of this chapter to discuss the fine points of the history of *Action Française*. For our purposes, it suffices to highlight the fact that Maurras's movement was in large measure a reaction to the excesses of France's Third Republic.

The Third French Republic

The Third Republic was born with France's humiliating defeat in the Franco-Prussian War of 1870. At the Battle of Sedan, Napoléon III was taken prisoner by the Germans. France was forced to surrender and, by way of the armistice, agreed to transfer Alsace and Lorraine to German control. The French Empire was dissolved, and a new republic proclaimed.

Ideologically, the new republic was decidedly anticlerical; it witnessed to a remarkable hostility to the Catholic Church. The anti-Catholic rhetoric of the French

28 Doering, *Jacques Maritain*, 8, 11.

29 Ibid., 11. Garrigou's stance, in turn, affected Maritain: "The opinion of such unworldly men and great scholars as Father Thomas Pègues and Réginald Garrigou-Lagrange, who saw only the single-minded opposition of *Action Française* to the worldly forces of modernism, certainly weighed heavily on the young philosopher." [Ibid., 15.]

30 Ibid., 17.

Revolution, made graphically clear with Diderot's dictum – "Humanity will not be free until the last king is strangled with the entrails of the last priest"[31] – was renewed. As a result, the more fervent one's Catholicism, the less likely one would be enamored of the Third Republic.

Garrigou-Lagrange, "fervent" by anyone's standard, was, like all conservative Catholic Frenchmen, scandalized by the Third Republic's overt hostility toward the Church. Adrien Dansette explains that the Third Republic carried out a clear-cut program of dechristianization – particularly through its education laws:

> Without reexamining these laws in detail, we should perhaps indicate the contribution to the dechristianization of the country made by the more important of them, which related to education. The law of 1880 forbade religious teaching in State schools, while that of 1886 removed from these schools the teachers belonging to religious orders. The teacher's training colleges were reorganized and increased in numbers and formed a new body of teachers with an entirely different spirit. Catholic teachers disappeared gradually from the field of public education and by 1914 the great majority of their successors owed no allegiance whatever to the Church. . . . In general terms the effect of the educational reforms in the various communes was to place alongside the representative of religion one who represented indifference or irreligion.[32]

From the Catholic perspective, the Third Republic was notorious for more than its education laws. Emile Combes, prime minister from 1902 to 1905, had as his ultimate goal the destruction of French Catholicism.[33] With this objective in mind, he took aim at France's religious orders and

31 *L'humanité ne sera pas libre avant que le dernier roi est étranglé dans les entrailles du dernier prêtre.*

32 Adrien Dansette, *Religious History of Modern France*, 2 vols., trans. John Dingle (New York: Herder & Herder, 1961), II, 415.

33 Ibid., II, 197.

used against them the 1901 law concerning associations. This law stipulated that "associations known as religious orders . . . were required to obtain an authorization from the *Conseil d'Etat*."[34]

> The superiors of the men's orders were warned as early as 1st April 1903 that the Chamber had refused their requests for authorization. The preaching orders, with a membership of 3,000 men, were ordered to close their principal houses within a fortnight. The teaching orders with nearly 16,000 members were given periods of grace of varying lengths. . . . The Dominicans, who had been promised authorization by Waldeck-Rousseau, tried to negotiate. . . . The superiors of other orders signed a protest in which they stated they would remain in their houses. Some of them were proceeded against in the courts.[35]

The Dominicans did not win their fight for authorization and were forced into exile. Their *studium*, as we have seen, found refuge in Le Saulchoir. Other orders also fled to Belgium, or to Italy or Great Britain; some went underground in France and tried to avoid secularization.[36]

A secularist ideology imbued all of French government. It held that to uphold the revolutionary ideals of liberty, fraternity, and equality, Catholicism must be destroyed and a rationalist religion must be taught – the human person must be put in the place of God.[37] This ideology informed foreign affairs as well as domestic politics: "Hardly had the law on . . . religious orders been passed than the government put an end to a period of quarrels with the Holy See by breaking off diplomatic relations."[38]

34 Ibid., II, 192.
35 Ibid., II, 202. (In this context, Dansette tells the dramatic story of the Third Republic's violent attack on the Grande-Chartreuse monastery.)
36 See: Ibid., II, 202 ff.
37 Ibid., II, 206.
38 Ibid.

The tumultuous story of Church-State relations in the France of the early twentieth century goes a long way toward accounting for the appeal of Charles Maurras's *Action Française* and how men like Jacques Maritain and Garrigou-Lagrange could react favorably to it.

Garrigou, in the less-than-friendly idiom of Congar's journal, was "held to be, alone among the French Dominicans, totally, virginally, faithful to St. Thomas and to have the grace of integral Thomism."[39] His fidelity to St. Thomas, witnessed in his preface to the Angelic Doctor's *De regimine principum*,[40] kept him from being friendly toward democracy. The call to restore the monarchy by putting Jean III, duc de Guise, on the throne and to restore the Catholic Church's traditional position in French society made it easy for him to overlook Maurras's own atheism and his purely pragmatic use of the symbols and ethos of Catholicism.[41]

Garrigou and Maritain: Estrangement

As the years went by, the relationship between Jacques Maritain and Garrigou-Lagrange became more and more strained. Ironically, the source of tension turned on overtly political matters: Maritain, the twentieth-century's most prominent Thomistic metaphysician, and Garrigou-Lagrange, Neo-Thomism's most eminent spiritual theologian, were to become estranged over contrary judgments concerning the contingent world of European politics.

Maritain, by the time of the founding of the Thomist Study Circles, had written several well-received works in Thomistic philosophy. However, he was not content to

39 Congar, *Journal d'un théologien*, 35–36. [. . . *il était estimé être, seul des dominicains français, totalement, virginalement fidèle à saint Thomas, et comme ayant une grâce thomiste intégrale.*]

40 St. Thomas Aquinas, *De regimine principum*, trans. Claude Roquet (Paris, 1926), vii–xxxi.

41 These were among the factors that eventually led Pope Pius XI to condemn *Action Française* in 1926.

remain in the world of abstract ideas. Slowly his reflection moved to considerations of social and political philosophy.[42]

Garrigou, who, through his work with the Thomist Study Circles, undoubtedly considered himself to be Maritain's chief mentor, did not take kindly to the philosopher delving into political matters. He was convinced that Maritain's most important talent was his ability to explicate the metaphysics of St. Thomas; he felt that Maritain should not use his time in dealing with political matters.

By 1937, the fifteenth anniversary of Garrigou's first retreat for the Thomist Study Circles, the relationship between the theologian and the philosopher was about to reach an impasse. The following passages from Maritain's *Notebooks*[43] offer a sense of the severity of the problem:

> I transcribe my notes of 1937 without attenuating anything in them. I insist only on remarking that our differences in political matters never diminished the affection and the gratitude which Raïssa and I had for him [i.e., Garrigou-Lagrange]. (And he for his part, even when he found fault with me, did what he could to defend me.)
>
> Friday the 24th of September
>
> Father G.-L. arrives in the evening; dines at our house with Charles Journet.
>
> Father is very worked-up against me; goes so far as to reproach me, a convert, with wanting to give lessons in the Christian spirit to "us who have been Catholics for three hundred years". . .
>
> This puts me in a black rage, which I do not hide. The retreat begins under a very bad sign. Father Garrigou would like to prohibit me from speaking on

42 On this development, see: Yves R. Simon, "Jacques Maritain: The Growth of a Christian Philosopher," in *Jacques Maritain: The Man and His Achievement*, ed. Joseph W. Evans (New York: Sheed & Ward, 1963), 3–24.

43 Maritain, *Notebooks*, 168–70.

> the philosophy of history, and from judging events, and from acting on young people in these matters. (He is not the only one in Rome to think like this, I know very well, and to be terrified of the 'political Maritain.') Metaphysics only! But he himself does not hesitate to pronounce in favor of Franco and to approve the civil war in Spain . . .
>
> Monday the 27th of September
>
> Mass by André Baron. Finally Father Garrigou loosens up a little. Up to now he has confined himself to platitudes. Arthur, the young Borgeaud, remarked that there was something, a hidden tragedy, which hindered everything. Father was obsessed by Spain. . . .[44]

This turned out to be the last of the Thomist Study Circle retreats. Garrigou informed the Maritains that he had accepted an invitation to speak in Brazil during September of 1938 and thus would be unavailable for 1938's retreat. As a result, the decision was made to transform that year's retreat "into study days bringing together a very small number of participants."[45] The days were marred by France's military mobilization in response to

44 Yves Simon provides the following explanation of the context: "Besides the slaughter, the Spanish Civil War brought about, and not in Spain alone, an extraordinary indulgence in hatred and in the most debased feelings the human soul ever conceived. . . . Spanish refugees who were pouring into France comprised all sorts of characters, from the most noble to the most undependable. We all felt that we had an urgent duty to do something about the misfortunes of our neighbors and its international consequences. Maritain stood for mediation between the parties at war. So did I. We met in committees with a faint hope that the crushing victory of one side and the slaughter of the other might be avoided." [Yves Simon, "Jacques Maritain," 18.] Garrigou, moved by the anti-clericalism of the Republicans – perhaps most vividly manifested in their atrocities against priests and nuns – hoped for an outright victory for Francisco Franco.

45 Maritain, *Notebooks*, 170.

the Third Reich's annexation of Czechoslovakia. Yet, says Maritain, the "hours spent together in metaphysics and theology at such a moment . . . [gave them] all a feeling of astonishing spiritual gaiety and an extraordinary calm."[46]

The meeting in 1938 would be the last annual gathering of the Thomist Study Circles: they "were killed by the war."[47] The war, too, provided an even deeper chasm between Garrigou and Maritain.

The Fall of France and the Rise of Vichy

By June of 1940, France had fallen to Hitler's Third Reich. Under the terms of the armistice signed on June 25, 1940, the northern part of the country, including Paris, would remain under direct German occupation. The rest of the country was allowed self-government, albeit within the ambit of Nazi Germany. This was a crushing blow to French pride – more humiliating than the Franco-Prussian War that had ushered in the Third Republic. Not a few members of the Catholic hierarchy expressed the view that "defeat is a Divine punishment for our anti-religious laws."[48] Now, the Third Republic was officially over and General de Gaulle had set up a government in exile in London – hoping to inspire resistance to the Nazi occupation and partition of France.

Alan Palmer provides the following explanation of what transpired in unoccupied France:

> On the defeat of France in 1940 the National Assembly was convened at the spa town of Vichy, in the unoccupied zone. There, on 10 July 1940, it authorized the Prime Minister, Pétain, to assume full powers, pending promulgation of a new constitution. Later in the day Pétain declared himself "Head of the

46 Ibid., 170–71.
47 Ibid., 171.
48 C. L. Mowat, ed., *The New Cambridge Modern History.* Volume 11: *The Shifting Balance of World Forces, 1898–1945* (New York: Cambridge University Press, 1968), 548.

> French State," and for four years France was administered by this interim autocracy, using Vichy as a capital.[49]

Vichy France under Marshal Philippe Pétain was fundamentally unrepublican and anti-democratic. *Famille, Travail, Patrie* officially took the place of *Liberté, Fraternité, Egalité*. What is most important to note for our purposes is that Pétain's rule overturned the anti-Catholic animus of the Third Republic. Calling his administration a *régime d'ordre moral*, Pétain suppressed the *Ecoles normales*, returned religious instruction to primary education, suspended legislation concerning religious congregations, and subsidized private schools.[50] In light of all these developments – and in spite of his fascism – Cardinal Gerlier would proclaim: "Pétain is France; and France is Pétain."[51] It is not an exaggeration to claim that not since the *ancien régime* had a French government been more hospitable to the institutional needs of the Catholic Church.

What of General de Gaulle? To many his Free French movement seemed a pipe dream. By late 1940 it did not appear that Britain would be able to hold out much longer against Hitler. At the same time, de Gaulle's rhetoric did not appeal to the conservative, *Action Française* wing of Catholicism.[52]

> De Gaulle's messages were addressed too blatantly to French republicans, and his calls for the revolt of the Army had rallied communists to him. Pétain, on the other hand, had declared himself in favor of monarchy in France, and not a liberal monarchy either. And so the sympathy of the *Action Française* for Pétain and

49 Alan Palmer, *The Penguin Dictionary of Twentieth Century History, 1900–1978* (New York: Penguin Books, 1979), 379.

50 Mowat, *The New Cambridge History*, 548.

51 Ibid.

52 Note: Pope Pius XII removed his predecessor's condemnation of *Action Française* in 1939.

> its hostility to de Gaulle and the British had stemmed in part . . . from the fact that British propaganda insisted on republican solidarity and traditions.[53]

Devout French Catholics found it difficult not to marvel with Charles Maurras at the appearance of Marshal Pétain. Maurras's famous exclamation, "*La divine surprise*," "did not refer to the country's defeat as some observers have charged, but to the miracle of the emergence of a man of destiny, a national savior, through the gift of the Marshal's gift of his person to France."[54] One notes that Maurras "had been asking for something along the lines of *Famille, Travail, Patrie* for many years; and the regal tone and bearing of the new head of state did his old monarchist heart good."[55]

While the overwhelming majority of the French lamented German hegemony, it bears repeating that not everyone was sorry to see the end of the Third Republic. The anticlericalism of the French government and its anti-Catholic policies inflamed many and fueled Maurras's *Action Française* movement. This situation raised a fundamental question *vis-à-vis* one's stance on the government of Marshal Pétain: where were one's loyalties to lie? Was, as Cardinal Gerlier proclaimed, Pétain equivalent to France? Did General de Gaulle have any claim to legitimacy?

Maritain and Garrigou-Lagrange found themselves on different sides of this question. Maritain's sympathies lay with de Gaulle and the Free French movement. He stood for principled resistance to Nazi Germany; he could find no justifying reason for collaborating with the Third Reich. There was no question in his mind that the regime at Vichy was illegitimate.

"Father Garrigou," wrote Maritain, was politically "a

53 Weber, *Action Française*, 458. Weber provides background information on Vichy France on pages 442–53.

54 Samuel M. Osgood, *French Royalism since 1870* (The Hague: Martinus Nijhoff, 1970), 161.

55 Ibid.

man of the right. . . ."[56] Having had no love for the Third Republic, Garrigou was moved to support Vichy. Maritain recounted that Garrigou found his position "decidedly too much for him."[57] Exasperated, Garrigou raised the stakes of the disagreement, casting it as a matter of faith and accusing Maritain of doctrinal deviations. For his part, Maritain reacted passionately against Garrigou's attempt "to transform contingent choices into quasi-articles of faith."[58] In a letter written six months after the war ended in Europe, Maritain said to Garrigou:

> In speaking like that, you risked making one believe that you deplored in me *concessions* to philosophical or theological error and doctrinal deviations, when all that you deplored was only what the Reverend Father Garrigou-Lagrange, 'man of the Right,' regarded as concessions and deviations from his own political positions and his own evaluation of political events.[59]

And, in a letter of 18 December 1946, Maritain continued:

> When you took the part of Marshal Pétain – to the point of declaring that to support de Gaulle would be a mortal sin – I thought that your political prejudices blinded you in a serious matter for the country; I did not think to suspect your theology nor to reproach you

56 Maritain, *Notebooks*, 168.

57 Ibid.

58 Fouilloux, *Une Eglise en quête*, 114. [. . . *d'avoir transformé des choix contingents en quasi-articles de foi.*]

59 Maritain to Garrigou-Lagrange, 12 December 1946, in Jacques and Raïssa Maritain, *Œuvres complètes*, IX, 1103–1104, cited by Fouilloux, *Une Eglise en quête*, 114–15. [*En parlant ainsi vous risquiez de faire croire que vous déplorez en moi des* concessions *à l'erreur philosophique ou théologique et une déviation doctrinale, alors que tout ce que vous êtes fondé à déplorer est seulement ce que le Révérend Père Garrigou-Lagrange, 'homme de droit,' regard comme des concessions et une déviation par rapport à ses propres positions politiques et à sa propre appréciation des événements politiques.*]

60 Maritain to Garrigou-Lagrange, 18 December 1946, in Jacques and Raïssa Maritain, *Œuvres complètes*, IX, 1115–16, cited by Fouilloux,

for a deviation in a doctrinal matter.[60]

Garrigou and Maritain would not be able to get beyond the rupture caused by this episode. It turned out to be a wound that would not heal. Both men were passionate in defense of their positions and strong emotions had co-mingled with reason and faith. From our vantage point it is impossible not to conclude that in this matter Garrigou was in the wrong: wrong in supporting Vichy and wrong in avoiding reconciliation with a long-time friend.

Before leaving this discussion, an issue raised by Maritain's letter of 18 December 1946 bears highlighting. Maritain said that in disagreeing with Garrigou, he had not thereby called into question Garrigou's theology. Nor had he reneged on his commitment to Thomism. His point was that one's theological commitments do not lead inexorably to specific choices in the real world of contingency. This is important to underline because one might be tempted to think that Garrigou's support for *Action Française* or Francisco Franco or Marshal Pétain is enough to show that his theology was corrupt. Even though Garrigou would attempt to justify his positions by appealing to the faith, it is safe to say that they rested upon his personal socio-political presuppositions.

Garrigou and M.-Dominique Chenu (1895–1990)

Teaching at the Angelicum for fifty years meant that Garrigou-Lagrange had a hand in forming a host of students. Moreover, his position gave him the opportunity to direct the doctoral dissertations of several generations of gifted students. As we have seen, some of the most well-

Une Eglise en quête, 115. [*Quand vous avez pris le part du Maréchal Pétain au point de déclarer que soutenir de Gaulle était un péché mortel, j'ai pensé que vos préjugés politiques vous aveuglaient en une matière grave pour le pays, je n'ai pas pensé à suspecter votre théologie ni à vous reprocher une déviation en matière de doctrine*.]

known included the Dominicans M.-Michel Labourdette, M.-Benoît Lavaud, and Louis-Bertrand Gillon and, of course, Karol Wojtyla – Pope John Paul II.[61] From Garrigou's perspective, his most gifted student, and, at the same time, his favorite, was his Dominican confrere M.-Dominique Chenu.[62]

Chenu, almost twenty years Garrigou's junior, entered the novitiate of the Paris province in 1913. At that time, the novitiate and the *studium* were united in one priory at Le Saulchoir. Due to the First World War and the fact that Belgium was sure to become coterminous with the front-line for the antagonists, the Dominican student brothers at Le Saulchoir were transferred to the Angelicum. It was there that they would encounter their fellow member of the Paris province, Garrigou-Lagrange, who, by 1914, had already published two books, eight articles in the *Revue thomiste* and two articles in the *Revue des sciences philosophiques et théologiques*.[63]

Chenu stayed for six years in Rome and wrote his doctoral dissertation – *Analyse psychologique et théologique de la contemplation* – under Garrigou's direction.[64] Olivier La Brosse, in his *Le Père Chenu: La liberté dans la foi*,[65] provides the following quotation from Chenu concerning his dissertation:

61 The following works all highlight Pope John Paul II's connection with Garrigou-Lagrange: Rocco Buttiglione, *Karol Wojtyla: The Thought of the Man Who Became Pope John Paul II*, trans. Paolo Guietti (Grand Rapids, Mich.: William Eerdmans, 1997); Jonathan Kwitny, *Man of the Century: The Life and Times of Pope John Paul II* (New York: Henry Holt, 1997); and George Weigel, *Witness to Hope: The Biography of Pope John Paul II* (New York: HarperCollins, 1999). Buttiglione's work has the most extended discussion.

62 Fouilloux, *Une Eglise en quête*, 130.

63 See: Zorcolo, *Bibliografia del P. Garrigou-Lagrange*, 200–205.

64 Chenu's dissertation was published in *RSPT* 75 (1991): 363–422.

65 Olivier La Brosse, ed. *Le Père Chenu: La liberté dans la foi* (Paris: Cerf, 1969).

> It was a new subject, for its time. From the spiritual and theological capital acquired at that time, I hope to have lost nothing; in any event, it has always been a safeguard for me against the temptation toward activism in Dominican life, where contemplation is the nourishing soil for theology as well as for the apostolate.[66]

Indeed, it was a new subject, and a subject which was well-suited to Garrigou's direction. Fouilloux notes that however much Chenu might eventually be led to disagree with Garrigou over Thomism and the meaning of theology, he would tenaciously hold to Garrigou's refusal to separate mysticism and asceticism.[67]

Garrigou had big plans for his protégé. He saw such promise in Chenu that after the defense of his dissertation he asked him to stay on at the Angelicum as his assistant and *chargé de cours*. Garrigou was ready to anoint his heir apparent.[68]

However, Chenu chose to turn down Garrigou's offer –

66 Chenu in La Brosse, *Le Père Chenu*, 31. [*C'était un sujet neuf, à l'époque. Du capital spirituel et théologique alors acquis, j'espère n'avoir rien perdu; en tout cas, ce me fut toujours une sauvegarde contre la tentation de l'activisme en vie dominicaine où la contemplation est la terre noutritive de la théologie comme de l'apostolat.*]

67 Fouilloux, *Une Eglise en quête*, 130.

68 See: La Brosse, *Le Père Chenu*, 31: . . . *le maître de l'Angelicum appréciait et aimait suffisamment son élève pour lui proposer, à sa sortie des études en 1920, de demeurer auprès de lui comme assistant et chargé de cours.* Chenu, commemorating his golden anniversary of profession in the Order of Preachers, wrote of his first years: *Ce ne fut cependant pas au Saulchoir que je fis mes études philosophiques et théologiques. Pour échapper à l'invasion allemande, je quittai avec les jeunes le territorire menacé et fus envoyé à Rome pour y poursuivre mes études, puisque ma santé, après les examens répétés, me tenait à l'écart du service militaire. Je fus alors, au collège Angélique, l'étudiant du Père Garrigou-Lagrange, entre autres maîtres fameux, étudiant qui jouit de la confiance de son professeur au point que le professeur le demandera comme collaborateur.* [M.-Dominique Chenu, "Regard sur cinquante ans de vie religieuse," in *L'hommage différé au Père Chenu*, ed. Claude Geffré (Paris: Cerf, 1990), 257–68, at 262.]

preferring to return to teach at Le Saulchoir. What accounts for this decision? Surely part of the answer is that after six years in Rome Chenu felt the need to reconnect with his home province and native land. But might his decision also have something to do with a growing dissatisfaction in him concerning Garrigou's overall stance as a theologian? Could it be that he accepted the conclusions of Garrigou's critics who found him rigid and altogether too polemical?[69]

Certainly years later Chenu's critique of Garrigou was severe. Olivier La Brosse quotes him as saying that Garrigou was "filled with a Wolffian scholasticism" and that he "demonstrated an ingenuous ignorance of history."[70] And the following quotation puts Chenu in a vastly different theological universe than Garrigou-Lagrange:

> . . . (P)urely philosophical truth cannot account for gospel truth, because there is an interiority to the truth of the faith which is not reducible to philosophical truth. To speak is to do. I do not understand a reality until I "do" that reality.[71]

69 See: Fouilloux, *Une Eglise en quête*, 47. Fouilloux says that at the Angelicum Garrigou *acquiert rapidement une réputation justifiée d'intransigeance thomiste, tant par son enseignement que par son abondante production imprimée où la polémique occupe une place non négligeable.*

70 La Brosse, *Le Père Chenu*, 30. [. . . *imprégné de scolastique wolfienne et affichant une candide ignorance de l'histoire*.] The charge that Garrigou was influenced positively by the German mathematician and rationalist philosopher Christian Wolff (1679–1754) is preposterous. Etienne Fouilloux claims that it originated in the polemics of Etienne Gilson: *C'était ainsi qu'il* (i.e., Gilson) *invente, semble-t-il, contre Garrigou-Lagrange, l'accusation de rationalisme wolffien, du nom d'un émule de Leibniz au XVIIIe siècle; accusation souvent reprise ensuite, mais énergiquement repousée par l'intéressé.* [Fouilloux, *Une Eglise en quête*, 124, n. 70.]

71 Chenu in La Brosse, *Le Père Chenu*, 31. [. . . *la vérité purement philosophique ne rend pas compte de la vérité évangélique, car il y a une intériorité de la vérité de foi qui n'est pas réductible à la vérité philosophique. Parler, c'est faire. Je ne comprends une réalité que quand je la fais.*]

It would take us too far a field to offer a complete exegesis of this text. Suffice it to say that the Neo-Thomists held for the unity of truth and that the truth of the Gospel is held to be accessible to people of goodwill through the exercise of their reason. They would tend to see elements of gnosticism in such a sharp distinction between 'philosophical truth' and 'gospel truth.' Concurrently, they would undoubtedly suspect that Maurice Blondel's philosophy of action was the basis for Chenu's last two lines; they would take exception to the idealism and subjectivism that appears to be celebrated in such a conception.[72]

We will have occasion to discuss the theological project of Garrigou-Lagrange at greater length. For now, we should emphasize that he held that one of the most significant functions of theology was to support and defend the truths of the faith. For Garrigou, theology exists in large measure to uphold orthodox faith and practice. Obviously, this is an archetypically conservative conception of theology's role.

Others might argue that theology's role is much more innovative: its function is to provide new ways of looking at human life, new ways of envisioning the living of the Gospel. And, following the ethos born in the late 1960s, one might be convinced that theology should begin with a critique of the Church's current teaching and practice.

It is clear that if the choice came down to the defense of orthodoxy or innovation and critique, Garrigou-Lagrange would have chosen the former and M.-Dominique Chenu would have chosen the latter. This fact alone would have been enough to ensure an eventual estrangement; however, forces external to their relationship saw to it that the estrangement would be greater than one would have imagined.

72 Chenu is open to a similar critique when he writes: *Il y a chez moi un dépassement de la dualité entre la contemplation et l'action, dans une unité plus profonde, qui est la réflexion théologique. . . . Il faut* faire *la vérité (Jn 3:21).* [Chenu in La Brosse, *Le Père Chenu*, 31.]

Chenu at Le Saulchoir

Etienne Fouilloux claims that the temptation of Le Saulchoir under the leadership of Ambroise Gardeil was to become lost in philosophical and theological speculation. Gardeil – one of his generation's most speculative thinkers – encouraged creative speculation on the mysteries of faith. However, under the leadership of Lemonnyer and Mandonnet, Le Saulchoir became known for its historical studies – particularly the history of the Middle Ages.[73] It would be the accomplishment of M.-Dominique Chenu "to bring together these two formulae in an original manner."[74]

Chenu became his province's Regent of Studies in 1932 and, following the Dominican practice of the time, took the helm of Le Saulchoir. His position afforded him the opportunity of publicizing his critique of so-called "Baroque Scholasticism" to a wider audience. He had, as Fergus Kerr remarks, "set himself the task of replacing what he took to be the non-historical exposition of the Thomist system by his teacher in Rome, R. Garrigou-Lagrange, with a reading of Thomas Aquinas in his historical context."[75]

Before long, Chenu began to believe that the historical approach to theology being worked out at Le Saulchoir should be documented and offered as a model for other theological institutes. Fouilloux provides the following reflection on Chenu's sentiments at the time:

> Rightly or wrongly, its successes persuaded the *studium* that it had become, not only a model for formation

73 See: Philippe Chenaux, *Entre Maurras et Maritain: une génération intellectuelle catholique (1920–1930)* (Paris: Cerf, 1999), 29–30. [Cf.: *Après 1919, sous l'influence du P. Mandonnet, les dominicains du Saulchoir se spécialisent dans l'étude historique du thomisme* (29). *L'application de la méthode historique à l'étude de saint Thomas devint ainsi un des traits caractéristiques du Saulchoir* (30).]

74 Fouilloux, *Une Eglise en quête*, 130. [. . . *à concilier les deux formules d'une manière originale.*]

75 Fergus Kerr, "Chenu, Marie-Dominique," in *New Catholic Encyclopedia* (Supplement, 1989).

> in the Order, but also the matrix for the only Thomist renewal worthy of the name: that which would reduce the religious detachment of intellectuals. Why keep this good news under a bushel basket? It must be propagated in the heart of the Order, if not beyond. It is from this perspective that the traditional discourse of the Regent for the Feast of St. Thomas in 1936 became, the next year, the brochure *Une école de théologie: Le Saulchoir.*[76]

Chenu's brochure was published privately in 1937 (and reprinted in 1985 by Editions du Cerf[77]) and immediately created a sensation in the Dominican world. Chenu could be every bit as polemical as Garrigou-Lagrange and was unable to resist including several "caustic asides about 'Baroque Scholasticism.'"[78] *Une école de théologie* was more or less a broadside on the "official" theological ethos of Roman Catholicism: it called into question the hegemony of the professors at the Roman universities. More importantly, it called into question the very truth of the principles of Neo-Thomist philosophy.

So overtly baited, the Roman authorities saw to it that the Master of the Order of Preachers would have to take action. Père Gillet established a commission to study *Une école de théologie* and to investigate Chenu's orthodoxy. Garrigou found himself appointed as the head of this commission.[79]

76 Fouilloux, *Une Eglise en quête*, 133. [*A tort ou à raison, ses succès persuadent le* studium *qu'il est devenu, non seulement un modèle de formation pour l'Ordre, mais aussi la matrice de seul renouveau thomiste digne de ce nom: celui qui doit réduire le détachement religieux des intellectuels. Pourquoi dès lors garder ces bonnes nouvelles sous le boisseau? Il faut les répandre au sein de l'Ordre, sinon au dehors. C'est dans cet optique que le traditionnel discours du régent pour la fête de saint Thomas 1936 devient, l'année suivante la brochure* Une école de théologie: Le Saulchoir.]

77 M.-Dominique Chenu, *Une école de théologie: Le Saulchoir*, with studies by Guiseppe Alberigo, Etienne Fouilloux, Jean Ladrière and Jean-Pierre Jossua (Paris: Cerf, 1985).

78 Kerr, art. cit.

79 See: Etienne Fouilloux, "Le Saulchoir en procès (1937–1942)," in

Garrigou left for posterity an unusual document pertaining to his involvement in this affair: "Pièces relatives à la condamnation du Père Chenu."[80] Contrary to what one might have expected, Garrigou was skittish about the whole matter. The fact that he belonged to the same province as Chenu and that he had been Chenu's mentor at the Angelicum and his doctoral dissertation director put him in a delicate position.[81] When the decision was eventually made to place *Une école de théologie* on the Index of Forbidden Books (in 1942), Garrigou made it clear that while he was in agreement with the decision, he had not instigated the investigation and had not been one of the prime movers behind the condemnation. Fouilloux remarks:

> All of the papers of the visitor [i.e., Garrigou-Lagrange] which have come down to us witness both to his disagreement with Chenu and his role in the instruction of the case; but they do not allow us to contest his oft-repeated claim that he was in no way the origin of the sanction which he approved . . .[82]

In the eyes of Garrigou-Lagrange, Chenu had, in Fouilloux's wonderfully evocative expression, committed

M.-Dominique Chenu, *Une école de théologie: Le Saulchoir* (Paris: Cerf, 1985), 37–60. Fouilloux says that by this time Garrigou had become for Chenu the very incarnation of everything that he wished to combat: Garrigou was the personification of a speculative and deductive Thomism, as well as a real-live watchdog of orthodoxy (40–41).

80 Garrigou's "Pièces" is kept in the archives of the Dominican province of France (Paris). Fouilloux quotes liberally from it in "Le Saulchoir en procès."

81 Cf.: Garrigou-Lagrange, "Pièces" (in Fouilloux, "Le Saulchoir en procès," 54): *La mission est particulièrement délicate pour moi, étant donné que l'un des deux livres condamnés a été écrit par un de mes anciens élèves, professeur dans ma province.*

82 Fouilloux, "Le Saulchoir en procès," 54. [*Tous les papiers du visiteur parvenus jusqu'à nous mettent en évidence et son désaccord avec Chenu et son rôle dans l'instruction du cas; mais ils ne permettent pas de contester l'affirmation répétée selon laquelle il ne serait en rien à l'origine d'une sanction qu'il approuve* . . .]

the crime of *lèse-thomisme*.[83] He had struck at a way of doing theology that had all but become "official"; it was believed that his manifesto would provide fuel for the enemies of the Church's teaching. Garrigou's following remark also highlights the embarrassment the Roman Dominicans felt in having one of their own attack Neo-Thomism:

> A professor at the Gregorianum [i.e., a Jesuit] said: "They [i.e., the Dominicans] cannot say that we are the ones who are destroying the doctrine of St. Thomas: they are destroying it themselves."[84]

Chenu would be under suspicion for the better part of two decades. He continued his historical-critical studies of the thought of St. Thomas, published several works of remarkable erudition,[85] and became the chief advisor to the worker-priest movement in France.[86] The tide turned in his favor when he was invited by some of the French-speaking African bishops to serve as a *peritus* at the Second Vatican Council. At the Council, Chenu "worked behind the scenes to have his ideas about Thomas Aquinas's 'evangelical humanism' incorporated into such conciliar texts as *Gaudium et spes*."[87]

Chenu was first and foremost a historian; he was a highly respected medievalist. His life's work of situating

83 Ibid., 43.

84 Garrigou-Lagrange, "Pièces," (in Fouilloux, "Le Saulchoir en procès," 43), parenthetical remarks added. [*Un professeur de la Grégorienne a dit: 'Ils ne peuvent pas dire que c'est nous qui détruisons la doctrine de saint Thomas, ils la détruisent eux-mêmes.'*]

85 See: *Introduction à l'étude de saint Thomas d'Aquin* (Paris: J. Vrin, 1950); *La théologie comme science au XIIIe siècle*, 3rd rev. ed. (Paris: J. Vrin, 1957); and *La théologie au XIIe siècle* (Paris: J. Vrin, 1957).

86 See: François Leprieur, *Quand Rome condamne: dominicains et prêtres-ouvriers* (Paris: Cerf, 1989).

87 Kerr, art. cit. Speaking of his experience at the Council, Chenu wrote: *Cette mise en route, cette entreprise d'*aggiornamento *est, à longeur des siècles, l'un des plus grands événements de l'histoire de l'Eglise. En avoir été le témoin, de près de loin, est une rare et bouleversante expérience*. (Chenu, "Regard sur cinquante ans," 268.)

St. Thomas in the context of the thirteenth century and exposing the genesis of the schools of Thomism had much in common with the historical-critical method of Scripture study. We might say that the "search for the historical Thomas" as undertaken by Chenu runs parallel to the "quest for the historical Jesus." And, in this, it shares in the latter's strengths and weaknesses. One the one hand, it could demonstrate that St. Thomas could not have held such and such a position which was in fact being held by a particular school of Thomism. On the other hand, it could not thereby show that such and such a position was *false*.

Garrigou-Lagrange was the beneficiary of a living tradition of thought. It was founded expressly upon the works of St. Thomas, but it had been augmented by St. Thomas's great Dominican commentators: John of St. Thomas, Cajetan, and Bañez. This living tradition was most concerned with the truth claims of its various positions – not the historical accuracy of attributing everything to St. Thomas himself.[88] It would be every bit as nonsensical to say "Let's only hold what St. Thomas himself held" as it would be to say "Let's only hold what scholars tell us the historical Jesus himself taught." Serge-Thomas Bonino, commenting on the Thomism of M.-Michel Labourdette, also a student of Garrigou-Lagrange, writes:

> For him, the history of theology is that of real progress, in the first place a maturation up to the thirteenth century, then an efflorescence. As a result, to claim that Western theology had, at a given moment,

88 Chenu the historian was scandalized by such an attitude. He derided what he called Garrigou's *candide ignorance de l'histoire, y compris l'histoire sainte*. (Chenu, "Regard sur cinquante ans," 262.) The following quote from Chenu succinctly states his deepest convictions concerning St. Thomas: *Ne pourrait-on enfin lire le Doctor angélique comme un théologien du XIIIe siècle, avec toutes ses racines culturelles, ses prédécesseurs païens ou arabes y compris, et non plus comme ce* Doctor perennis, *à jamais figé, hors du temps, sur le double piédestal de l'orthodoxie et de la sainteté?* (Chenu, in La Brosse, *Le Père Chenu*, 38).

> taken the wrong path and that consequently we must return to an understanding of the faith anterior to this error, appeared to him as an inadmissible regression, a betrayal of the very essence of Christian theology and the meaning of its history.[89]

In Chapter 7 we will see that Garrigou's critique of the *nouvelle théologie* follows the same line as that of Labourdette.

One of the most frequent critiques of Garrigou-Lagrange is his alleged failure to understand the basics of history and the importance of history for theology.[90] He certainly was no historian; yet, he was keenly aware of the dangers of historicism:

> We must use the historical method in the history of doctrines, and this is indeed of great help in understanding the state and difficulty of the question, so as to give us, as it were, a panorama of the solutions of any great problem. But in philosophy we must employ the analytic and synthetic method proportionate to it. In theology, however, we rely first upon proofs taken from the authority of Holy Scripture or divine tradition, or even the writings of the holy Fathers, and in the second place on arguments drawn from reason,

89 Serge-Thomas Bonino, "Le thomisme du P. Labourdette," *Revue thomiste* 92 (1992), 97. [*Pour lui, l'histoire de la théologie est celle d'un réel progrès, d'une maturation d'abord, jusqu'au XIIIe siècle, puis d'une efflorescence. Par conséquent, prétendre que la théologie occidentale a pu, à un moment donné, s'égarer gravement et qu'il faut, par conséquent, revenir à une époque de l'intelligence de la foi antérieure à cet égarement lui apparaît comme une régression inadmissible, une trahison de l'essence même de la théologie chrétienne et du sens de son histoire.*]

90 We have seen how Chenu accused him of a *candide ignorance de l'histoire* – including *l'histoire sainte*. However, it bears noting that Garrigou, in his *Our Savior and His Love for Us* (St. Louis: B. Herder, 1951), included an entire chapter on "The Prophetic Announcement of the Savior" in which he deals with salvation history. What is more, he quotes approvingly from Catholicism's father of the historical-critical method – M.-Joseph Lagrange, O.P. (See: n. 25, p. 61 and n. 37, p. 64.)

> while, of course, not neglecting the history of problems and their solutions.[91]

Always and everywhere, the Neo-Thomists were most interested in truth claims; their zeal rarely encompassed the historical development of various teachings within the schools of Thomism. They were scandalized that determining that a proposition belong to, say, "Baroque Scholasticism," was enough for some to dismiss any truth claims it might be making. They were inclined to argue that uncovering a proposition's historical pedigree does not provide one with data pertaining to its veracity.

All of this is to underscore that the condemnation of *Une école de théologie: Le Saulchoir* was not without an objective foundation and need not be attributed to Garrigou's alleged resentment that Chenu did not stay on as his assistant at the Angelicum.[92] And the controversy surrounding this episode in the relationship between Garrigou and Chenu remains an important one for contemporary

91 Réginald Garrigou-Lagrange, *The One God: A Commentary on the First Part of St. Thomas' Theological Summa*, trans. Bede Rose (St. Louis: B. Herder, 1943), 13. In this, Garrigou takes his cues from St. Thomas: "If we consider . . . the works of St. Thomas, we shall see that the common Doctor of the Church did not despise history, as was the case with Descartes, but, so far as possible in his time, he made use of the history of doctrines, appropriating whatever truth he found in the writings of the ancient philosophers, especially Aristotle, as well as in the works of the Fathers and other Doctors of the Church. Often, too, with very keen mental perception, St. Thomas has recourse to the history of errors in formulating his objections, since Providence permits errors so that the truth may become more apparent, and permits evils so that greater good may result therefrom." (Ibid.)

92 *Pace* La Brosse, *Le Père Chenu*, 31: *Il n'est peut-être pas téméraire de penser que la déception alors éprouvée par le professeur romain ne se manifesta pas, en d'autres circonstances, sans un certain ressentiment.* See also: Fouilloux, "Le Saulchoir en procès, 41: *Mais Chenu ne fera pas la carrière romaine apparement tout tracée. Par une bifurcation décisive, dont on peut légitimement penser qu'elle a heurté le P. Garrigou, ses supérieurs lui demandent de compléter l'équipe du Saulchoir. . . .*

Catholic theology. As Guiseppe Alberigo concludes: "In my opinion, the problem which has kept a great timeliness and which has even grown in importance, is that which pertains to the recognition of the historical status of Christianity."[93]

Conclusion

M.-Dominique Chenu used to speak of there being two Chenus: one was thought to be "an old medievalist . . . completely occupied with the reading of old texts, nourished by erudition, attached to the former centuries of Christendom," the other was "frisky, skipping like a kid in front of the entrenchments of the Church, living fully with the conflicts of the contemporary world."[94] The former was highly respected in his field; the latter was rather suspect in some people's minds.[95] Of course, there was but one Chenu; his individuality, however, was not without its complexities and paradoxes.

One can readily posit the same duality for Réginald Garrigou-Lagrange. On the one hand, he appears as the epitome of the Dominican friar-scholar: he is learned and vigorously prolific, religiously observant, a venerable member of his Order. On the other hand, he is embroiled in political controversies and seems to collude with apparently repressive instances of ecclesiastical discipline. Yet there was but one Garrigou-Lagrange: one individual whose life witnessed to a complex set of values and contingent judgments concerning those values.

93 Guiseppe Alberigo, "Christianisme en tant qu'histoire et 'théologie confessante,'" in *Une école de théologie: Le Saulchoir*, 26. [*A mon avis, le problème qui a conservé une grande actualité, et qui a même vu s'accroître sans cesse son importance, est celui relatif à la reconnaissance du statut historique du christianisme.*]

94 Chenu in La Brosse, *Le Père Chenu*, 7. [*. . . un vieux médiéviste . . . tout occupé de la lecture des textes anciens, nourri d'érudition, attaché aux vieux siècles de chrétienté . . . .frignant, gambadant comme un cabri en avant des tranchées de la Sainte Eglise, vivant en plein mêlée du monde contemporain.*]

95 Ibid.

In conclusion, the last word will be given to Jacques Maritain. To his journal entry for 24 September 1937, Maritain years later added a parenthetical comment concerning Garrigou-Lagrange:

> This great theologian, who was little versed in the things of the world, had an admirably candid heart, which God finally purified by a long and very painful physical trial, a cross of complete annihilation, which, according to the testimony of the faithful friend who assisted him in his last days, he had expected and which he had accepted in advance. I pray to him now with the saints of Heaven.[96]

In such a stance, Maritain witnessed as much to his own sanctity as to that of Garrigou-Lagrange.

The next chapter begins the second half of this work – the systematic presentation of aspects of Garrigou's thought. We will begin by highlighting the main themes and the fundamental principles of the Thomism that Garrigou espoused throughout his Dominican life. A number of these we have touched upon in our discussion of his disputes with Bergson and Blondel and in the relationships recounted in this chapter.

96 Maritain, *Notebooks*, 169. The "faithful friend" of whom Maritain speaks was M.-Rosaire Gagnebet, O.P.

6. The Thomism of Garrigou-Lagrange

When we will have received the light of glory and see all things in God, we will have . . . a vertical view of things according to the true scale of values, starting with the Supreme Truth and the Sovereign Good and ending with the divagations of error and evil. We will see the prize of divine revelation and below it the first principles *of natural reason, which also, in their way, come from God.* Réginald Garrigou-Lagrange, *Le réalisme du principe de finalité*[1]

When Réginald Garrigou-Lagrange professed his vows in 1900, Pope Leo XIII's *Aeterni Patris* was just over twenty years old. Leo, then an old man, would live another three years; his ordinances concerning the teaching of the doctrine of St. Thomas were firmly in place. It had all but

1 Réginald Garrigou-Lagrange, *Le réalisme du principe de finalité* (Paris: Desclée de Brouwer, 1932), frontispiece. [*Quand nous aurons reçu la lumière de gloire et verrons toutes choses en Dieu, nous aurons . . . une vue verticale des choses selon la véritable échelle des valeurs, depuis la Vérité suprême et le Souverain Bien jusqu'aux dernières divagations de l'erreur et du mal. Nous verrons alors le prix de la Révélation divine et au-dessous d'elle celui des* premiers principes *de la raison naturelle, qui elle aussi, dans son ordre, vient de Dieu.*]

become "traditional" that the thought of the Angelic Doctor would guide seminary students and, *a fortiori*, Dominican student brothers. In this chapter, we will discuss the general parameters of the Thomism of Garrigou-Lagrange. We will begin by highlighting two of most influential figures in Garrigou's early Dominican life – Ambroise Gardeil, O.P. and M.-Benoît Schwalm, O.P. In large measure, these two account for the general parameters of the brand of Thomism that Garrigou-Lagrange appropriated for himself, as well as the style that marked his career.

Ambroise Gardeil (1859–1931)

When the Paris province was forced to move its *studium* from Flavigny to Le Saulchoir, Ambroise Gardeil was its Regent of Studies. The Dominican custom of the time made the Regent both the chief administrator of the school and the one entrusted with overseeing the intellectual life of the province. Gardeil, the one who first guided Garrigou and his fellow student brothers in the study of St. Thomas's *Summa*, "was a Thomist who had steeped himself thoroughly in the *Summa theologiae*, and who had absorbed the metaphysics of knowledge, free will, and beatitude which Thomas had worked out in the *Summa's Pars Secunda*."[2] He was a significant force in the Neo-Thomism of the opening decades of the twentieth century. In testimony of this, Garrigou would write at Gardeil's death:

> He leaves us the example of a theologian who was steady, original, profound and fearless, who knew how to unite the understanding of the intellectual and spiritual needs of his time with a great respect for the past.[3]

2 McCool, *The Neo-Thomists*, 45.

3 Réginald Garrigou-Lagrange, "In memoriam," *Revue thomiste* 15 (1931): 808; in Henri-Dominique Gardeil, *L'œuvre théologique du Père Ambroise Gardeil* (Etiolles: Le Saulchoir, 1954), 8. [*Il nous laisse l'exemple d'un théologien sûr, original, profond et hardi, qui*

Gardeil had entered the Dominican Order at the very beginning of the Thomistic revival. His earliest mentor in the Order was Réginald Beaudouin, O.P.[4] Gardeil, writes Gerald McCool, was confident that in St. Thomas's "metaphysics of intellect and will and in the traditional Dominican theology of the act of faith, he had found the resources needed to meet the exigencies of contemporary thought . . ."[5] Like many others, Gardeil believed that those theologians who were enamored of Bergson and Blondel were running the risk of falling into doctrinal error. Here, as we have seen in Chapter 4, his influence on Garrigou was enormous.[6]

Ambroise Gardeil is best known for two works: *Le donné révélé et la théologie*[7] *and La structure de l'âme et l'expérience mystique*.[8] In the former, he presented his contribution to the defense of the Church's teaching during the

savait unir à un grand respect du passé l'intelligence des besoins intellectuels et spirituels de son temps.]

4 It was to Beaudouin, after the reestablishment of the Order of Preachers in France, "que revient l'honneur principal d'avoir reconstitué les études à Flavigny et formé le personnel enseignant." [Daniel-Antonin Mortier, *Histoire abrégée de l'Ordre de Saint-Dominique en France* (Tours: Alfred Mame et fils, 1920), 371; See Mortier's section "Action dominicaine française. L'enseignement doctrinal," 370–73.]

5 McCool, *The Neo-Thomists*, 56.

6 McCool underscores the fact that Gardeil argued the Thomistic position by focusing on St. Thomas's metaphysics of causality. He explains: "If it is to be known, the extramental object must first act upon consciousness. In that case, the dynamic activity of the consciously willing agent must be a *reaction* to the metaphysically prior action of real being on it. Therefore, Gardeil continued, the ultimate solution of the problem of the immanence of consciousness cannot be reached on the level of consciousness itself, as Blondel thought. The answer is found on the deeper level of St. Thomas' realistic metaphysics in which both action and the will's dynamic response to it are grounded in being – *agere sequitur esse*." [*The Neo-Thomists*, 58.]

7 (Paris: Victor Lecoffre, 1910).

8 (Paris: Gabalda, 1927).

Modernist crisis.[9] In the latter, from late in his career, Gardeil undertook a discussion of mystical theology. Following St. Thomas, he held that "the human mind, through *intellectus* (insight), has an immediate awareness of its own activity in its knowledge of the extramental object."[10] In this awareness, by which the human soul – "the radical principle from which man's spiritual actions spring"[11] – "comes to act" or "actualizes itself."[12] The upshot of this, says Gardeil, is that the human person can have an intuition of his own spiritual activity. McCool offers the following explanation: "Dim and imperfect though it may be, man's intuitive grasp of his own spiritual activity is a veiled and imperfect intuition by the soul of its own essential reality."[13]

Gardeil's influence on Garrigou-Lagrange is probably best seen in the following quotation from Garrigou's memorial to his mentor:

> Father Gardeil was one of those who thought that the explication of the *Summa theologiae* of St. Thomas consisted especially in underlining the great principles which enlighten the whole thing, in calling attention to the most elevated summits of this mountain chain, that is to say, to some fifty articles which serve as the key to the entire work. . . . So it was that Father Gardeil attached the whole treatise on grace to this principle from Ia, q. 20, a. 2: *Amor Dei est infundens et creans bonitatem in rebus*, the uncreated love of God for us, far from supposing in us lovability, puts it in us, and makes us better. From this is deduced the reality of sanctifying grace and the efficaciousness of

9 H.-D. Gardeil, *L'œuvre théologique*, 69. In his preface to *Le donné révélé*, Ambroise Gardeil had written: *Mon ambition est moins de réfuter le modernisme que d'essayer, sur le point choisi, de le remplacer* (xxvii). [Cited in H.-D. Gardeil, *L'oeuvre théologique*, 71.]

10 McCool, *Neo-Thomists*, 61.

11 Ibid.

12 Ibid.

13 Ibid.

> actual grace followed by the salutary act. Father Gardeil gave an excellent commentary on the *Summa theologiae* . . . which consisted especially in underlining its principles. . . . This view of principles, this was primarily what the students formed by Father Gardeil received from him.[14]

M.-Benoît Schwalm (1860–1908)

Ambroise Gardeil was indisputably the chief intellectual formator of Garrigou-Lagrange. Much of what Garrigou would eventually defend in his voluminous writings can be linked to his having learned from the founder of Le Saulchoir. Indeed, "With Garrigou-Lagrange the tradition of Gardeil reached its full maturity."[15]

If Garrigou was the heir of Gardeil's intellectual heritage, he was, almost as significantly, the heir of M.-Benoît Schwalm's fighting spirit. Garrigou tended to model Schwalm's strenuous critiques of Maurice Blondel and Henri Bergson. Gardeil's serenity and calm in the midst of theological controversy did not take root in Friar Réginald. Rather, he shared with Schwalm a love for argumentation

14 Garrigou-Lagrange, "In memoriam," 800–801; cited by H.-D. Gardeil, *L'oeuvre théologique*, 152–53. [*Le P. Gardeil était de ceux qui pensent que l'explication de la* Somme théologique *de saint Thomas consiste surtout à souligner les grands principes qui éclairent tout, à attirer l'attention sur les sommets les plus élevés de cette chaîne de montagnes, c'est-à-dire sur une cinquantaine d'articles, qui donnent la clef de l'oeuvre tout entière. . . . C'est ainsi que le P. Gardeil rattachait tout le traité de la grâce a ce principe de* Ia Pars, *q. 20, a. 2:* Amor Dei est infundens et creans bonitatem in rebus, *l'amour incrée de Dieu pour nous, loin de supposer en nous l'amabilité, la pose en nous, et nous rend meilleurs. De là se déduit la réalité de la grâce sanctifiante et l'efficacité de la grâce actuelle suivie de l'acte salutaire. Le P. Gardeil donnait ainsi à entendre qu'un excellent commentaire de la* Somme théologique *peut être très bref et consiste surtout à souligner les principes. . . . Cette vue des principes, voilà surtout ce que les élèves formés par le P. Gardeil ont reçu de lui."*]

15 McCool, *The Neo-Thomists*, 69.

as well as an ardent zeal for defending the teachings of the Church.

M.-Benoît Schwalm, professor at Flavigny and later at Le Saulchoir, published "Les illusions de l'idéalisme et leurs dangers pour la foi" in 1896.[16] It was one of the first published critiques of the work of Maurice Blondel; Schwalm found no fewer than fifty statements made by Blondel which he considered to be heterodox.[17] The fundamental problem, of course, was Blondel's Kantianism. Schwalm's critique of this approach is made manifest in the following explanation:

> Post-Kantian idealism, which served as Blondel's model, was a philosophy of immanence. This meant that it was cut off from the world of being and the normative guidance of the teaching Church. Protestants might ignore that teaching in their individualistic approach to faith, but at least they acknowledged the Bible as faith's authoritative norm. Idealists on the other hand, would recognize no norm beyond their own consciousness. This came down to saying that every idealist could be his own Pope. How then could idealism and Catholicism be compatible?[18]

Schwalm's was "the first expression of a negative attitude toward Blondel's philosophy"[19] by a Neo-Thomist. It was far from the last: as we have seen, the career of Garrigou-Lagrange assured as much.

Strict-Observance Thomism

The first chapter of Helen James John's *The Thomist Spectrum*[20] is entitled "Garrigou-Lagrange and Strict-Observance Thomism." She notes that the qualifier "strict-

16 *Revue thomiste* 4 (1896): 413–41.
17 McCool, *The Neo-Thomists*, 54.
18 Ibid., 54.
19 Ibid., 55.
20 Helen James John, *The Thomist Spectrum* (New York: Fordham University Press, 1966).

observance" was coined in "a half-joking fashion many years ago, but has now become a standard way of speaking about the Thomism taught in the Roman universities up to the Second Vatican Council";[21] it is a double-entendre – playing on the strict-observance faction present in many religious orders. In her judgment, St. Pius X's condemnation of Modernism in *Pascendi* was the single-most important factor to highlight for the explanation of this type of Thomism because, in its wake, "the reaction against Modernism became the leit-motif for a total interpretation of the thought of St. Thomas."[22] Garrigou-Lagrange would become the leading proponent of Strict-Observance Thomism; and with the Sacred Congregation for Studies' publication of its "Decree of Approval of Some Theses Contained in the Doctrine of St. Thomas Aquinas and Proposed to the Teachers of Philosophy" on 27 July 1914,[23] this version of Thomism "found a quasi-official formulation."[24]

To simplify a host of issues, Strict-Observance Thomism is at great pains to protect the metaphysical foundations of Catholic theology; part and parcel of this "protection" is a demonstration that the Aristotelian heritage in metaphysics has neither been transcended nor shown to be seriously wanting. In this section, we will examine the philosophical underpinnings of Strict-Observance Thomism; we will see that many of the issues that we explored in reference to Garrigou's disputes with the philosophies of Henri Bergson and Maurice Blondel will come into clearer focus. Since Strict-Observance Thomism is most interested in combatting Modernism, the following insight is helpful in

21 Ibid., 5. McCool refers to "French Dominican Thomism"; others prefer "Aristotelian Thomism."

22 Ibid., 4–5.

23 This is the document wherein the so-called Twenty-four Thomistic Theses are to be found. See especially Edouard Hugon, *Les vingt-quatre thèses thomistes* (Paris: Téqui, 1926).

24 John, *Thomist Spectrum*, 5.

setting the stage for understanding Garrigou's passionate engagement with the question:

> The philosophical aspect of Modernism lay in the position that the doctrines of faith must be regarded not as stable truths of the speculative order, but as "symbolic" expressions of man's religious needs, whose content required radical reformulation to adapt it to the changed circumstances of successive eras of Christianity. The import of this position, which retained the traditional expressions of faith while denying their truth, has been aptly, if flippantly, summed up in the proposition that 'There is no God and the Blessed Virgin is His mother.'[25]

Of utmost importance is that Strict-Observance Thomism holds that the truths of Christian faith are expressions of realities that transcend the religious longings of the human person. These truths are held to have been revealed by God: they are not accounted for by a mere inspection of the workings of the human heart. This point must be insisted upon: Strict-Observance Thomism, while employing what might today strike many as obscure philosophical concepts, places its priority squarely on revelation. There is no equivocation in its doctrine that God has revealed certain truths and that these truths cannot be known apart from the gratuity of divine revelation. While it is true that these truths can be rationally analyzed and can be shown to be "reasonable" and can even be shown to *respond to* the deepest needs of the human person, they cannot be accounted for without reference to the God who has deigned to reveal them.

René Latourelle, long-time professor at the Gregorian University in Rome, gives significant attention to this is his magisterial *Théologie de la révélation*.[26] He notes that Garrigou-Lagrange, in his *De revelatione per Ecclesiam*

25 Ibid., 4.

26 René Latourelle, *Théologie de la révélation* (Paris: Desclée de Brouwer, 1963).

catholicam proposita, wrote that revelation is "essentially supernatural, a free, divine action by which God, in order to lead the human race to its supernatural end (which consists in the vision of the divine essence), speaks to us through the prophets and in these last days through Christ."[27] When it came to a formal definition of revelation, Garrigou settled on the following: "the word of God in the mode of teaching."[28] Latourelle explains that Garrigou grounded this especially on the following passages of Scripture: Hebrews 1:1, Isaiah 50:4, Hosea 2:4, Psalm 84:9, and on "the passages . . . where it is said that the crowds gave to Christ the title 'Master' and that Christ claimed this title as being proper to himself (Matthew 8:28; John 8:13)."[29] Also, he is quick to point out that the condemnation of the following Modernist proposition in *Lamentabili* guided Garrigou's approach: "Christ did not teach a body of doctrine applicable to all times and to all peoples, but he rather inaugurated a religious movement adapted, or capable of being adapted, to different times and places."[30]

The Modernist position was a denial that Christ taught a stable and substantial body of doctrines; their idea was that he initiated a new religious movement by witnessing to the in-breaking of the kingdom of God. To Garrigou, such a proposition defied the clear witness of the Gospels: Jesus's public ministry was dominated by a three-fold

27 Ibid., 218; citing Garrigou-Lagrange, *De revelatione*, I, 132. [. . . *l'action divine, libre et essentiellement surnaturelle par laquelle Dieu, pour conduire le genre humain à sa fin surnaturelle, qui consiste en la vision de l'essence divine, nous parlant par les prophètes et en ces derniers temps par le Christ* . . .]

28 Ibid., 219; citing Garrigou-Lagrange, *De revelatione*, I, 143. [. . . *la parole de Dieu par mode d'enseignement.*]

29 Ibid. [. . . *les passages . . . où il est dit que les foules donnaient au Christ le titre de Maître et que le Christ lui-même revendiquait ce titre comme lui étant propre (Matthieu 8:28; Jean 8:13).*]

30 Ibid., citing *Denz.*, n. 2059. [*Le Christ n'a pas enseigné un corps de doctrine applicable à tous les temps et à tous les hommes, mais il a plutôt commencé un mouvement religieux adapté ou capable d'être adapté aux différents temps et lieux.*]

attention to preaching, teaching, and healing. The significance of the content of Jesus's preaching and teaching is witnessed to by the fact of its having been scrupulously preserved by the Christian community and by each successive generation's self-critique in reference to this teaching.

At its heart, Garrigou's preference was to conceive of revelation as "the word of a very wise superior manifesting to his inferior sublime truths."[31] Here, of course, one encounters Thomism's distinctive espousal of a high Christology. Jesus of Nazareth is the God-man – the Word-made-flesh – the only Son sent by the Father to save the fallen human race. He is one with us in his assumption of a human nature, yet he is infinitely superior to us as a Divine Person. Jesus's words and deeds are God's words and deeds in human history. Simply put: in coming to save us the Son of God revealed all that we need to know for our eternal beatitude. To say otherwise is an offense against his saving mission; it would be tantamount to accusing the Messiah of incompetence.

T. J. Walshe's *The Principles of Catholic Apologetics*[32] is substantially a translation of Garrigou's *De revelatione*. Walshe points to the importance of Christology in the distinction that Garrigou would make between human and divine teaching:

> . . . when the teaching is Divine, inasmuch as many supernatural statements are beyond human comprehension, the authority and infallibility of the teacher are the guarantee of their truth. Here, too, two conditions are necessary: (1) The proposition of the truth; (2) Supernatural light. And the proposition must enunciate: (a) A *hidden* truth, because Revelation is distinct from Inspiration. (b) The truth must be taught in a determinate sense. (c) The divine origin of the

31 Latourelle, *La théologie de la révélation*, 219. [. . . *la parole d'un supérieur très sage manifestant à son inférieur des vérités sublimes*.]

32 T. J. Walshe, *The Principles of Catholic Apologetics* (St. Louis: B. Herder, 1926).

> Revelation must be clearly manifested. Finally, if intellectual light is needed for the comprehension of the truths of nature, supernatural light will be needed for the acceptance of truths divinely proposed.[33]

This accords with St. Thomas's teaching in the *Summa theologiae* (Ia, q. 117, a. 1). As Latourelle remarks: "There must be, according to St. Thomas, an objective proposition of the truth and an interior light in order to judge the proposed truth, or, at least, the authority of the master."[34] Following St. Thomas, Garrigou emphasized the objective and supernatural reality of divine revelation, its utter gratuity, and the fact that since it is principally "word," "it is unlike the infusion of the light of faith."[35]

As we will see, Pope John Paul II, in his encyclical *Fides et ratio* strenuously upholds the tradition of giving priority to faith in the question of the relationship between faith and reason. To do otherwise, of course, would be to flirt with rationalism. Faith, however, must be understood; it is always, to borrow from St. Anselm, "seeking understanding." What rational tools will one use to understand one's Christian faith? Of the many philosophies that human culture knows and has known, which one ought to be chosen to aid in the comprehension of faith? Is every philosophy equal to this task?

As is well-known, St. Thomas chose the philosophy of Aristotle for this task. He found that Aristotle's thought served the faith well; he found, most precisely, that the metaphysics of Aristotle provided a strong foundation upon which to "think the faith." In light of this, and in light of Pope Leo XIII's Thomistic revival, theologians began to ask if Catholic theology must be forever wedded to the philoso-

33 Ibid., 110. Cf.: Latourelle, *La théologie de la révélation*, 220.

34 Latourelle, *La théologie de la révélation*, 220. [*Il y faut, selon saint Thomas, une proposition objective de la vérité et une lumière intérieure pour juger de la vérité proposée ou, tout au moins, de l'authorité du maître*.]

35 Ibid., 219. [. . . *elle diffère de l'infusion de la lumière de foi*.]

phy of Aristotle. Many said no and attempted to change the philosophical foundations of Catholic theology – none with great success.

The University of Fribourg's eminent philosopher, I. M. Bochenski, sets the stage for an answer as to why this was so. He explains that modern philosophy, that is, philosophy during the time between 1600 and 1900,

> came into being with the decline of scholastic philosophy. Characteristic of scholasticism is its pluralism (assuming the plurality of really different beings and levels of being), personalism (acknowledging the pre-eminent value of the human person), its organic conception of reality, as well as its theocentric attitude – God the Creator at its center of vision. Detailed logical analysis of individual problems is characteristic of scholastic method. Modern philosophy opposes every one of these tenets. Its fundamental principles are *mechanism*, which eliminates the conception of being as integral and hierarchical, and *subjectivism*, which diverts man from his previous concentration of God and substitutes the subject as the center. In point of method modern philosophy turned its back on formal logic. With some notable exceptions, it was characterized by the development of great systems and by the neglect of analysis.[36]

The mechanistic and subjectivist *a prioris* of modern philosophy, along with a whole set of reductionisms in contemporary philosophy, simply do not provide a solid enough grounding for Christian faith.

In some presentations of the question, one is given the impression that St. Thomas chose the philosophy of Aristotle because it was the most avant-garde of the day. Or, that he chose it because it was the most *actuelle* – the philosophy most holding sway in his milieu. The implication in all of this is the supposition that fidelity to St.

36 I. M. Bochenski, *Contemporary European Philosophy*, trans. Donald Nicholl and Karl Aschenbrenner (Berkeley and Los Angeles: University of California Press, 1957), 1–2.

Thomas in any age consists in forging a theological synthesis with the philosophy or philosophies most current in one's time and place – notwithstanding overt hostilities toward Christian faith in these schools of thought.

Aidan Nichols, commenting on the approach of Garrigou's student, M.-Michel Labourdette, analyzes this dynamic:

> The idea that what one should take from Thomas is, for example, the spirit of openness which led him to welcome the work of Aristotle Labourdette stigmatized as a *sottise* that betrays a complete lack of understanding what theology is. Thomism cannot just be a state of mind of openness to modernity since by itself this does not answer the question as to what doctrinal, philosophical, and theological principles could make such an openness fruitful precisely for Christian faith.[37]

St. Thomas's choice of Aristotle came from his Christian intuition that Aristotle's thought would help Christ to be better known and better loved. It is simply wrong to think that he felt the need to create a theological synthesis with the wildest or woolliest philosophy that he could find. St. Thomas was convinced of the basic truth of Aristotle's metaphysics; he believed that Aristotle's thought was in fundamental conformity with the way things *really are*. And so did Réginald Garrigou-Lagrange.

The basics of Thomistic metaphysics

The Neo-Thomism of Garrigou-Lagrange is witnessed to by an unwavering adherence to the Twenty-four Thomistic Theses approved by the Sacred Congregation of Studies in 1914. They are a summary statement of "the principles and more important thoughts of the holy Doctor."[38] They were proposed as guidelines for the teaching of philosophy

37 Aidan Nichols, "Thomism and the *Nouvelle Théologie*," *The Thomist* 64 (2000): 14.

38 Sacred Congregation for Studies, "Decree of Approval of Some

in Catholic institutions throughout the world. In this, of course, they were part of St. Pius X's bulwark against Modernism. As Helen James John remarks, it is clear that "the citadel to be defended against Modernism was the objective and stable value of man's intellectual knowledge of being."[39]

In this project, a significant hurdle to be surmounted was the fact that St. Thomas did not write a full-blown epistemology. He "had never considered that the mind's power to know must be established before metaphysics could justifiably set to work."[40] John continues:

> Historical scholars had catalogued the wealth of the scholastic heritage and demonstrated the perfection of its complex yet rigorously coherent logical structure, so frequently and so aptly compared to that of Gothic architecture. Yet if the medieval heritage was to have for the twentieth century more than archeological value, Thomists realized, it was in dire need of epistemological foundations.[41]

The major philosophical figure to be reckoned with was Immanuel Kant. Kant, attempting to uphold the possibility of scientific knowledge in light of David Hume's scathing skepticism, had denied "the claim of the human mind, in the speculative order, to understand reality as such."[42] The Neo-Thomists, whose ultimate goal was to salvage the possibility of "a valid, though inadequate, rational knowledge of God,"[43] were duty-bound to contend with the epistemological difficulties surrounding the espousal of a realist metaphysics.

Theses contained in the Doctrine of St. Thomas Aquinas and Proposed to the Teachers of Philosophy," 27 July 1914. [. . . *eas plane continere sancti Doctoris principia et pronuntiata maiora*.]

39 John, *Thomist Spectrum*, 6.

40 Ibid., 3.

41 Ibid.

42 Ibid.

43 Ibid.

In this regard, Garrigou-Lagrange and the Neo-Thomists seized upon the principle of contradiction (sometimes called the principle of noncontradiction or the principle of identity). This principle appeared to Garrigou-Lagrange "as the key to the whole structure of Thomistic realism, for in the confrontation of the notion of being with the experience of multiplicity and change, this principle serves as basis for the capital assertion that being is necessarily prior to becoming."[44]

In its simplest form, the principle of contradiction holds that being is not non-being. One is hard-pressed to find a more elemental principle in philosophy. Garrigou explains:

> It is the declaration of opposition between being and nothing. It may be formulated in two ways, one negative, the other positive. The first may be given thus: "Being is not nothing," or thus: "One and the same thing, remaining such, cannot simultaneously both be and not be." Positively considered, it becomes the principle of identity, which may be formulated thus: "If a thing is, it is: if it is not, it is not." This is equivalent to saying: "Being is not non-being."[45]

Helen James John, as we have seen, highlights the principle of contradiction as the key to Garrigou's thought. Garrigou, following Aristotle, held that it is the first principle of any thought and the prerequisite for the existence of meaningful discourse. Garrigou cites the following passage from Aristotle's *Metaphysics* to make the point:

> No one can ever conceive that one and the same thing can both be and not be. Heraclitus, according to some, differs on this point. But it is not necessary that what a man says be also what he thinks. . . . To think thus would be to affirm and deny in the same breath. It would destroy language, it would be to deny all substance, all truth, even all probability and all degrees of probability. It would be the suppression of all desire,

44 Ibid., 6.
45 Garrigou-Lagrange, *Reality*, 33.

> all action. . . . Even becoming and beginning would disappear, because if contradictories and contraries are identified, then the point of departure in motion is identified with the terminus and the thing supposed to be in motion would have arrived before it departed.[46]

For Garrigou and the Neo-Thomists, the principle of contradiction is "simultaneously a law both of thought and of being. It excludes not only what is subjectively inconceivable, but also what is objectively impossible."[47] One notes with Garrigou that René Descartes had held that the principle of contradiction depends on God's free will, "that God could have made a world wherein two contradictories would be simultaneously true."[48] Descartes's position is imbued with the voluntarism of the nominalists; Descartes's "idea of divine liberty," says Garrigou, "is an idea gone mad."[49] Garrigou's position is that the principle of contradiction holds objectively and absolutely:

> [W]e are speaking . . . of the real impossibility of a contradictory thing, a squared circle, for example. And we say that this impossibility is real and absolute, and that even by miracle it can have no exception. This necessity is not hypothetical as when we say: It is necessary to eat, even though we know that by a miracle a man could live without eating. The necessity we speak of is objective and absolute.[50]

Garrigou's epistemological claim is that the principle of contradiction is accounted for by our "intellectual intuition of the objective extramental impossibility of a thing which, remaining the same, could simultaneously be and not be. . . ."[51] This Aristotelian and later, Thomistic, realism refuses to accept the minimalism of Parmenides' "Being is,

46 Aristotle, *Metaphysics*, IV, 3; cited in Ibid., 373.
47 Garrigou-Lagrange, *Reality*, 373.
48 Ibid., 372.
49 Ibid.
50 Ibid., 373, n. 6.
51 Ibid., 373.

non-being is not" and the agnosticism of nominalism's "If something exists, then of course it exists, but perhaps our notion of being does not allow us to know the fundamental law of extramental reality."[52]

Four principles flow directly from the principle of contradiction: the principle of sufficient reason, the principle of substance, the principle of efficient causality, and the principle of finality. "All these principles are the principles of our natural intelligence. They are first manifested in that spontaneous form of intelligence which we call common sense, that is, the natural habitude of intelligence, before all philosophic culture, to judge things sanely."[53] A brief explanation of each of these principles is now in order.

Garrigou formulates the principle of sufficient reason in the following fashion: "Everything that is has its *raison d'être* in itself, if of itself it exists, in something else, if of itself it does not exist."[54] In other words, the existence of a contingent being does not provide a sufficient explanation for its existence.

The principle of substance is defined as "That which exists as the subject of existence is substance, and is distinct from its accidents and modes."[55] It is derived immediately from the principle of identity; as Garrigou explains, "that which exists as subject of existence is one and the same beneath all its multiple phenomena, permanent or successive."[56]

The principle of efficient causality says that "Every contingent being, even if it exists without a beginning, needs an efficient cause and, in the last analysis, an uncreated cause."[57] The existence of a being that does not exist of

52 Ibid.
53 Ibid., 35.
54 Ibid., 33.
55 Ibid., 34.
56 Ibid.
57 Ibid., 35. See: *Summa theologiae*, I, q. 2, a.2.

itself is accounted for by the efficient causality of another: beings do not bring themselves into being.

The principle of finality, according to Garrigou, "is expressed by Aristotle and Aquinas in these terms: 'Every agent acts for a purpose.'"[58] Another way of stating the matter is to say that "the agent tends to its own good."[59]

At this juncture, the following quotation from Garrigou's *Reality* will help to frame the discussion that surrounds Thomistic realism:

> Thomistic realism is founded, not on a mere postulate, but on intellectual grasp of intelligible reality in sense objects. Its fundamental proposition runs thus: The first idea which the intellect conceives, its most evident idea into which it resolves all other ideas, is the idea of being. Grasping this first idea, the intellect cannot but grasp also the immediate consequences of that idea, namely, first principles as laws of reality. If human intelligence doubts the evidence of, say, the principle of contradiction, then – as Thomists have remarked since the seventeenth century – the principle of Descartes (*Cogito ergo sum*) simply vanishes. If the principle of contradiction is not certain, then I might be simultaneously existent and non-existent, then my personal thought is not to be distinguished from impersonal thought, nor personal thought from the subconscious, or even from the unconscious. The universal proposition, Nothing can simultaneously both be and not be, is a necessary presupposition of the particular proposition, I am, and I cannot simultaneously be and not be. Universal knowledge precedes particular knowledge.[60]

58 Ibid.

59 Ibid. Garrigou adds: "On this principle of finality depends the first principle of practical reason and of morality. It runs thus: 'Do good, avoid evil.' It is founded on the idea of good, as the principle of contradiction on the idea of being. In other words: The rational being must will rational good, that good, namely, to which its powers are proportioned by the author of its nature" (Ibid.).

60 Ibid., 35–36. [Cf.: *Cognitio magis communis est prior quam cognitio minus communis*. See: *Summa theologiae*, I, q. 85, a. 3.]

Garrigou and the Neo-Thomists held that man's first thought is being and that the supreme reality is not – contra Bergson – "creative evolution, but Being itself."[61] This is not to say that the ordinary person, or even the philosopher "is gifted with an intellectual intuition of the Supreme Being."[62] Rather, "the first intelligible object grasped by our intellect joined to the senses is the intelligible being of sensible things, their essence indistinctly apprehended, which has only an analogous resemblance to the highest Being."[63]

Strictly allied to these considerations is the fundamental distinction within being between act and potency. Indeed, it is so fundamental that it constitutes the first of the Twenty-four Thomistic Theses:[64] "Potency and act so divide being that whatever is, either is pure act, or is necessarily composed of potency and act as primary and intrinsic principles."[65]

The following example states the case for the Thomistic position admirably well:

> The child was not the hero who comes victorious from battle, and yet there was a real transition from the one state to the other. There was, then, a real capacity or potency for such an evolution; there likewise must have been an energy, an activity, i.e., an act to realize the transition. Whence, to deny the reality of potency and act is to deny the reality of life, of progress among

61 John, *Thomist Spectrum*, 9.

62 Ibid.

63 Ibid.; citing Garrigou-Lagrange's *Le réalisme du principe de finalité* (Paris: Desclée de Brouwer, 1932), 30: . . . *le premier objet intelligible, que connaît notre intelligence unie au sens, c'est l'être intelligible des choses sensibles, leur essence confusément connue, qui n'a qu'une ressemblance analogique avec l'Etre suprême.*

64 See: Hugon, *Les vingt-quatre thèses thomistes*, 3. [*Potentia et actus ita dividunt eus, ut quidquid est vel sit actus purus, vel ex potentia et actu tamquam primis atque intrinsecis principiis necessario coalescat.*]

65 John, *Thomist Spectrum*, 8; translating Thesis 1.

> men, to deny experience, to deny oneself, to deny the universe and common sense.[66]

Helen James John remarks that the distinction between potency and act coincides with "the key distinction of all Christian philosophy: that between infinite and finite being, between the Absolute, the Necessary, and the relative and contingent."[67] Only God is pure Act; only God is without potency. "[T]o be composed of potency and act is the mark of the creature."[68]

The distinction between potency and act undergirds the Thomistic principle of causality, viz., "nothing is brought from potency to act except by a being in act."[69] Garrigou's exploitation of this principle is an important defense of St. Thomas's Five Ways of demonstrating the existence of God.

In the first place, Garrigou's formulation of the principle of causality is stated in the following way: "Anything that exists, if it does not exist of itself, depends in the last analysis on something that does exist of itself.[70] This position, in turn, can be defended by reference to the principle of contradiction: its denial entails a denial of the principle of contradiction. "To say 'a thing contingent, that is, a thing which of itself does not have existence, is nevertheless uncaused' is equivalent to saying: A thing may exist of itself and simultaneously not exist of itself."[71]

John provides the following point that serves as support for the demonstrations of God's existence:

> If we add to the principle of causality so understood the assertion that contingent beings exist (allowing that the contingency of finite beings is demonstrated

66 Hugon, *Les vingt-quatre thèses thomistes*, 6; cited and translated in Ibid., 8.

67 John, *Thomist Spectrum*, 8.

68 Ibid.

69 Ibid., 10.

70 Ibid., 10.

71 Ibid.

> by the distinction already pointed out between act and potency), then we have, at least in skeletal form, the basic proof for the existence of God, of which the famous 'five ways' may be regarded as simple variations.[72]

Garrigou, witnessing to the importance of the distinction between act and potency, devoted an entire chapter to it in his *Reality*.[73] Strict Observance Thomism conceives of potency as really distinct from act unlike some Thomists, notably the Suarezians, for whom potency "is conceived as an imperfect act . . . a virtual act, merely impeded in its activity, as, for example, in the restrained force of a spring."[74] As is frequently his wont, Garrigou fashions a *reductio ad absurdum* argument against this idea:

> The reality of potency is . . . a necessary prerequisite if we are to harmonize the data of sense (e.g., multiplicity and mutation) with the principle of contradiction or of identity, with the fundamental laws, that is, of reality and thought. That which begins, since it cannot come either from actuality or from nothing, must come from a reality as yet undetermined, but determinable, from a subject that is transformable. . . .[75]

The final principle to be enunciated is the analogy of being. Helen James John, commenting upon a passage in Garrigou's *Le réalisme du principe de finalité*, writes:

> . . . when the metaphysician seeks to deepen his understanding of the first object of the mind, to determine the exact nature, not merely of this or of that being but of being as being, *ens in quantum ens*, he is faced with a most delicate task. For the slightest mistake as regards the relation of our idea of being to the different realities to which it applies will lead him

72 Ibid., 10; cf.: Garrigou-Lagrange, *Reality*, 76 ff.

73 See: "Act and Potency," *Reality*, 37–57.

74 Garrigou-Lagrange, *Reality*, 37.

75 Ibid., 40.

> directly either to *pantheism*, which would place the being of God on the same level as that of a man or a stone, or to *agnosticism*, which would set an unbridgeable abyss between the being given in our experience and that of God, so as to render the latter completely unknowable. Only the true notion of universal being will escape these errors.[76]

The "analogy of being" is the only way out of the problem of pantheism and agnosticism. Ironically, the importance of this principle is shown by the number of contemporary theologians who fail to recognize it. John is right: they tend to veer off into pantheism or agnosticism. For one, God is as directly experienced as any other datum of human experience. For another, God is utterly and unequivocally unknowable. The first, a version of pantheism, undercuts the transcendence of God; the second, agnostic in its ethos, denies the immanence of God.

These points provide a segue to our next chapter – Garrigou-Lagrange on the nature of theology. We will see that his theology, informed by Thomistic philosophical principles, and guided by the first question in St. Thomas's *Summa theologiae*, is a robust example of "faith seeking understanding."

76 John, *Thomist Spectrum*, 10–11; referring to Garrigou-Lagrange, *Le réalisme du principle de finalité*, 225–26.

7. Garrigou-Lagrange: What Is Theology?

What reason cannot discover, Christ has revealed to us. St. Paul says that He has show us God's excess of love for us and taught us that our love ought to be a response and be modeled on the very love God has for us. "We are to love, then, because God loved us first" (1Jn 4:19). We must meditate together on what God's love for us has been, on what has been the response of the saints, and on what our response should be. Réginald Garrigou-Lagrange, *The Last Writings*

In his *Thomas Aquinas, Theologian*, Thomas O'Meara sets out to "introduce Thomas Aquinas in the vocation and profession he chose for himself: theologian."[1] He explains: "He was first and always a theologian: in the university and in the Dominican *studium*, in the pulpit and in his room writing."[2] O'Meara recognizes that the approach to St. Thomas which most exemplified the neo-Thomist revival from 1850 to 1960 was to see him primarily as a

1 Thomas Franklin O'Meara, *Thomas Aquinas, Theologian* (Notre Dame, Ind.: University of Notre Dame Press, 1997), xi.

2 Ibid.

philosopher – the Christian philosopher *par excellence*.[3] By and large, the insight that St. Thomas must be seen as a theologian has gained pride of place in interpreting the man and his work.[4]

Granting that St. Thomas must be seen first of all as a theologian, what exactly is a theologian? Indeed, what is theology? How does the theologian "do" theology? At first glance, these questions might seem self-evident; one might assume that they have been answered with something approximating unanimity. Nothing could be farther from the truth.[5]

In this chapter, we will examine the nature of theology as Garrigou-Lagrange understood it. To this end, we will focus attention on his article on Thomism in the *Dictionnaire de théologie catholique* and his "La nouvelle théologie: où va-t-elle?"[6] We will then show how his teaching contrasts with the work of two representative theologians in contemporary fundamental theology. We will conclude by suggesting what Garrigou's approach might be able to offer to the theological project in our day.

What is theology?

Garrigou broaches the topic of theology in his article on

3 Ibid., xi–xii, 192–95.

4 This is witnessed in Jean-Pierre Torrell's magisterial *L'Initiation à Saint Thomas d'Aquin: Sa personne et son oeuvre* (Fribourg: Éditions Universitaires Fribourg Suisse), 1993. This work has appeared in English as *Saint Thomas Aquinas: The Person and his Work*, trans. Robert Royal (Washington, D.C.: Catholic University of America Press, 1996).

5 O'Meara, for his part, will say that a theologian is "a theoretician of life and history within the mystery of the presence of the divine" (xviii) and that for St. Thomas theology "was not a search for shocking theories or a condemnation of people but a sharing in God's view of earth" (xx). O'Meara does not offer an in-depth commentary on the first question of the *Prima pars*, that is not within the scope of his work. See, however, pages 42–43 for his appreciation of the questions.

6 Réginald Garrigou-Lagrange, "La théologie nouvelle: où va-t-elle?," in *La synthèse thomiste* (Paris: Desclée de Brouwer, 1946): 699–725.

Thomism in a rather circuitous fashion: he begins by exposing a divergence of opinion within the Thomist school. At issue is "the definability of theological conclusions properly called, obtained by a discourse which is truly illative coming from a premise of faith and a premise of reason."[7] The disagreement is best exemplified by the proposals of two Dominican theologians, Francisco Marín-Sola and Louis Charlier.

Marín-Sola's *L'évolution homogène du dogme catholique* held that theological conclusions that had been deduced from a premise of faith and a premise of reason could be defined as infallible teaching of the Church. "Marín-Sola held that strictly illative theological reasoning could discover truths capable of being defined as dogmas of faith."[8] By and large, Marín-Sola's proposal would severely limit the existence of different schools of thought in Catholic theology.

Louis Charlier's position is diametrically opposed to that of Marín-Sola. In fact, Charlier's *Essai sur le problème théologique*[9] strikes at the very question of certainty in theology. Garrigou offers the following quote from Charlier's work: "Demonstration, in the strict sense of the word, does not apply to theology."[10] Garrigou explains that for Charlier, "theology itself is not able to reach certitude in its conclusions which belong more to the metaphysics of which the theologian makes use, than to theology properly so-

7 Garrigou-Lagrange, "Thomisme," in *DT*, XV.1, 847. [. . . *la définibilité des conclusions théologiques proprement dites, obtenues par un discursus vraiment illative en partant d'une prémisse de foi et d'une prémisse de raison*.]

8 F. D. Nealy, "Marín-Sola, Francisco," in *NCE*.

9 (Thuillies: Ramgal, 1938).

10 Garrigou-Lagrange, "Thomisme," 847. [*La demonstration au sens rigoureux du mot ne peut s'appliquer en théologie.*]

11 Ibid. [*...la théologie elle-même ne pourrait pas parvenir avec certitude à de telles conclusions, qui appartiendraient plutôt à la métaphysique dont se sert le théologien, qu'à la théologie proprement dite.*]

called."[11] Charlier refused to admit that certitude could be reached by deductive reasoning from the givens of theology.

Garrigou, by calling attention to Marín-Sola and Charlier, set forth the extreme positions:

> Whereas Fr. Marín-Sola thinks that theological reasoning that is properly illative can discover truths that are capable of being defined as dogmas of faith, Fr. Charlier believes that theology itself is not able to reach with certainty such a conclusion.[12]

Garrigou held that neither Marin-Sola nor Charlier are in conformity with the mind of St. Thomas and his major commentators. He writes: "We judge that the true Thomistic doctrine rises in the middle and above these extreme positions."[13] To make his case, Garrigou turns to St. Thomas's *Summa theologiae*, I, q. 1.

Under the subheading of the proper object of theology, Garrigou writes:

> We will suppose here that which St. Thomas speaks of in question I of the *Summa theologiae* – that, properly speaking, theology is a science which proceeds under the light of divine revelation, and presupposes, therefore, infused faith in revealed truths and which has as its proper object God considered in his intimate life, as author of grace, God as revelation and faith make him known to us, and not only God as author of nature, accessible to the natural power of our reason.[14]

12 Ibid. [*Tandis que le P. Marin-Sola pense que le raisonnement théologique proprement illative fait découvrir des vérités susceptibles d'être définies comme dogme de foi, le P. Charlier estime que la théologie elle-même n'est pas capable de parvenir avec certitude à de telles conclusions.*]

13 Ibid. [*Nous estimons que la extrêmes doctrine Thomiste s'élève au milieu et au-dessus de ces positions extremes.*]

14 Ibid., 848. [*Nous supposons ici ce qu'expose saint Thomas dans la q. I de la* Somme théologique *– que la théologie est à proprement parler une science qui procède sous la lumière de la Révélation divine, qui suppose donc la foi infuse aux vérités révélées et qui a pour objet propre Dieu considéré en sa vie intime, comme auteur de*

Theology is a science – a field of human enquiry – that, by virtue of the light of divine revelation, has for its object the study of God considered in himself.[15] The theological project supposes faith and gives priority to faith.

Of course, says Garrigou, the theologian does not have direct access to God: he or she is not yet participating in the beatific vision. The theologian does not see God *clare visa* but rather *obsure per fidem cognita*.[16] How, then, is theology distinguished from faith? Garrigou explains that faith is the foundation of theology, because theology is the science that is concerned with the truths of the faith, which it must explain and defend by way of analogy. Theology seeks to discover the relationship between the various truths of the faith, to connect them into a body of doctrine, and to deduce from them other truths contained virtually within them.[17] Garrigou adds that theology cannot do its work without recourse to metaphysics since the explication of the truths pertaining to the intimate life of the Godhead is dependent upon what metaphysics says of God as First Cause.[18]

What does Garrigou mean by calling theology a science? Following Aristotle's definition, *scire est cognoscere causam*

la grâce, Dieu tel que la révélation et la foi nous le font connaître, et non seulement Dieu auteur de la nature, accessible aux forces naturelles de notre raison.]

15 Garrigou, following St. Thomas (*ST*, I, Q. 6), explains that theology is concerned with God *sub ratione Deitatis*, not simply *sub ratione entis et primi entis* (Ibid.).

16 Ibid.

17 Garrigou writes that in relationship to theology, faith is *comme sa racine, parce qu'elle est une science des vérités de la foi qu'elle doit expliquer et défendre par la méthode d'analogie. Elle cherche à découvrir leur subordination en un corps de doctrine et à déduire les vérités qu'elle contiennent virtuellement*. (Ibid.)

18 Cf.: Ibid., 848: *En ce travail la théologie ne peut se servir de la méthode d'analogie dans l'explication des vérités relatives à la vie intime de Dieu* ad ipsam Deitatem ut sic, *sans recourir à ce que la métaphysique nous dit de Dieu comme premier être,* sub ratione entis.

propter quam res est et non potest aliter se habere,[19] theology is a science because it is called to determine the nature and the properties of the various articles of Christian faith. For instance, theology must offer a reflection on something as foundational as the nature of the human person and his or her call to beatitude; it also must comment on something as technical as the differences between the infused virtues and the acquired virtues.[20] Moreover, theology is a science because like all sciences, it concerns drawing conclusions from principles and thus arrives at certain knowledge. The difference, of course, is that theology is the only science whose formal principles are divinely revealed.[21]

What is at stake here? Garrigou, faithful to the Thomistic tradition, holds that theology is a rational undertaking; it proceeds by way of rational argumentation; it has recourse to the general principles of rational discourse. Theology, grounded in the divinely revealed truths of the faith, interprets human life and existence in light of that faith. Theology is not an audacious creation of the theologian; utterly linked to divine revelation, theology is not a freewheeling, artistic enterprise.[22]

At the same time, theology is not the fullness of truth. It is a systematization of divinely revealed truths, yet it

19 Garrigou is quoting from Aristotle's *Posterior Analytics* 1. I, lect. 4 (Ibid.).

20 Ibid.

21 Ibid. (Cf.: *La science se dit au sens plus large de toute connaissance certaine; elle se dit au sens proper de la connaissance des conclusions par les principes.*)

22 *Pace* Monika Hellwig, "Theology as a Fine Art," in *Interpreting Tradition: The Art of Theological Reflection*, ed. Jane Kopas (New York: Scholars Press, 1983), 3–10. Hellwig writes: "Theology is, when all is said and done, an attempt to find ultimate meaning in life, to find a purpose that makes it all worthwhile. Theology does not set out to invent that meaning and purpose but to discover it, and the road to discovery is essentially a road inward into the subjective dimensions of human experience as well as outwards into interpersonal and intramundane history" (5).

never attains the status of "revelation." Theology is a human work; as such, it is not even an approximation of the beatific vision.[23] Garrigou insists strongly that "in heaven theology will exist in the state of perfection, with its principles fully evident, here and now it exists in an imperfect state, it has not yet reached the state of adulthood."[24] Theology as we know it is not in a state of perfection; indeed, the "perfect theology" remains elusive.[25]

Garrigou writes that for St. Thomas and his school, theology is a science that is subordinated to God and the blessed. It is a wisdom that is superior to that of metaphysics but inferior to faith. It is a *habitus* acquired by work, but its root is essentially supernatural.[26]

The various operations of theology

Having discussed the nature of theology according to St. Thomas, Garrigou moves to enumerate the various operations of theology, the tasks that theology is called upon to undertake. He notes that these operations are indicated by St. Thomas in the *Summa*, especially at I, q. 1, aa. 6, 8, 9, and most clearly in the questions concerning such revealed truths as eternal life, predestination, the Holy Trinity, and the mysteries of the Incarnation, the Redemption, the Eucharist, and the other sacraments.[27]

23 Garrigou writes: *Lorsque le théologien ne sera plus* viator, *lorsqu'il aura reçu la vision béatifique, il verra immédiatement* in Verbo, *la vie intime de Dieu, la Déité ou essence divine; il atteindra en pleine lumière les vérités qu'il connaissait d'abord par la foi, et il pourra encore voir* extra Verbum *les conclusions qui peuvent s'en déduire. Au ciel la théologie existera à l'existence parfait avec l'évidence des principes*. ("Thomisme," 848.)

24 Ibid. [*Au ciel la théologie existera à l'état parfait avec l'évidence des principes,* in via *elle existe à l'état imparfait, elle n'a pas encore l'âge adulte pour ainsi parler*.]

25 This is of capital importance. The Neo-Thomists are frequently accused of holding that their theology is the perfect expression of theology.

26 Garrigou-Lagrange, "Thomisme," 848.

27 Ibid., 849.

Garrigou is able to isolate eight theological operations according to the mind of St. Thomas.[28] They are as follows:

1. "Theology gathers together the various revealed truths contained in the deposit of faith, Scripture and Tradition, in the light of the magisterium of the Church that proposes to us these revealed truths."[29] This is the work of positive theology and it "includes the study of biblical theology, of the documents ... of the tradition, of the various forms of the living magisterium."[30] This is fundamentally a *descriptive* task.
2. Theology institutes a conceptual analysis of each revealed truth "in particular the most fundamental, in order to specify clearly the subject and the predicate of these truths."[31] This is theology's *analytic* task; it is an important preamble to all creative theology. Garrigou gives an elemental example: "Take, for example, this sentence: The Word was made flesh. Theological analysis shows that the sentence means: The Word, who is God, became man."[32]
3. Theology defends the faith against its adversaries by either showing how each revealed truth is part of the deposit of faith or by showing how they do not involve a contradiction in terms. This is the *apologetic* task that pertains to theology.
4. Theology proposes arguments of fittingness to demonstrate the truth of its revealed mysteries. This *manifesting* task is made clear in the following reflection: "it is appropriate that God, the supreme Good, communi-

28 See: Ibid., 849–53.

29 Ibid., 849. [*La théologie recueille les différentes vérités révélées contenues dans le dépôt de la Révélation, Ecriture et Tradition, à la lumière du magistère de l'Eglise qui nous propose ces vérités révélées.*]

30 Garrigou-Lagrange, *Reality*, 64.

31 Garrigou-Lagrange, "Thomisme," 849. [. . . *en particulier des plus fondamentales, pour bien préciser la signification du sujet et du prédicat de ces vérités.*]

32 Garrigou-Lagrange, *Reality*, 64.

cate His entire nature in the eternal generation of the Word and that the Word be incarnate for our salvation" because "God is by nature self-diffusive; and the more elevated the good is, the more intimately and abundantly does it communicate itself."[33]

5. Theology has recourse to explicit reasoning, to show "that which is implied in a revealed truth, without thereby creating a new truth."[34] This *explicative* task "passes from a confused formulation of the truth to a more distinct formulation of the same truth."[35]
6. Theology uses a discourse that is "not only explicative but properly and objectively illative, in order to deduce from two revealed truths a third truth revealed elsewhere, often explicitly, in Scripture or in Tradition."[36]
7. Theology deduces "by way of a discourse which is properly illative, from two revealed truths a third truth not revealed elsewhere, that is, not revealed in itself, but only in the two others of which it is the fruit."[37]
8. Finally, theology deduces "by a discourse properly illative from one truth of the faith and one truth of reason (not revealed), a third truth that is not simply or properly revealed, but only virtually, in its cause."[38]

33 Ibid., 65; cf. *ST*, I, q. 32, a. 1, ad. 2 and III, q. 1, a. 1.

34 Garrigou-Lagrange, "Thomisme," 850. [*...ce qui est impliqué dans une vérité révélée, sans passer encore à une vérité nouvelle.*]

35 Garrigou-Lagrange, *Reality*, 65.

36 Garrigou-Lagrange, "Thomisme," 850. [*. . . non pas seulement explicatif, mais proprement et objectivement illative, pour déduire de deux vérités révélées une troisième vérité* aliunde revelata *contenue, souvent même explicitement, dans l'Écriture ou la Tradition divine.*]

37 Ibid., 851. [*. . . par* discursus *proprement illative, de deux vérités révélées une troisième vérité* non aliunde revelata, *qui n'est pas révélée en elle-même, mais seulement dans les deux autres dont elle est le fruit.*]

38 Ibid. [*... par* discursus *proprement illative d'une vérité de foi et d'une vérité de raison non révélée, une troisième vérité qui n'était pas* simpliciter *ou proprement révélée, mais seulement* virtualiter, *dans sa cause.*] Garrigou explains that *cette troisième vérité, du domaine, si elle est rigoureusement déduite, est non pas de la foi, mais de la science théologique.*

Garrigou wrote a commentary on the first part of the *Summa* that was published in English as *The One God.*[39] A brief look at Garrigou's comments on St. Thomas's question, "Whether sacred doctrine is a science" (*ST*, I, q.1, a. 2), will serve as a conclusion to this section.

The first thing to note is the following difficulty: "every science proceeds from principles directly known and evident, whereas sacred theology proceeds from principles of faith, which are obscure and not admitted by all."[40] What is more, St. Thomas says that science refers to universal principles but theology treats of particulars "namely, of Christ, the apostles, the patriarchs, and the prophets."[41] How, then, can theology be fittingly called a science?

The answer to these problems is that the science of theology is subordinated to a higher science, indeed, the highest science, that which is possessed by God and the blessed. Garrigou explains:

> A subordinated science proceeds from principles known by the light of a higher science, as the science of perspective (optics) proceeds from principles established by geometry. Now sacred theology proceeds from principles transmitted by God through revelation. Therefore sacred theology is a science subordinated to the science of God and the blessed.[42]

There are three corollaries that must be highlighted. First, "[t]he principles of a subordinated science can be known in two ways: either by faith and without evidence of reason, or by a higher science already acquired, and then there is evidence of reason."[43] Thus, writes Garrigou, the theologian "believes the principles transmitted by God

39 Réginald Garrigou-Lagrange, *The One God: A Commentary on the First Part of St. Thomas' Theological Summa*, trans. Bede Rose (St. Louis: B. Herder, 1943).

40 Garrigou-Lagrange, *The One God*, 43.

41 Ibid.

42 Ibid., 44.

43 Ibid.

revealing and proposed by the Church; and thus his theology is truly a subordinated science. . . ."[44]

The second corollary is that the theologian "will have the same theological habit in heaven as he now has on earth; just as the optician does not lose his science of optics when he becomes a geometer."[45] The import of this is to highlight that the higher science does not obliterate the lower.

The third corollary, proceeding from the first two, is of great significance: "[t]herefore what is substantially a true science is sometimes imperfect under certain conditions."[46] Thus theology is substantially a true science because it rests on evident principles. The example that Garrigou uses is that of an optician who does not know the geometric foundation of his science. He writes: "The optician who is not a geometer has good grounds for thinking that his optics is a science and not merely an opinion."[47]

Disputing with the "new theology"

In "La théologie nouvelle: où va-t-elle?" Garrigou brings his understanding of the nature of theology to bear on what was then a new trend in theology: the *ressourcement* of Jesuit theologians Jean Daniélou, Henri de Lubac, and Henri Bouillard. These theologians were calling for a "return to the sources" of theology – Scripture and the Fathers of the Church. They were dissatisfied with Scholasticism; their explicit goal was to undo the hegemony of Neo-Thomism. Even though none of these theologians was enamored with the term, their work became know as the "*nouvelle théologie*" – "the new theology."

Garrigou's article asks, "Where is the new theology going?" It is best to reveal Garrigou's judgment immediately: he believed that the new theology was headed

44 Ibid.
45 Ibid., 45.
46 Ibid.
47 Ibid.

toward Modernism.[48] He expressed grave reservations and issued serious warnings. In the judgment of at least one interpreter, Garrigou's article was "hasty and unjust."[49] It is safe to say that for many, to warn that a particular theology or theological proposition is tending toward Modernism is tantamount to casting aspersions. For instance, Karl Rahner and Herbert Vorgrimler's otherwise dispassionate *Dictionary of Theology* ends its article on Modernism with the following *ad hominem* display: "To this day 'Modernism' unfortunately remains a term used for spiteful invective by arrogant people in the Church who have no idea how difficult faith is for men of our time."[50]

Garrigou, we can be sure, would not have agreed with such an opinion. For him, Modernism had become a perennial tendency in Catholic circles since at least the end of the nineteenth century: he agreed with St. Pius X that it was the synthesis of all heresies.

We have already discussed the parameters of Catholic Modernism and the Church's response to it. J. J. Heany offers a helpful summary by focusing on the following three points – what he calls the "triple thesis of Modernism:"

> (1) a denial of the supernatural as an object of certain knowledge (in the totally symbolic nonobjective approach to the content of dogma, which is also related to a type of agnosticism in natural theology); (2) an exclusive immanence of the divine and of revelation ("vital immanence") reducing the Church to a simple social civilizing phenomenon; (3) a total emancipation of scientific research from Church dogma, which would allow the continued assertion of faith in dogma

48 Garrigou's oft-quoted line is: *Où va la nouvelle théologie? Elle revient au modernisme*. See: "Où va-t-elle?," 721.

49 Jacques Guillet calls this work an *amalgame hâtif et injuste*. See: *La théologie catholique en France de 1914 à 1960* (Paris: Médiasèvres, 1988).

50 Karl Rahner and Herbert Vorgrimler, *Dictionary of Theology* (New York: Crossroad, 1985), 313.

> with its contradiction on the historical level, as understood in certain presentations of the "Christ of faith, Christ of history," "Church of faith, Church of history" distinctions.[51]

The proximate cause of Garrigou's article and his judgment that the *nouvelle théologie* was heading toward Modernism was his reading of Henri Bouillard's *Conversion et grâce chez saint Thomas d'Aquin.*[52] The following passage caused him great distress:

> When the mind evolves, an immutable truth does not persist except due to a simultaneous and correlative evolution of all the ideas, maintaining between them the same relationship. A theology that does not belong to the present moment [i.e., *actuelle*] is false.[53]

This passage, more than any other, sounded a clarion call for both sides of the growing debate. The "reformers" found in it the rationale for their intuition that Neo-Thomism's hold on theology must be broken. The "traditionalists" took it as it was intended: a frontal assault on their most sincerely held positions.

A more remote cause of Garrigou's article was his knowledge of the growing disagreement between the Dominican friars of the province of Toulouse and the Jesuits of Fourvière. The Dominicans of the *studium* of St-

51 J. J. Heany, "Modernism," in *NCE*.

52 Henri Bouillard, *Conversion et grâce chez saint Thomas d'Aquin* (Paris: Aubier [Editions Montaigne], 1944).

53 Bouillard, *Conversion et grâce*, 219, cited in Garrigou-Lagrange, "Où va-t-elle?," 699. [*Quand l'esprit évolue, une vérité immuable ne se maintient que grâce à une évolution simultanée et correlative de toutes les notions, maintenant entre elles un même rapport. Une théologie que ne serait pas actuelle serait une théologie fausse.* For effect, Garrigou underlined the phrase *une vérité immuable* and the entire last sentence.] Jacques Guillet, in an understatement, remarks: *La formule faisait choc: on ne l'oublia pas.* [*La théologie catholique en France*, 42.] It bears noting that Bouillard would be the author of a work highly complimentary of Blondel: *Blondel et le christianisme* (Paris: Editions du Seuil, 1961).

Maximin were led by Garrigou's former student, M.-Michel Labourdette, O.P., editor of the *Revue thomiste*.[54] The Jesuits were led by Henri de Lubac and Jean Daniélou; they were best known for their project – *Sources chrétiennes*.

Labourdette published his "La théologie et ses sources" in the May-August 1946 volume of the *Revue thomiste*. It was a critical study of the work of de Lubac and Daniélou with *Sources chrétiennes*. Labourdette, while praising the effort to bring the Fathers of the Church to modern Catholics, was concerned with the underlying rationale of the project. He explained:

> Fr. Daniélou characterizes very well the intention of this new collection as opposed to the one formerly directed by Hemmer and Lejay: "For these latter, it was ultimately about the publishing of historical documents, witnesses to the faith of those of former times. This new project believes that there is more to ask of the Fathers. They are not only true witnesses from a state of things now changed; they are still the most current [i.e., *actuelle*] nourishment for the men and women of today because we find in them precisely a certain number of categories which are those of contemporary thought and of which scholasticism has lost."[55]

54 Labourdette studied under Garrigou at the Angelicum, receiving his doctorate in theology in 1935. Garrigou directed his thesis on the meaning of faith in St. John of the Cross (it was entitled *La foi théologale et son rôle dans la connaissance mystique d'après saint Jean de la Croix et saint Thomas d'Aquin*). It is noteworthy that Pope John Paul II, also under Garrigou's direction at the Angelicum, chose a similar topic for his dissertation. Labourdette reviewed the Pope's work (in French: *La foi selon saint Jean de la Croix*) in *Revue thomiste* 83 (1983): 85–86.

55 M.-Michel Labourdette, "La théologie et ses sources," *Revue thomiste* 46 (1946), reprinted in *Dialogue théologique*, eds. M-Michel Labourdette, M.-J. Nicholas and R.-L. Bruckberger (Var, France: St-Maximin, Les Arcades, 1947), 25. [*Le R. P. Daniélou caractérise très bien l'intention de la nouvelle collection par opposition à celle que dirigeaient autrefois Hemmer et Lejay: 'Pour cette*

The Thomist critique, as worked out by the Toulouse Dominicans, claimed that in turning to the Fathers for their theology, the Jesuits were leaving behind essential "source material" for theology, viz., the development of doctrine during the Middle Ages and beyond, up to the present-day. De Lubac and Daniélou were judged to be choosing more inchoate expressions of Christian doctrine than is healthy for Catholic faith. In seeking answers to theological questions from the Fathers – answers presumed to be more in line with the thought patterns of contemporary men and women – the directors of *Sources chrétiennes* were not allowing themselves to see the whole truth. Labourdette writes:

> It is a permanent temptation for contemporary thought to judge every intellectual system of expression not essentially on its conformity with "that which is" (how could one attain this?), but primarily and definitively on its relationship with that which the author and his time thinks, with what they have experienced. The mystery of subjectivity interests them more than impersonal truth.[56]

At the same time, the Jesuits were engaged in a strenuous critique of Thomism, noted, in the eyes of the Dominicans, more for its hyperbole than for its accuracy.

dernière, il s'agissait avant tout de publier des documents historiques, témoins de la foi des anciens. La nouvelle pense qu'il y a plus à demander aux Pères. Ils ne sont pas seulement les témoins véritables d'un état de choses révolu: ils sont encore la nourriture la plus actuelle pour les hommes d'aujourd'hui, parce que nous y retrouvons précisément un certain nombre de catégories qui sont celles de la pensée contemporaine et que la théologie scolastique avait perdues.']

56 Ibid., 38–39. [*C'est une tentation permanente pour l'intelligence contemporaine de juger tout système d'expression intellectuelle, non essentiellement sur sa conformité avec ce qui est (comment l'atteindre?), mais d'abord et en définitive sur son rapport avec ce que son auteur et son temps ont pensé, avec ce qu'ils ont éprouvé. Les mystères de la subjectivité l'intéressent plus que la vérité impersonelle.*]

Labourdette is at great pains to counter the charges raised by Daniélou in his article "Les orientations présentes de la pensée religieuse."[57] It is important to note that there is a direct link between Daniélou's critique of Thomism and the general parameters of contemporary critiques of Thomism. Here, in Daniélou's words, is a summary:

> These two abysses, historicity and subjectivity, to which one must add the perception of the coexistence by which each of our lives reverberates in those of all others and which is common to Marxism and existentialism, these two abysses demand that theological thought be expanded. It is very clear that scholastic theology is a stranger to these categories. Its world is the static world of Greek thought where its mission was to incarnate the Christian message.[58]

The critique of the directors of *Sources chrétiennes* rested on the accusation that Thomism cannot speak to contemporary men and women because it is irremediably tied to a static Greek world view and because it cannot respond to the questions raised by historical consciousness and human subjectivity.[59]

Labourdette denied the major premises of Daniélou's critique. Daniélou had created a straw man, a caricature of Thomism drawn from the most debased of the scholastic manuals. It is disingenuous to identify Thomism with what

57 Jean Daniélou, "Les orientations présentes de la pensée religieuse," *Etudes* no. 249 (April-May-June 1946): 5–21.

58 Ibid., 14; cited in Labourdette, "La théologie et ses sources," 36. [*Ces deux abîmes, historicité, subjectivité, auxquels il faut ajouter la perception de la coexistence par laquelle chaucune de nos vies retentit dans celle de tous les autres et qui est commune au marxisme et à l'existentialisme, ces deux abîmes obligent donc la pensée théologique à se dilater. Il est bien clair en effet que la théologie scolastique est étrangère à ces catégories. Le monde qui est le sien est le monde immobile de la pensée grecque où sa mission a été d'incarner le message chrétien.*]

59 This judgment appears in practically every theological work that eschews a Thomistic framework; it has become one of contemporary theology's foundational truisms.

everyone would agree was a second-rate expression. The Thomism that Labourdette defends is

> a way of thinking which is perfectly alive, at the same time ambitious and able to enter into the new problems of the day and to understand them, and to assimilate all that is authentic in their doctrines, but that is too respectful of the truth, too concerned to protect its scientific rigor that it avoids facile conformities to agree to separate immediately ideas and categories that it had not first closely examined and critiqued.[60]

The debate between the Dominicans of St-Maximin and the Jesuits of Fourvière was published in 1947 as *Dialogue théologique: pieces du débat entre "La Revue Thomiste" d'une part et les R.R.P.P. de Lubac, Daniélou, Bouillard, Fessard, von Balthasar, S.J. d'autre part.*[61] Garrigou, hoping to add his commentary to the problematic initiated by his confreres, submitted his article to the *Revue thomiste* for publication. Labourdette feared that bringing Garrigou into the discussion would dangerously increase the tensions; he judged it best to decline to publish Garrigou's work.[62] Garrigou turned to the Angelicum's theological journal to get "La théologie nouvelle: où va-t-elle?" published.

60 Labourdette, "La théologie et ses sources," 37. [*...une façon de pensée parfaitement vivante, à la fois ambitieuse et capable d'entrer dans les problèmes nouveaux et de les comprendre, de s'assimiler tout ce que contiennent d'authentique les doctrines les plus modernes, mais trop respectueuse de la vérité, trop soucieuse de garder sa rigueur scientifique et d'éviter les conformismes faciles, pour accepter de séparer immédiatement d'idées et de catégories qu'elle n'aurait pas au préalable mûrement examinées et critiquées.*]

61 M.-Michel Labourdette, M.-J. Nicolas, R.-L. Bruckberger, eds., *Dialogue théologique* (Var: Les Arcades, St-Maximin, 1947). It is worth noting a rather ironic state of affairs (from the Dominican point of view): Henri de Lubac, Jean Daniélou, and Hans Urs von Balthasar were eventually made cardinals (Daniélou by Pope Paul VI and the other two by Pope John Paul II). None of the Dominicans were so honored.

62 Aidan Nichols, "Thomism and the Nouvelle Théologie," *The Thomist* 64 (2000): 12.

Are dogmatic formulations immutable?

Garrigou's foray into the debate is divided into two parts. The first is signaled by the question: "Do dogmatic formulations themselves keep their immutability?"[63]

Once again the work of Henri Bouillard figures prominently in Garrigou's mind. He quotes the section of *Conversion et grâce chez saint Thomas d'Aquin* where Bouillard writes, in reference to the Council of Trent's use of the concept of formal causality in its "Decree on Justification," that the Council "had used to this end the common notions of the theology of the time. But one can substitute others for them without changing the meaning of the teaching."[64]

Garrigou replied that the Council of Trent did not canonize the Aristotelian notion of "form" "with all of its connections to the Aristotelian system. But it did approve of it as a *stable human notion*, in the sense of our speaking about that which formally constitutes something (here, justification)."[65] Garrigou explains that the Council of Trent speaks of sanctifying grace as distinct from actual grace when it teaches that it is an infused, supernatural gift, which inheres in the soul and by which the human person is justified.[66] Garrigou asks: "But how can one maintain the meaning of this teaching of the Council of Trent, 'sanctifying grace is the formal cause of justification,' if 'one substitutes for it a notion other than that of formal causality'?"[67]

63 I.e., *Les formulas dogmatiques elles-mêmes gardent-elles leur immutabilité?*

64 Garrigou-Lagrange, "Où va-t-elle?" 702, quoting Bouillard, *Conversion et grâce*, 221. [. . . *a utilisé à cette fin des notions communes dans la théologie du temps. Mais on peut leur en substituer d'autres, sans modifier le sens de son enseignement.*]

65 Ibid. [. . . *avec toutes ses relations aux autres notions du système aristotélicien. Mail il l'a approuvée comme une notion humaine stable, au sens où nous parlons tous de ce qui constitue formellement une chose (ici la justification).*]

66 Ibid. Garrigou cites Denz. 799 and 821.

67 Ibid. [*Mais comment peut-on maintenir le sens de cet enseignement*

Garrigou notes that Bouillard claims that substituting another *notion* is necessary to explain justification; he does not say that finding "a verbal equivalent" is what the theologian must do.[68] Because of this, he feels free to put these words on Bouillard's lips: "One must be content to say: At the time of the Council of Trent, grace was thought of as the formal cause of justification, but today we must think of it differently. This concept from the past is no longer *actuelle* and hence it is no longer true, because a doctrine which is no longer *actuelle* is false."[69]

Garrigou recognizes that nothing short of the definition of truth is at stake in all of this. Bouillard has given up the time-honored *adaequatio rei et intellectus* for Maurice Blondel's *conformitas mentis et vitae*.[70] Garrigou holds that the choice of a new definition of truth makes all the difference in Bouillard's proposal. And, he asks, with the Blondelian definition, how can one distance oneself from this fundamental proposition of Modernism: *Veritas non est immutabilis plusquam ipse homo, quippe quae cum ipso, in ipso, et per ipsum evolvitur.*[71]

Not only does the *nouvelle théologie* rely on a different definition of truth, it relies, argues Garrigou, on a new definition of theology itself: "Theology is nothing other than a spirituality or religious experience that has found intellectual

du Concile de Trente 'la grâce sanctifiante est la cause formelle de la justification,' si 'l'on substitue une autre notion à celle de cause formelle'?] Garrigou assumes that all Catholic theologians would agree that maintaining the meaning of the conciliar teaching is the goal.

68 Ibid., 702–703.

69 Ibid., 703. [Cf.: *Il faut se contenter de dire: la grâce a été conçue à l'époque du Concile de Trente comme la cause formelle de la justification, mais aujourd'hui il faut la concevoir autrement, cette conception passée n'est plus actuelle et donc elle n'est plus vraie, car une doctrine qui n'est plus actuelle, a-t-il été dit, est une doctrine fausse.*]

70 Ibid., 704.

71 Ibid., 705, citing Denz. 2058: "Truth is no more immutable than man himself, inasmuch as it is evolved with him, in him, and through him." [English trans. of Denz. by Roy J. Deferrari, *The Sources of Catholic Dogma* (St. Louis: B. Herder, 1955), 512.]

expression."[72] This definition in turn is the foundation for the following sentiment: "If theology can help us to understand spirituality, spirituality in its turn in many cases can explode our theological framework and oblige us to conceive of many other types of theology. . . . To each great spirituality there corresponded a great theology."[73] Garrigou was afraid that this could go so far as undermining the principle of noncontradiction. Two theologies could potentially hold contradictory positions, with truth being defined in reference to different religious experiences. And "that would, in a singular fashion, bring us nearer to Modernism."[74]

Applications to original sin and the Eucharist

In the second section of his article, Garrigou focuses his attention on the Church's doctrines concerning original sin and the Eucharist. He is concerned that the *nouvelle théologie*, with its espousal of new definitions for truth and for theology will lead to a radical diminishment of the fundamental teachings of the Church. Garrigou's fear was not unfounded for he had seen some of the unpublished works of the new theologians – typewritten, unsigned works that were circulated between themselves and that were shared with certain members of the French clergy. One of the things that most disturbed Garrigou about these underground works was the deformed way of thinking about the Christian faith. The *fides quae* had become "an assemblage of probable opinions."[75] The act of Christian faith, the *fides*

72 Ibid. [*La théologie n'est autre qu'une spiritualité ou expérience religieuse qui a trouvé son expression intellectuelle.*]

73 Garrigou-Lagrange, "Où va-t-elle?," 705–6. [*Si la théologie nous peut aider à comprendre la spiritualité, la spiritualité à son tour fera, dans bien des cas, éclater nos cadres théologiques, et nous obligera à concevoir divers types de théologie. . . . A chaque grande spiritualité a correspondu une grande théologie.*]

74 Ibid., 706. [*Cela nous rapproche singulièrement du modernisme.*] Garrigou cites the Holy Office's condemnation of twelve postulates of the "philosophy of action" on December 1, 1924.

75 Ibid., 711. [... *un ensemble d'opinions probables*]

qua, was no longer thought of as a supernatural adherence to revealed truths *propter auctoritatem Dei revelantis*, but as an adherence of the spirit to a "general perspective of the universe."[76]

Garrigou judged that the doctrine of original sin was being all but denied[77] and that the doctrine of the Real Presence was being eviscerated of its meaning. Since the question of the Real Presence seems to be the most burning one in Garrigou's mind, we will focus our attention on this part of "La théologie nouvelle: où va-t-elle?"

As one might expect, the Aristotelian concepts of substance and accident were judged to be problematic by the new theologians. Curiously, however, it was not because they were no longer *actuelle*; rather, the Aristotelian language was judged to be too clear, not respectful enough of the mystery of the Eucharistic Presence.[78] With this judgment, of course, the language of transubstantiation was deemed equally unacceptable.[79]

According to Garrigou, some of the new theologians explained transubstantiation in the following manner:

76 Ibid. [... *une adhésion de l'esprit à une perspective générale de l'univers*]

77 Garrigou believed that many of the ideas adduced in these secret communiqués concerning original sin came from Teilhard de Chardin. It is instructive to note that once, at "a reception for new French books at the Centre S. Louis-des-Français, Teilhard came face to face with Garrigou who visited with him briefly about the Auvergne. The Dominican left and the Jesuit observed to a French diplomat: 'There goes the man who wants to burn me at the stake.'" [Thomas O'Meara, "A Neo-Thomist Theology of Grace: Reginald Garrigou-Lagrange," unpublished manuscript, 4; citing M. and E. Lukas, *Teilhard: The Man, the Priest, the Scientist* (New York: Bantam, Doubleday, Dell, 1977), 272.]

78 Garrigou-Lagrange, "Où va-t-elle?," 717. Garrigou offers a direct quote from one of the new theologians: *Ajoutons que dans sa clarté trompeuse, elle supprime le mystère religieux. A vrai dire, il n'y a plus là un mystère, il n'y a plus là qu'un prodige.*

79 Ibid. Transubstantiation is taken to be *la manière dont les scolastiques conçoivent cette transformation et leur conception est inadmissible.*

> According to our current perspectives . . . when, in virtue of the offering which is done according to the rite determined by Christ, the bread and the wine have become the efficacious symbol of the sacrifice of Christ, and in consequence of his spiritual presence, their religious being has changed. . . . This is what we understand by 'transubstantiation.'[80]

Garrigou states that this is a far cry from the Council of Trent's definition of transubstantiation.[81] For Garrigou, an "efficacious symbol" with its "spiritual presence" is simply not the same notion as a change of substance.[82]

In light of these opinions, Garrigou writes that he does not think that the new theologians have technically abandoned the teaching of St. Thomas; rather, they never really held the Thomistic teaching and they certainly never understood it.[83]

Concerning this lack of understanding, a great deal turns on the definition of truth. An unidentified professor of theology had written Garrigou the following message:

> This debate concerns the very definition of truth, and, without a clear understanding of this, one will return

80 Ibid., 718. [*Dans nos perspectives actuelles. . . lorsqu'en vertu de l'offrande qui en a été faite selon un rite déterminé par le Christ le pain et le vin sont devenus le symbole efficace du sacrifice du Christ, et par consequent de sa présence spirituelle, leur être religieux a changé.... C'est là ce que nous pouvons désigner par la transubstantiation.*]

81 He gives the Tridentine definition from Denz. 884: *conversio totius substantiae panis in Corpus et totius substantiae vini in Sanguinem, manentibus duntaxat speciebus panis et vini*. See: Ibid., 719.

82 Garrigou notes that the new theologians take a similar tack when it comes to explaining the Incarnation. They held that *(b)ien que le Christ soit vraiment Dieu, on ne peut pas dire que par lui il y avait une présence de Dieu sur la terre de Judée. . . . Dieu n'était pas plus présent en Palestine qu'ailleurs. Le* signe efficace *de cette présence divine s'est manifesté en Palestine au premier siècle de notre ère, c'est tout ce que l'on peut dire*. See: Ibid.

83 Ibid., 720. Garrigou remarks that this state of affairs is *douloureux et inquiétant*.

> to Modernism in thought as in action. The writings of which you have spoken to me are read by many in France. They exercise a powerful influence over those of average intelligence, it is true: the more serious are not taken in by them. You must write for those who have the sincere desire to be enlightened.[84]

It is clear that the traditional definition of truth, *adaequatio rei et intellectus*, was being substituted with the subjective *adaequatio realis mentis et vitae*. As Garrigou explains: "Truth is no longer the conformity of judgment with extramental reality and its immutable laws, but the conformity of judgment with the demands of action and human life which is always evolving."[85] For Garrigou, to change the definition of truth in this way is to embrace a total relativism. If the true is not that which is, but rather that which is becoming and thus always changing, then there is no rational foundation for the Church's theology. To hold such an opinion is, says Garrigou, a very serious error.[86]

We have seen that this new definition of truth comes from the thought of Maurice Blondel. What, however, is driving the new theologians to embrace it and with it, a radical interpretation of Catholic dogma? Garrigou opines:

> Where do these tendencies come from? A good judge of these matters has written to me the following: 'We are

84 Ibid. [*C'est en effet sur la notion même de vérité que porte le débat, et, sans bien s'en render compte, on revient vers le modernisme dans la pensée comme dans l'action. Les écrits dont vous me parlez sont très lus en France. Ils exercent une grosse influence, sur les esprits moyens il est vrai: les gens sérieux n'accrochent pas. Il faut écrire pour ceux qui ont le sincère désir d'être éclairés*.]

85 Ibid., 721–22. [Cf.: *La vérité n'est plus la conformité du jugement avec le réel extramental et ses lois immuables, mais la conformité du jugement avec les exigences de l'action et de la vie humaine qui évolue toujours*.] It bears repeating that this change of definition had been condemned some years earlier. See: Denz. 2058 and 2080.

86 Cf.: *Or cesser de défendre la définition traditionelle de la vérité, laisser dire qu'elle est chimérique, qu'il faut lui en substituer une autre vitaliste et évolutioniste, cela conduit au relativisme complet, et c'est une très grave erreur.* See: Ibid., 723.

> reaping the fruit of the frequentation of university courses without the necessary precautions. One wishes to frequent the thought of the masters of modern thought in order to convert them and one ends up being converted by them. One accepts, little by little, their ideas, their methods, their disdain for scholasticism, their historicism, their philosophical idealism, and all of their errors. If this frequentation is useful for those who are already formed, it is surely perilous for those who are not.'[87]

What is so scandalous for many today is that Garrigou, understanding as he did the currents of modern philosophy, did not attempt to build a theology upon their foundations. This is taken to be scandalous because it is a truism in certain circles that if St. Thomas were alive today, he would do just that. It is as if St. Thomas chose the philosophical framework of Aristotle because it was the most avant-garde or the most difficult with which to reconcile Christian faith. Rather, Garrigou's position was that St. Thomas chose to use Aristotle because he believed Aristotle's philosophy to be *true* and because he saw that its truth was helpful in bringing forth the truth of the Christian faith. Garrigou judged modern philosophy to be wanting; he considered many of its propositions to be unhelpful in explaining the Christian mysteries – unhelpful because most were devised in conscious opposition to Christian faith.[88] Garrigou held that the philosophical foundations of Thomism best describe the way things are;

87 Ibid., 721. [*D'où vient ces tendances? Un bon juge m'écrit: 'on recueille les fruits de la fréquentation sans précautions des cours universitaires. On veut fréquenter les maîtres de la pensée moderne pour les convertir et l'on se laisse convertir par eux. On accepte peu à peu leurs idées, leur méthodes, leur dédain de la scolastique, leur historicisme, leur idéalisme et toutes leurs erreurs. Si cette fréquentation est utile pour des esprits déjà formés, elle est sûrement périlleuse pour les autres.'*] One notes that Garrigou knows of what he speaks. He had himself studied at the Sorbonne; he attended the lectures of Émile Durkheim, Lévy-Bruhl, Henri Bergson, and Alfred Loisy. [See: Gagnebet, "L'œuvre du P. Garrigou-Lagrange," 11.]

88 This position is strenuously argued by John Milbank in *Theology*

he "stoutly maintained the interpretation of Aquinas of the pre-Cartesian commentators,"[89] seeing no need to adapt his thought to that of Kant or Hegel or Bergson or Blondel.

Two Representatives of Contemporary Fundamental Theology

In 1950 Pope Pius XII warned of new trends in theology in his encyclical *Humani generis*. The pope was leery of the very things that Garrigou found problematic in the *nouvelle théologie*; he wrote:

> In theology some want to reduce to a minimum the meaning of dogmas; and to free dogma itself from terminology long established in the Church and from philosophical concepts held by Catholic teachers, to bring about a return in the explanation of Catholic doctrine to the way of speaking used in Holy Scripture and by the Fathers of the Church. They cherish the hope that when dogma is stripped of the elements that they hold to be extrinsic to divine revelation, it will compare advantageously with the dogmatic opinions of those who are separated from the unity of the Church. . . . Moreover they assert that when Catholic doctrine has been reduced to this condition, a way will be found to satisfy modern needs, that will permit of dogma being expressed also by the concepts of modern philosophy, whether of immanentism or idealism or existentialism or any other system. Some more audacious affirm that this can and must be done, because they hold that the mysteries of faith are never expressed by truly adequate concepts but only by approximate and ever changeable notions, in which the truth is to some extent expressed, but is necessarily distorted.[90]

and Social Theory: Beyond Secular Reason (Cambridge, Mass.: Blackwell, 1991).

89 Benedict Ashley, *The Dominicans* (Collegeville, Minn.: Liturgical Press, 1990), 219.

90 Pope Pius XII, *Humani generis*, nn. 14–15, in *The Papal Encyclicals, 1939–1958*, ed. Claudia Carlen (Raleigh: McGrath, 1981), 177.

For some fifteen years official Church policy worked to hold back the developments in theology envisioned by men like de Lubac and Daniélou. Through the intervention of an assertive Holy Office and the collaboration of theologians like Garrigou-Lagrange, the more extravagant fears of Pope Pius XII did not see the light of day.

It is a truism that Pope John XXIII's *aggiornamento* and the Second Vatican Council had far-ranging effects on the Church's theological landscape.[91] In this section we will examine the contours of these changes through a study of the work of two contemporary Catholic theologians: Roger Haight and Monika Hellwig. Haight will focus our attention on the nature of theology,[92] and Hellwig will offer a reflection on what it means to be a theologian.[93] It will become clear that most of Garrigou's most firmly held convictions are no longer taken to be germane.

Roger Haight, *Dynamics of Theology*

Haight's preface to his *Dynamics of Theology* could have been written by de Lubac, Daniélou, or Bouillard. The problematic that grounded the disagreements between the Dominicans and the Jesuits in post-World War II France is

91 Joseph Komonchak remarks that "[I]n the wake of the Council, Catholic theology . . . was quite transformed. Historical critical method was applied with growing skill and rigor to the Scriptures and the monuments of the tradition. The anthropological turn was widely embraced in order to overcome the extrinsicism of the manuals. The unitary method of an imposed neo-Scholasticism gave way to a plurality of methods, languages, and conclusions. The habitual recourse to the latest Roman document was challenged by widely claimed rights to dissent and to theological autonomy or even by simple indifference. The primary reference to the needs of the Catholic subculture was often replaced by methods of correlation, critical or not, which conceived theology primarily as an engagement with contemporary culture." See: "The Ecclesial and Cultural Roles of Theology," *CTSA Proceedings* 40 (1985): 15–32, at 27.

92 Roger Haight, *Dynamics of Theology* (New York: Paulist, 1990).

93 Monika Hellwig, *The Role of the Theologian* (Kansas City: Sheed & Ward, 1987).

Haight's starting point. He writes: "My goal is to provide grounds for the creative interpretation or reinterpretation of traditional doctrines."[94] Of course this is not merely for the sake of novelty:

> Unless the church in its ministers and ministries can find the freedom that is engendered by historical consciousness to dramatically reinterpret its message, it will not preserve that message but surely compromise and even contradict it by default.[95]

Haight will proceed throughout his text by highlighting the significance of history and historical consciousness and by challenging the Church to rethink its fundamental beliefs in light of what is taken to be a paradigm change. Paradoxically he remarks that "[w]hat is required then is a conscious release from traditionalism in order to keep the tradition alive and meaningful."[96]

How does Haight define theology? He writes: "Theology today may be understood as a discipline which seeks to understand and determine the underlying truth of all reality."[97] This is obviously in contrast to the definition given by Garrigou-Lagrange and the Thomist tradition.[98]

94 Haight, *Dynamics of Theology*, ix. Unfortunately, he does not say what he sees the differences to be between 'creative interpretation' and 'reinterpretation.'

95 Ibid., x.

96 Ibid.

97 Ibid., 1. Haight gives a variation of this definition later in his text: "[T]heology is a discipline that interprets all reality – human existence, society, history, the world, and God – in terms of the symbols of Christian faith" (216).

98 Haight's definition also contrasts with definitions of other contemporary theologians. For instance, John Macquarrie defines theology as "the study which, through participation in and reflection upon a religious faith, seeks to express the content of this faith in the clearest and most coherent language possible" [See: *Principles of Christian Theology* (New York: Charles Scribner's Sons, 1977), 1]. Gerald O'Collins and Edward Farrugia claim that theology is the "methodical effort to understand and interpret the truth of revelation. As *fides quaerens intellectum*, theology uses the resources of reason, drawing in particular on the disciplines of history and

What accounts for Haight's all-encompassing definition? He explains: "Christian theology does not merely talk about God. Rather theology attempts to construe all things, the world, human existence, human history and society, as well as God from within the vision that is mediated to the Christian community through its religious symbols."[99] He then proceeds to argue that a theologian like Aquinas had a similar vision of theology: "Aquinas too conceived of theology as dealing with the whole of reality."[100]

Haight is certainly exaggerating when he claims that St. Thomas's *Summa theologiae* "treated every imaginable question and subject matter from the perspective of Christian revelation."[101] Not only are there questions that St. Thomas did not treat, there are many questions that are treated in their own right and according to their own logic – not in light of Christian revelation.

At the same time, one is allowed to question if the content of divine revelation as St. Thomas understood it is equivalent to "the vision that is mediated to the Christian community by its religious symbols." Semantically Haight actually strikes a less than global tone: his vision is of a radically contextualized and perspectival revelation. The "vision" of which he speaks is tied to the particular religious symbols of a particular human group. By definition it would be inaccessible for those outside the group.

This is curiously out of step with the vision of St. Thomas in the *Prima Pars*, questions 2–26. Here St. Thomas set out to examine the question of God through a

philosophy. In the face of the divine mystery, theology is always 'seeking' and never reaches final answers and definitive insights" [*A Concise Dictionary of Theology* (New York: Paulist, 1991), 240]. Richard McBrien says that theology is the "ordered effort to bring our experience of God to the level of intelligent expression" [*Catholicism* (Minneapolis: Winston, 1981), 1258].

99 Haight, *Dynamics of Theology*, 1. Haight defines a symbol as "that through which something other than itself is made present and known" (130).

100 Ibid., 2.

101 Ibid.

study of his effects. None of this is necessarily "mediated through Christian symbols." St. Thomas holds that human reason – with its intrinsic engagement with reality – is equal to the task.[102]

As one might expect, Haight is not employing the metaphysics of Aristotle nor is he espousing the critical realism of the Thomist tradition.[103] With what we have seen with Garrigou, it is perhaps surprising to note that Haight rests his theological reflections on the philosophy of action espoused by Maurice Blondel in his 1893 *Action: Essay on a Critique of Life and Science of Practice*. He writes:

> This dynamic concept of action is operative throughout this essay [i.e., his *Dynamics of Theology*]. It will help to define the very nature of faith, the purpose of revelation, the dynamics of religious symbol, the communication of scripture, and the logic of theological method. Finally, it provides the foundational concept for an integral conception of spirituality. Since spirituality is the Christian life in action, and the purpose of theology is to nurture spirituality, the perspective defined by a philosophy of action may be seen as a principle that coordinates the whole work.[104]

Our brief exposure to the use of Blondel by the Modernists gives us pause. Nowhere does Haight discuss the inherent difficulty in using Blondel's thought as a foundation for Catholic theology.[105] With this undergirding and

102 Cf. *Catechism of the Catholic Church*, n. 36 (quoting Vatican Council I, *Dei Filius* 2): "Our holy mother, the Church, holds and teaches that God, the first principle and last end of all things, can be known with certainty from the created world by the natural light of human reason."

103 Concerning the dialectical structure of concrete religious symbols and the traditional account of the distinction between matter and spirit, he writes: "One can bypass Thomistic metaphysics and by a phenomenological or descriptive experiential account of the human person arrive at a *similar* conception" (137, emphasis added). The important theological question, of course, is how much similarity is required for there to be continuity in faith.

104 Haight, *Dynamics of Theology*, 9.

105 Haight also insinuates the ideas of George Tyrell and Lucien

employing the theological categories of Paul Tillich and Karl Rahner, Haight can assert that "[t]he object of faith . . . is transcendent and beyond knowledge of this world;"[106] that "Christian revelation . . . is a subjective existential phenomenon" and that the "objective sense of the term is really derivative and in the long run causes confusion;"[107] and "[u]ltimately the response to the question of how concepts participate in God can only be existential, subjective, and experiential."[108] These points lead him to posit what probably most distances him from the Thomism of Garrigou:

> One cannot arrive at further knowledge of the object of faith on the basis of an objective deduction from the first expressions of revelation. The expressions of revelation are not first premises for objective reasoning. . . . Revelation is not objective knowledge, but an experience of encounter with God. "The data of revelation," then, is a phrase that refers back to content that emerged out of a heightened experience *of* but not *about* God.[109]

And, in a related vein, Haight adds: "There are no revealed doctrines as such, for revelation is personal encounter with a personal God and not an historically

Laberthonnière into his text. On page 245, n. 19, for instance, he writes: "The idea of the moral substance of Christian doctrine is borrowed from Lucien Laberthonnière, a colleague of Blondel." On pages 81–82, he says: "using Tyrell's conception, the experience that is mediated by Jesus is one that encompasses the whole of human personality eliciting a total response. The wholeness of this experience transcends its mental impression and imaginative interpretation. This encompassing experience of encounter remains the primary referent of revelation." Is it catering to *odium theologicum* to note that Tyrell died excommunicate and that Laberthonnière's works were put on the Index of Forbidden Books?

106 Haight, *The Dynamics of Theology*, 10.

107 Ibid., 69. Cf.: "Revelation, then, is first of all a form of human consciousness. Revelation is human experience and not other than human experience because it is the experience of human beings."

108 Ibid., 141.

109 Ibid., 79.

relative interpretation of that encounter in the form of an objective proposition."[110]

Joseph Komonchak helps to situate Roger Haight's approach in the landscape of contemporary theology:

> A most dramatic change since the Council is the unwillingness of many theologians to accept a primarily or exclusively ecclesial role. Theology has even been *defined* as the mediation between a religion and a culture. It involves a critical correlation between a text and a situation, between the claims of a tradition and the challenges of modernity. . . . [M]any, perhaps most, theologians regard as at least inadequate the definition of their role as simply the defense of magisterial teaching; they refuse the notion that systematic theology, if they retain it even as an ideal, can be carried out simply as a meditation on Church doctrines . . . ; and they claim standards and criteria for their work which cannot be reduced simply to obedience to the magisterium.[111]

Monika Hellwig, *The Role of the Theologian*

Komonchak's remarks on the role of the theologian in the framework of much of contemporary theology leads to a discussion of the work of Georgetown theologian, Monika Hellwig.

In 1987, fulfilling her role as president of the Catholic Theological Society of America, Hellwig delivered an address entitled "The Role of the Theologian." Sheed & Ward subsequently published it under the same title.

110 Ibid., 83.

111 Komonchak, "The Ecclesial and Cultural Roles of Theology," 27. One notes that "magisterium" does not even figure as an entry in Haight's *Dynamics of Theology*. His section headings are titled: "Faith," "Revelation," "Scripture," "Religious Symbols," and "Method" – one looks in vain for the teaching authority of the Church as a topic for theology. He will remark: "Some theologians are narrowly confessional and tie Christian theology to their particular church community" (190).

Hellwig begins her remarks by noting that the past year had been a difficult one for Catholic theologians.

> It has not been an easy year for theologians in North America whose work is in the Catholic community and tradition. Several members of our society have been deprived of scholarly positions or prevented from taking them by hierarchic intervention. . . .What has become central in all these cases and in all the questions that have been raised about them is the timid but persistent question coming from many quarters: how can there be any discussion among Catholic theologians on a point on which Rome has already spoken?[112]

Hellwig sees that the issue is none other than "the dissemination of greater understanding of the task of the theologian within the Church."[113]

Hellwig fears that many would wish to reduce "the role of the theologians in the Church to that of a severely restricted type of catechist – one who repeats the finished formulae and teaches others to do so with greater or lesser comprehension but with little or no critical reflection and little or no curiosity over new questions about old assumptions."[114] This is utterly important because it turns upon how one conceives the Church's teaching. Hellwig believes that the critics of contemporary theologians seem to be assuming that "the teaching of the Church is essentially finished and static, needing only to be explained to different generations, but retaining the form that was definitively established during the ages up to and including the Council of Trent."[115]

Not surprisingly, Hellwig remarks that this "classical view" is incompatible with our "historical experience of reality in which it becomes clear that there cannot be any

112 Hellwig, *The Role of the Theologian*, 1, 3.
113 Ibid., 3.
114 Ibid.
115 Ibid., 5–6.

teaching which is not culturally, temporally, and linguistically conditioned."[116]

So, what is the theologian's role? How does the theologian undertake the task of theology? Hellwig, "indulging a little whimsy" writes that

> in the case of the theologians each scholar's career is likely in a life-time to include all or several of the following roles: the theologian is sometimes myth-maker, sometimes the fool; sometimes the comforter and sometimes the builder; sometimes the archivist and sometimes the critic; sometimes the archeologist and sometimes the ghost.[117]

To discuss each of these metaphors would take us too far afield. We will focus attention on Hellwig's first dyad: the theologian as myth-maker and the theologian as fool. These two images possess the dynamism that informs the others.

For Hellwig, the motif of myth-maker pertains to the creative and constructive role of theologians. "Because all language about God and divine presence and action in creation is necessarily analogical, there is always a quiet process of myth-making at work where theology is being done."[118] This, in large measure, accounts for a fundamental and perennial dynamic of theology: ". . . the myth-making process cannot stop, because it must respond to cultural contexts so as to be intelligible in changing societies, and because contrast and plurality are needed if the process is not to become idolatrous."[119]

In this "myth-making," what are the criteria for fidelity to Scripture and Tradition?[120] She writes:

116 Ibid., 6.
117 Ibid., 9.
118 Ibid., 11.
119 Ibid., 14–15.
120 Ibid., 12. Oddly, Hellwig speaks of fidelity to "*gospel* and tradition." (emphasis added).

> First and foremost, we need to judge the appropriateness of shifts in the underlying myths in the light of the gospel of Jesus Christ as it merges from Scripture. But there is, as it were, another dimension to the question, namely the historical development within the life of the community in the course of the centuries. Therefore, we also have to judge by considering the long-term development of the mythic base of the tradition.[121]

The "theologian as fool" is the other side of the story: rather than myth-making, it is myth-breaking that becomes the role of the theologian. "The theologian is called upon . . . to play the role of the fool, the court jester, who must find a way to challenge prejudices and ill-considered assumptions in a manner that entertains or attracts before it offends."[122]

In describing this role, Hellwig marshals a host of historical examples: St. Paul challenging the ritual prescriptions of the Law, Irenaeus and the gnostics, Augustine and Pelagius, Leo the Great and monophysite Christology, and St. Thomas and "the myth underlying Platonically based theology and pseudospirituality."[123] The difficulty with these examples, of course, is that from our vantage point – knowing how doctrines did indeed develop – we lack the appreciation of the upheavals caused by "myth-breaking." This is made apparent when Hellwig writes: ". . . one might suggest that there are myths underlying our institutional ecclesiology that should be examined and challenged in the name of the gospel, of the tradition, and of the consciousness of believers."[124]

Hellwig concludes this section with the following reflection:

121 Ibid., 14–15.
122 Ibid., 17–18.
123 Ibid., 19.
124 Ibid., 19–20.

> There is no doubt that, no matter how fondly various elements of such myths are reiterated and reinforced by voices of authority, theologians would not be faithful to their calling if they did not bring such elements into question. Yet it is the task of the myth-breaker, the delicate and dangerous task of the fool. We should not really expect to be thanked for it.[125]

The other three sets of images carry the basic dynamic as does the juxtaposition of "myth-maker" and "fool." For lack of better terms, one tends to be "constructive" and other tends to be "deconstructive." It bears noting that of all the images, "the theologian as comforter" best describes the vision which informs the Thomist school: "Perhaps the most appreciated role of the theologian is the pastoral role when the tradition and its reflective formulation are applied in ways that are non-controversial and also happen to be helpful to people in interpreting the meaning of their lives, in resolving doubts and problems, and in coming to practical decisions."[126]

Garrigou-Lagrange: A Critical Retrieval

Catholic theology has witnessed a sea change since the days of Garrigou-Lagrange's disputes with the practitioners of the *nouvelle théologie*; Garrigou's understanding of the nature of theology and the theological enterprise provides a striking contrast with the way they tend to be understood today. From matters as elemental as how one defines theology to the question of the relationship of philosophy to the doing of theology, Garrigou and contemporary theologians are at odds.

There are at least four categories to highlight. The first concerns the definition of theology. What is it? How does it relate to other fields of inquiry? And, most important, what are its sources?

125 Ibid., 22.
126 Ibid., 23–24.

Second, in examining the historical development of Christian doctrine, how does one account for the continuity of Christian faith through the ages? In making proposals for "creative reinterpretations" of Christian symbols, what exactly does one think that one is doing? (Unveiling a truth that has always been present in an inchoate fashion? Creating a new meaning which helps to make sense of our experience?)

Third, what is the status of the theological conclusions that the theologian eventually arrives at? Are all theologies equally true? How does one evaluate a theological proposition?

Finally, and perhaps most significantly, what are the operative theologies of revelation and the Church that inform one's answers to the above questions?

Garrigou and the Neo-Thomist school had clear and distinct answers to all these questions. (Indeed, their clarity and their eye for distinctions at times earned them the epithet of "rationalism.") They would say: Theology is the science which treats of God and God's relationship to humankind; it is a rational reflection on divine revelation (Scripture and Tradition); it proceeds by way of an explicit metaphysic, and theological conclusions are judged by reference to theology's sources and, ultimately, by the Church's magisterium. Moreover: God has deigned to explicitly reveal truths concerning both Himself and what is necessary for salvation; these truths can be expressed (adequately, but not perfectly) in propositional form – indeed for their intelligibility they must be. Finally: the Church is the guardian of this "deposit of faith"; the theological task is to work at the systematization of these truths so that their overall coherence can be better appreciated, always keeping in mind that theology is not revelation and is never in a state of perfection.

In an examination of the ethos of contemporary Catholic theology, one finds a significantly different set of propositions. In the first place: theology is much more about *us* than it is about God; Feuerbach's anthropological critique and the Enlightenment's turn to the subject usually set the stage for all that follows. Secondly: God's revelation takes place everyday and everywhere; one must look at and listen to one's own experience if one would see and hear God. So: one should not place undo emphasis on a particular time and place where God has revealed Himself in the past – what matters is developing a critical reflection on one's experience and correlating it with a critical reflection on one's culture.

What conclusions can we make in the face of these wildly different approaches to theology and the theological enterprise? It is not enough to remark that the Church's magisterium, as witnessed to by the *Catechism of the Catholic Church*, remains more inclined to side with Garrigou than with the contemporary spirit of theology. The most pressing distinction that must be made concerns the *fides qua* and the *fides quae*. The subjective experience of radical trust in a personal God (*fides qua*) must be distinguished from the faith of the Church (*fides quae*) – the body of beliefs to be believed. Determining what those beliefs are, how they are related, and how they are to be expressed properly and in fidelity to the apostolic witness ought to remain a primary work of the theologian. In this regard, there is no good reason to argue for the radical autonomy of theology – it is a "subordinate science" – always in a receptive posture vis-à-vis God's truth.[127]

What is one to make of contemporary theology's espousal of the historical-critical method? How ought one to understand the role of historical consciousness in theology? Most pointedly: has the recognition of "historical development" sounded the death knell for Thomism?

127 See: Aidan Nichols, *The Shape of Catholic Theology* (Collegeville, Minn.: Liturgical Press, 1991), chapter 2: "The Task of Theology," for a fine discussion of these points.

To say that "all theologies are historically conditioned artifacts of particular cultures" doesn't really tell one something particularly significant: *everything* that one can point to is "historically conditioned." For the Thomist school, *when* an idea came into existence and *where* it developed are not as interesting as its particular truth claims. The Thomist is always more interested in the truth or falsity of an idea than its historical pedigree. To identify where an idea appeared and when it was formulated, say the Thomists, does not help you evaluate its truth claims. To say otherwise is blatant chauvinism.

Much has changed since the days when Neo-Thomism was all but the official theology of the Church and Réginald Garrigou-Lagrange was its principal Dominican expositor. The Second Vatican Council rightfully returned the Church to a posture of acceptance toward a plurality of theological approaches. Nonetheless, it is our contention that Garrigou's answers to the most elemental questions pertaining to theology are important correctives to some problematic trends in contemporary Catholic theology.

In this regard, one might expect that Garrigou himself would be allowed the last word in this chapter. However, that honor will be given, ironically perhaps, to Jean Daniélou and Henri de Lubac. Garrigou's antagonists in the 1940s and 1950s lived long enough to see what they considered to be problematic developments in Catholic theology. The two who were among those most responsible for the Council's openness to other theologies judged that things were going too far – beyond the boundaries set by the *fides quae*.

First, Jean Daniélou. In his memoir, *Et qui est mon prochain?* he writes:

> Personally, in the present situation, I think that we are more threatened by the danger of Modernism than by the danger of integralism and, after the great conciliar effort to adapt to the modern world – an effort

> which must be continued – I believe that it is primordial to affirm the necessity of fidelity to fundamental values. Certain traditionalists consider me to be their ally, while my position does not align with theirs at all: it expresses a fundamental defense against a threat which weighs on the constitutive elements of the faith.[128]

He explains further:

> . . . it is urgent to specify the points to which all Catholics must give their assent; which would put outside the Church all those who do not accept them, who would deny, for instance, the virginity of Mary, the Eucharist. . . . There are, in the Church, many things that are debatable, things that allow for very diverse opinions, which will be perhaps modified, but it is very important today to place the accent on those fundamental elements that are constitutive of the faith.[129]

In 1969, four years after the closing of the Second Vatican Council, Henri de Lubac published *L'Eglise dans la crise actuelle*.[130] Like his Jesuit confrere, he was concerned about certain interpretations of the Council that he

128 Jean Daniélou, *Et qui est mon prochain,?* (Paris: Stock, 1974), 200–201. [*Personellement, dans la situation actuelle, je considère que nous sommes plus menacés par le danger moderniste que par le danger intégriste et, après le grand effort conciliare d'adaptation au monde moderne – effort qui doit être poursuivi – je crois primordial d'affirmer la nécessité d'une fidelité aux valeurs fondamentales. Certains traditionalistes me considèrent comme leur allié, alors que ma position ne s'aligne nullement sur la leur: elle exprime une défense vitale contre une menance qui pèse sur les éléments constituitifs de la foi.*]

129 Ibid., 201. [. . . *il est urgent de préciser les points sur lesquels tout catholique doit donner son accord; se mettraient par là même en dehors de l'Église tous ceux qui les refuseraient, qui nieraient la virginité de Marie, l'Eucharistie. . . . Il y a, dans l'Église, beaucoup de choses discutables sur lesquelles peuvent s'exprimer des opinions très diverses, qui seront peut-être modifiées, mais il est très important, aujourd'hui, de mettre l'accent sur les éléments fondamentaux et constitutifs de la foi.*]

130 Henri de Lubac, *L'Eglise dans la crise actuelle* (Paris: Cerf, 1969).

judged to betray the spirit of the Council Fathers. In particular, he sensed a hypercritical and destructive *Zeitgeist* at work in many theologians. He noted that faced with the Tradition of the Church, they

> hold up superbly individual "reflection," and humble "faithfulness" before that which is facilely called "the truth." When such a state of affairs dominates, the authority of the Church becomes the preferred target of critics. It is now seen only as an external power, indeed as an enemy, the exercise of which is judged to be tyrannical, oppressive. The Church's magisterium is no longer supported, except impatiently; its declarations are held to be abusive – harshly discussed, indeed, entirely rejected.[131]

Faced with this hostility, de Lubac asks:

> Isn't it necessary, when the seriousness of the hour calls for it, that the theologian know to suspend for a time his historical research, his "constructions" and his personal research . . . to remember that his existence as a theologian and all the authority that his profession can mean to him are founded before all else on the charge he has received in light of the defense and explanation of the faith of the Church?[132]

131 Ibid., 26–27. [. . . *oppose alors superbement la 'réflexion' individuelle et l'on humilie la 'fidelité' devant ce qu'on nomme bien facilement la 'vérité.' Lorsque domine un tel état d'esprit, l'autorité de l'Eglise devient la cible préférée des critiques. Elle n'est plus envisagée que comme une puissance extérieure, voire ennemie, dont tout exercise est jugé tyrannique, 'oppresseur.' Son magistère n'est plus supporté qu'avec impatience; ses déclarations sont tenues pour abusives, âprement discutées, voire entièrement rejetées.*]

132 Ibid., frontispiece. [*Ne faut-il pas, lorsque la gravité de l'heure le demande, que le théologien sache suspender pour un moment ses enquêtes historiques, ses constructions et ses recherches personnelles,–auxquelles il aurait d'ailleurs tort en tout temps d'attacher une importance excessive,– pour se souvenir que toute son existence de théologien et toute l'autorité que cette profession peut lui valoir sont fondées avant tout sur la charge qu'il a reçue, en vue de la défense et de l'illustration de la foi de l'Eglise?*]

Henri de Lubac's reflection touches upon a serious lacuna in contemporary theology: there is little by way of classical apologetics. He notes that historical criticism is unequal to this basic theological task.[133]

In the 1940s and 1950s Daniélou and de Lubac were vigorous in their defense of doing theology in a way other than that of the Neo-Thomists. They were correct in insisting that there have always been a variety of theological traditions in the Church and that this plurality is a good thing.[134] Within a decade and a half from the publication of *Humani generis* they had the validation of an Ecumenical Council for most of their positions. However, by the end of their lives they were calling for an emphasis on limits to theological pluralism, sensing that the Church's theological enterprise was slipping into anarchy.

Where does all this leave us? It is our contention that the Thomism of Garrigou-Lagrange and particularly his way of defining theology and the theological task could provide helpful parameters for determining the nature and scope of the theological enterprise in the twenty-first century. It is not a matter of proscribing pluralism or of mandating an Aristotelian metaphysic for all theologies. It is simply a matter of fidelity to the *spirit* of Vatican II and in particular the *letter* of *Optatam totius*: "Under the light of faith and with the guidance of the Church's teaching authority, theology should be taught in such a way that students will accurately draw Catholic doctrine from divine revelation, understand that doctrine profoundly, nourish their own spiritual lives with it, and be able to proclaim it, unfold it, and defend it. . . ."[135]

133 Ibid., 74. De Lubac is dependent upon the conclusions of H. Zahrnt's *Aux prises avec Dieu, la théologie protestante au XIXe siècle*.

134 One can still maintain that Daniélou's critique in "Les orientations présentes de la pensée religieuse" was an unfair caricature of Thomism. Perhaps an overstatement was necessary in order to create space for his own approach.

135 Second Vatican Council, *Optatam totius*, n. 16.

In the next chapter we move to a discussion of what might be termed Garrigou's most lasting contribution: his spiritual theology. We will see that, in large part, it was born of a synthesis of St. Thomas's theology and the spirituality of St. John of the Cross.

8. The Spirituality of Garrigou-Lagrange

The elect will become part of the very family of God as they enter into the circle of the Holy Trinity. In them the Father will generate his Word; the Father and the Son will issue forth Love. Charity will assimilate them to the Holy Spirit and meanwhile the vision will assimilate them to the Word, who in turn will make them similar to the Father whose expression He is. At that time we will be able to say truly that we know and love the Trinity that dwells in us as in a temple of glory, and we shall be in the Trinity, at the summit of Being, Thought, and Love. This is the glory; this is the goal to which our spiritual progress tends – configuration to the Word of God. Réginald Garrigou-Lagrange, *The Last Writings*

As we have noted, Réginald Garrigou-Lagrange came to hold the first chair of Catholic spiritual theology in the Church's history. He lectured on spirituality at the Angelicum from 1917 until Christmas, 1959. It is safe to say that in the preconciliar Church no one had a higher profile than he when it came to expertise in Catholic spirituality; certainly no one was better versed in the classical Dominican approach to the question. In this chapter, we will outline Garrigou's contribution to spirituality in the Catholic tradition. If his form of dogmatic theology failed to win the day at the Second Vatican Council, we will see that his most passionately held spiritual propositions were incorporated into official Catholic teaching by the Council Fathers.

What is Spirituality?

Before proceeding, it is necessary to ask the obvious question: What is spirituality? How is one to understand the significance of this branch of theology? Especially in recent years, with the proliferation and commercialization of numerous "spiritualities," it is important to define our terms carefully.

As a starting point, we should recognize that Catholic spirituality is ultimately concerned with the interaction between the human person and God. As a branch of theology, it aims at understanding God's actions in the lives of human persons and the individual's call to respond to God's loving presence. Because of this, every Catholic spirituality implies a theology of grace, a more or less coherent explanation of how God comes to the individual to heal, forgive, justify, and sanctify. Garrigou held that "this part of theology is, above all, a development of the treatise on the love of God and of that on the gifts of the Holy Spirit, to show how they are applied to lead souls to divine union."[1]

Since God calls human beings into relationship with himself, Catholic spirituality is also concerned with the human person's response to the divine offer of intimacy.

1 Réginald Garrigou-Lagrange, *The Three Ages of the Interior Life: Prelude of Eternal Life*, 2 vols., trans. M. Timothea Doyle (St. Louis: B. Herder, 1947), I, 10. Ultimately, Garrigou held that spirituality is an application of moral theology: "Moral theology ought to treat, not only of sins to be avoided, but of virtues to be practiced, and of docility in following the inspirations of the Holy Spirit. From this point of view, its applications are called ascetical and mystical theology." (Ibid.)

Because of this, the various dispositions that ought to be encouraged and nurtured, as well as those which ought to be avoided and censored play a key role in Catholic spirituality.

In a closely related vein – yet secondarily – spirituality is concerned with the practices that one ought to undertake to dispose oneself to the self-giving of God. Here one would find, for instance, the three archetypical practices counseled by the Gospels: prayer, fasting, and almsgiving. Here, too, would be found the *lectio divina*, mortifications, contemplation, and any number of other practices.

In his *summa* of spirituality, *The Three Ages of the Interior Life*,[2] Garrigou writes:

> We shall consider first of all the foundations of the interior life, then the elimination of obstacles, the progress of the soul purified and illuminated by the light of the Holy Spirit, the docility which it ought to have toward Him, and finally the union with God which the soul attains by this docility, by the spirit of prayer, and by the cross borne with patience, gratitude, and love.[3]

Catholic spirituality deals with God's gracious gift of himself through his Holy Spirit; it is concerned with the human person as potential and actual recipient of utter Gratuity. When all is said and done, Catholic spirituality is about the profound living of the Gospel of Jesus Christ – recognizing with Garrigou that "no religion that is profoundly lived is without an interior life, without that intimate and frequent conversation which we have not only with ourselves but with God."[4]

2 It first appeared, of course, in French: *Les trois âges de la vie intérieure: prélude de celle du ciel*, 2 vols. (Paris: Cerf, 1938).

3 Garrigou-Lagrange, *The Three Ages*, I, 3. [Note: In her translation, M. Timothea Doyle translated *Saint-Esprit* as "Holy Ghost." In light of contemporary Catholic usage, I have taken the liberty of changing this to "Holy Spirit" whenever quoting directly from *The Three Ages*.]

4 Ibid., I, 8.

The Universal Call to Holiness

Since the closing of the Second Vatican Council, Catholics have generally become more aware of the radical dimensions of the following of Christ. It has become a commonplace for people to hear that Christian discipleship is "countercultural"; it would come as no surprise for many to hear that following Jesus calls them to more than simply keeping the Ten Commandments. This is a development that has its roots in one of the Council's key teachings in *Lumen gentium*: "Thus it is evident to everyone that all the faithful of Christ of whatever rank or status are called to the fullness of the Christian life and to the perfection of charity."[5] And again, "In the various types and duties of life, one and the same holiness is cultivated by all who are moved by the Spirit of God, and who obey the voice of the Father, worshipping God the Father in spirit and in truth."[6]

This teaching was the result of a long – and at times acrimonious – discussion among the experts in the Catholic spiritual tradition. We will see that Garrigou-Lagrange's position, informed by the classical Dominican tradition and bolstered by the reflection of Juan Arintero, O.P., eventually became the Church's official teaching. To demonstrate what was at stake in all of this, we will begin by discussing the history of the interpretation of what is rightly called the "Charter of the Christian Life" – Jesus's Sermon on the Mount. It will become clear that one's interpretation of the Lord's words inevitably set the stage for a number of important conclusions in spirituality.

Servais Pinckaers,[7] Dominican professor emeritus of moral theology at the University of Fribourg, devoted

5 Second Vatican Council, *Lumen gentium*, n. 40. [Cf.: *Catechism of the Catholic Church*, n. 2013.]

6 Ibid., n. 41.

7 Pinckaers was directed in his doctoral studies at the Angelicum by Louis-Bertrand Gillon, O.P. Gillon, the author of the groundbreaking *Christ and Moral Theology*, trans. Cornelius Williams (Staten Island, N.Y.: Alba House, 1967) had himself been directed by

years of study to the question of the interpretation of the Sermon on the Mount. In his masterpiece, *The Sources of Christian Ethics*,[8] Pinckaers shows that Christian history has witnessed five basic approaches to the interpretation of the Sermon. These interpretations, each of which inform a particular vision of the Christian moral life and thus Christian spirituality, are enumerated as follows:

1. The "Catholic" Interpretation
2. An Idealistic Moral Theory
3. An Interim Morality
4. The Sermon, A Social Program
5. The Lutheran Interpretation[9]

The "Catholic" interpretation – "Catholic" only in the sense of being an approach which has known hegemony in recent centuries – "rests on the distinction between a moral code designed for all Christians, expressed in the Decalogue, and a more spiritual and exacting doctrine reserved for an elite group such as religious, who have freely chosen to strive for evangelical perfection."[10] In this conception, the Sermon on the Mount is the domain of *counsels*, not *commands*.

The second interpretation is inspired by the thought of Immanuel Kant and nineteenth-century idealism. "In contrast to Judaism's obsession with works, the Sermon presents us, they would say, with a new morality of sentiment, where benevolence and one's personal intentions are central."[11] At the same time, the Sermon is an expression of "an ideal – unworkable no doubt, but still useful on the practical level, since we need to ask a great deal of people in order to obtain even a little effort and progress."[12]

Garrigou. During his time at the Angelicum, Fr. Pinckaers attended any number of lectures by Garrigou.

8 Servais Pinckaers, *The Sources of Christian Ethics*, trans. Mary Thomas Noble (Washington, D.C.: Catholic University of America Press, 1995).

9 Ibid., 136–39.

10 Ibid., 136.

11 Ibid., 137.

The third interpretation, inspired in large measure by Albert Schweitzer, takes its starting point in eschatology. Accepting the hypothesis that Jesus and the first disciples expected the imminent dawn of the parousia, this interpretation holds that the Sermon on the Mount "proclaimed a very demanding doctrine approaching heroism, but it was valid only for the short space of time before the imminent return of Christ."[13] Accordingly, the Sermon represents an impossible morality and spirituality. It may be possible to live according to its vision in the short term – especially if one expects a cataclysmic end to be just around the corner. However, was not designed with the "long haul" in mind.

The fourth interpretation, identified by Pinckaers with the position of Leon Tolstoy, does not see the sublime spirituality of the Sermon on the Mount, and chooses to see it as "a blueprint for a new society ruled by love and enjoying peace."[14] Tolstoy's interpretation was social and political; he envisioned "as the logical result of the Sermon the abolition of armies, courtrooms, and oaths."[15] Its intent was never directed toward providing the individual Christian with moral or spiritual guidance.

Finally, the classical Lutheran approach holds that the Sermon is to be read in light of St. Paul's Letter to the Romans and its critique of the Law. Martin Luther believed that "the Sermon confronts us with the impossible . . . in order to make us aware of our sins and lead us through this revelation to repentance and faith."[16] Pinckaers comments:

> Luther's interpretation of the Sermon was merely an application of his teaching on justification and the Law. The Sermon was treated as the Old Law. It

12 Ibid.
13 Ibid., 138.
14 Ibid.
15 Ibid.
16 Ibid., 139.

> played the same role of prosecutor, with still stronger demands. . . . The Sermon was viewed as a law that promised justice in return for works. No matter how excellent, such a text would be considered inferior to the Pauline doctrine of justification by faith and would be interpreted in its light.[17]

Pinckaers, informed by research in the thought of the Fathers of the Church and biblical exegesis, is at great pains to underline that these five interpretations of the Sermon on the Mount all seriously miss the mark. They each fail to convey the sense of the Lord's teaching in Matthew's gospel. He explains that when it comes to this teaching, we are dealing with "the earliest authentic sources of catechesis and Christian moral theology."[18]

> We should note that the Sermon, like the entire Gospel, is addressed to all, beginning with the poor and humble. St. John Chrysostom and St. Augustine knew this well and said it to the people. It can hardly be viewed therefore as a counsel reserved for the chosen few. The teaching is unequivocal: if you wish to enter the Kingdom of heaven, you must practice Gospel "justice." If you do this you are building on rock; if not, on sand.[19]

The central problem is whether the Sermon is addressed to all or to a religious elite. Concurrently, one must ask if the Sermon counsels an impossible ideal – values to be aimed at yet never really acquired – or, rather, a description of what is truly possible through God's grace.

The "traditional" Catholic approach, the approach that held sway since the time of the Counter-Reformation, accepted the idea that Jesus' words were not addressed to all his disciples and that therefore he was envisioning at least two tiers among his disciples. The majority would be held to the bare minimum – most often conceived as being

17 Ibid.
18 Ibid., 164.
19 Ibid.

the keeping of the Ten Commandments. A select few, specially graced by God, would be responsible for maximizing the Gospel message: they would be called to live out the Beatitudes. Catholicism's two-fold structure of laity and clergy/religious provided a ready-made framework for this distinction. The laity – at work "in the world" – is working toward achieving moral rectitude; only those in religious life and members of the clergy are called explicitly to holiness.

The Second Vatican Council overturned this long-standing approach to the question. In this, the Council Fathers were indebted, in the first place, to the Spanish Dominican, Juan González Arintero, one of the first theologians to challenge the traditional vision.[20] Since Arintero's impact on the thought of Garrigou-Lagrange was so significant, we will move now to outline his contribution to spiritual theology.

Juan González Arintero (1860–1928)[21]

Juan Arintero was born in 1860 in Lugueros, Spain. He entered the Dominican Order in 1875 and did his studies in the *studium* in Corias. He was sent to study the natural sciences at the University of Salamanca and, by the end of his initial formation, he would receive the licentiate in philosophy and the lectorate in theology. From 1909 until 1912, Arintero taught apologetics at the Angelicum. He returned to Salamanca in 1912 and spent the rest of his life dealing with the questions raised by mysticism. Arintero is best known for his four-volume work in spirituality, *Desenvolvimento y vitalidad de la Iglesia*.[22]

20 One notes that Arintero's challenge did not come directly from biblical exegesis or Patristic studies. His perspective came from a close reading of mystical theology, particularly that of St. John of the Cross.

21 See especially: "Biographical Note," in Juan González Arintero, *The Mystical Evolution in the Development and Vitality of the Church*, trans. and ed. Jordan Aumann (St. Louis: B. Herder, 1950), xi–xiii.

22 The four volumes are as follows: *Evolucion organica*, *Evolucion doc-*

Evolucion mistica, volume three of Arintero's masterwork, contains his mature reflection on Catholic spirituality. What is most important for our narrative – and which parallels the discussion of Fr. Pinckaers on the Sermon on the Mount – is to highlight that from the beginning Arintero rejected the traditional "two-tier" approach in Catholic spirituality.

M.-M. Gorce, in his article in the *Dictionnaire de spiritualité*, explains:

> The author considers that the spiritual evolution of the whole Church is like the covering of the spiritual growth that all true Christians are realizing. Is there not even in this consideration the principal foundation for one of the most cherished theses of Fr. Arintero: the coextension of mysticism with the Christian life; mysticism being an element of the life of the Church and the Church living in each Christian? *L'Evolucion mistica* threw into disarray the well-informed partisans of ancient and respectable mysticisms.[23]

Not only are all Christians called to explicit holiness, Arintero held that they are also offered by God the gift of contemplation: they are addressed by "the generality of the call to the mystical life."[24]

Garrigou himself reviewed the second edition (1920) of Arintero's *Cuestiones misticas* in *La vie spirituelle*.[25] In this

trinal, *Evolucion mistica*, and *Mecanismo divino de las factores de l'evolucion Eclesiastica*.

23 M.-M. Gorce, "Arintero (Juan González)," in *DS*, I, 856. [*L'auteur considère que l'évolution spirituelle de l'ensemble de l'Eglise est comme l'enveloppe des accroissements spirituels que réalisent tous les vrais chrétiens. N'y a-t-il pas dans cette considération même le fondement principal d'une thèse chère entre toutes au P. Arintero: la coextension de la mystique à la vie chrétienne; la mystique étant un élément de la vie de l'Eglise et l'Eglise vivant en chaque chrétien?* L'Evolucion mistica *jetait en désarroi bien des partisans éclairés de diverses mystiques anciennes et respectables.*]

24 Ibid., 857. [. . . *de la généralité de l'appel à la vie mystique.*]

25 Réginald Garrigou-Lagrange, review of Juan Arintero, *Cuestiones misticas o sea las alturas de la contemplacion accesibles a todos* in *La vie spirituelle* 3 (1920): 158–60.

work Arintero revisited the themes that he had explored in *Evolucion mistica* some twenty years earlier. At the very beginning of the review, Garrigou underscored Arintero's most potent claim:

> According to the Dominican master, mystical or infused contemplation can be desired without presumption and can be obtained by those who seek it sincerely and generously; if there are few contemplatives, it is not that contemplation is properly an extraordinary gift, in a miraculous sense, it is because of our lack of perseverance, abnegation, and love for the Cross . . .[26]

Garrigou's review is, as one might expect, congratulatory; he does not find a single point with which to take exception. He concludes by highlighting that the last section of *Cuestiones* is "the substance of that which Fr. Arintero has best written and is most useful for the direction of souls who desire truly to make progress in their union with God."[27]

Besides teaching that mysticism is an aspect of the "ordinary" features of living the Christian life, Arintero was a strenuous critic of the distinction that had gained currency in the modern period between infused and acquired contemplation.

This distinction is now little more than a footnote in the annals of Catholic spirituality.[28] However, it was a significant

26 Ibid., 158–59. [*Selon le maître dominicain, la contemplation mystique ou infuse peut bien être désirée sans présomption, et obtenue par ceux qui la cherchent sincèrement et généreusement;—s'il y a peu de contemplatifs, ce n'est pas que la contemplation soit un don proprement extraordinaire, au sens de miraculeux, c'est à cause de notre défaut de persévérance, d'abnégation et d'amour de la croix . . .*]

27 Ibid., 160. [. . . *la substance de ce que le P. Arintero a écrit de meilleur et de plus utile pour la direction des âmes qui désirent vraiment progresser dans l'union à Dieu.*]

28 It is telling that the *Catechism of the Catholic Church* has 11 paragraphs devoted to contemplation (nn. 2709–19) and that the distinction between acquired and infused contemplation does not appear.

issue in the first half of the twentieth century. Was contemplation the result of a divinely infused gift or was it a human achievement?[29] Arintero's position, more or less assured by the Dominican tradition's long-standing emphasis on the priority of God's grace, was to deny the very existence of acquired contemplation. In chapter 10 of his *La verdadera mistica tradicional* (1925), "he applies himself to destroy the modern notion of acquired contemplation. The explication of this innovation appeared to him to harbor hidden contradictions, the supernatural order being always the order of the infused and never the order of the acquired."[30] In all of this, Arintero held that the mystical life – the interior life of the individual Christian – is to be identified with "that which St. Thomas Aquinas profoundly analyzed according to the classical objective considerations of states, gifts, and theological virtues."[31]

In this regard, M.-M. Gorce summarizes the significance of Arintero's work by highlighting its Thomistic foundation:

> The mystical life is grounded in the very foundation of the human being by the theological realities studied by the *Summa* of St. Thomas. . . . The *Weltanschauung* of the spiritual world brings to Thomism a very clear doctrinal economy. In order to edify a mystic, its theoreticians do not have to look beyond the habitual preoccupations of St. Thomas Aquinas.[32]

29 It is not too far afield to see this question as a logical extension of the Jesuit and Dominican disagreements on grace – the *De auxiliis* controversy.

30 Gorce, art. cit., 857.

31 Ibid. [. . . *telle que saint Thomas d'Aquin l'a profondément analysée selon les considérations objectives classiques des états, des dons, des vertus théologales.*]

32 Ibid., 858. [*La vie mystique est constituée au tréfond de l'être humain par ces réalités théologiques qu'étudie la* Somme *de saint Thomas. . . . Cette* Weltanschauung *du monde spirituel apporte au thomisme une très appréciable économie doctrinale. Pour édifier une mystique, ses théoriciens n'ont pas besoin de chercher en dehors ou à côté des préoccupations habituelles de saint Thomas d'Aquin.*]

As one might expect, Arintero's position did not win universal acclaim. One particularly strong critic was the French Sulpician, Albert Farges (1848–1926). Farges, professor in Bourges, Nantes, Paris, Issy, and finally in the seminary at Angers (1898–1905), waged battle with Arintero and Auguste Saudreau[33] in his courses on asceticism and mysticism.[34]

In the controversy surrounding contemplation, Farges declared himself an enemy of the idea that there is a universal call to infused contemplation. He writes:

> What are the reasons that so many souls stop in the ways of mysticism? The first is most often their own fault since they do not respond generously enough to grace. . . . The second is that they lack – very frequently, alas! – a good spiritual director. . . . But the third, and beyond any doubt the principal, is that God, who is master of his gifts, does not call them any higher.[35]

33 Auguste Saudreau (1859–1946), priest of the diocese of Angers, was the author of many works on spirituality. In *Les degrès de la vie spirituelle* (1896), he taught *que les grâces mystiques étaient les conditions normales de la perfection, largement offertes à quiconque s'y dispose généreusement*. See: Irénée Noye, "Saudreau (Auguste)," in *DS*, XIV, 359–60.

34 His lectures were published as *Les phénomènes mystiques distingués de leurs contrefaçons humaines et diaboliques* (Paris: Librairie Saint-Paul, 1923) and *Les voies ordinaires de la vie spirituelle, traité de théologie ascétique* (Paris: Librairie Saint-Paul, 1924). The following English translations are extant: *Mystical Phenomena Compared with their Human and Diabolical Counterfeits*, trans. S. P. Jacques (London: Burns, Oates & Washbourne, 1926) and *The Ordinary Ways of the Spiritual Life*, trans. not given (New York: Benzinger, 1927).

35 Albert Farges, *Les phénomènes mystiques*, 275; cited in Irénée Noye, "Farges (Albert)," in *DS*, V, 96. [*Quelles sont les raisons de l'arrêt de tant d'âmes dans les voies mystiques? La première, c'est le plus souvent la faute de ces âmes qui ne correspondent pas assez généreusement à la grâce. . . . La seconde, c'est qu'elles manquent – trop souvent, hélas! – d'un bon directeur. . . . Mais la troisième, et sans aucun doute la principale, c'est que Dieu, qui est le maître de ses dons, ne les appelle pas plus haut.*]

The reason that the majority does not reach the heights of mystical contemplation is simply that God does not wish them to. God chooses to reserve this gift to a select few.

Farges describes the kind of contemplation – i.e., acquired contemplation – that the majority of Christians are called to in the following terms:

> The second contemplation of God without infused species is done by the concepts of reason and faith, normally by abstracting from sensible things. It is therefore ordinary, active, or acquired by human effort, assisted by grace and the light afforded by the gifts of the Holy Spirit.[36]

Farges's work upheld the *status quo* within Catholicism created in the early modern period. It validated the two-tier theory: there is an "ordinary" Christian majority and an "extraordinary" religious elite. One might be tempted to say that from one point of view, Farges's position was more pastorally sensitive than that those of Arintero and Saudreau. Undoubtedly it would be reassuring to most Christians to hear that the reason that they have not reached the heights of the spiritual life is because God has not given them the graces necessary for such progress. They would be able to take heart that it was not due to any moral failure on their part: they were, after all, called to "ordinariness." At the same time, they would be warned that to seek the higher gifts could mean that they were falling into the sin of presumption – acting as if they knew better than God what they needed.

To this line of reasoning, Arintero, Saudreau, and eventually Garrigou-Lagrange,[37] would say that such was not

36 Albert Farges, *Autour de notre livre 'Les phénomènes mystiques'* (Paris, 1921), 91–92; cited in Noye, art. cit., 96. [*La seconde contemplation de Dieu sans espèces infuses se fait par les concepts de la raison et de la foi, normalement abstraits des choses sensibles. Elle est donc ordinaire, active ou acquise par l'effort humain, secondé de la grâce et des lumières des dons du Saint-Esprit.*]

37 In his *Perfection chrétienne et contemplation selon S. Thomas d'Aquin et S. Jean de la Croix* (Var: Saint-Maximin, 1923), for

the teaching of the Angelic Doctor – let alone the teaching of the Lord Jesus in the Gospels.

The Spirituality of Garrigou-Lagrange

The spiritual teaching of Garrigou-Lagrange is found primarily in his articles for *La vie spirituelle* and three of his books: *Perfection chrétienne et contemplation*, *L'Amour de Dieu et la croix de Jésus*, and the two volumes of *Les trois âges de la vie intérieure*. There is, as one might expect, a strong genetic link between these works: they all can be traced back to Garrigou's course on spirituality at the Angelicum.[38] Moreover, his articles in *La vie spirituelle* formed a good part of *La perfection chrétienne*[39] and *L'Amour de Dieu*. As was the case with his philosophical and theological work, Garrigou's spiritual writings reveal a fundamental constancy that might at first glance appear repetitive. In fact, he was examining the one sublime mystery – God's intimate relationship with the human person – from several different vantage points. One finds, therefore, a constant reiteration of fundamental themes from the Dominican tradition's reflection on spirituality: charity as the heart of the Christian life;[40] the utter gratuity of

example, Garrigou cites his former mentor, Benoît Schwalm: *Concluons avec le P. Schwalm, qui rappelait ainsi en 1905 "l'unanimité d'une tradition:" "Saint Thomas ne classe jamais la contemplation parmi les grâces extraordinaires. Faire des miracles, prophétiser, discerner l'Esprit de Dieu ou le mauvais esprit dans les coeurs . . , telles sont les grâces que le Docteur Angélique signale comme en dehors des voies communes. . . . La contemplation rentre au contraire dans le développement normal de la vertu et de la perfection chrétienne . . ."* [713–14; Garrigou is citing Schwalm's preface to P. Faucillon's *La vie d'union à Dieu* (Paris, 1905).]

38 In the *avant-propos* to *Les trois âges*, for instance, he writes: *Cet ouvrage est comme le résumé d'un cours d'ascétique et mystique que nous avons fait depuis vingt ans à la Faculté de Théologie de l'Angelico à Rome* (ix).

39 In its introduction, Garrigou writes: *Ces pages sont l'abrégé d'un cours latin de théologie ascétique et mystique fait ces dernières années à la Faculté de théologie du Collège Angélique à Rome; elles ont paru en grande partie dans* La vie spirituelle (i).

40 Cf. his remark toward the end of *Perfection chrétienne: . . . j'ai*

God's grace and humanity's complete dependence on God's gift of his divine life to accomplish any good; the recognition that St. Thomas is as much a guide in spirituality as he is in dogmatic and moral theology;[41] and, the emphasis, forcefully argued in the early years of the twentieth century by Juan Arintero that the distinction between acquired and infused contemplation is a false one.[42]

Granting that Garrigou's spiritual teaching is remarkably consistent, we will focus our exposition of his thought on his most acclaimed work – *The Three Ages of the Interior Life*. This work, a veritable *summa* of spirituality, is now considered a classic and has been rightly called "the fullest theological analysis of spiritual life from a Dominican perspective."[43]

In *The Three Ages*, as in *Perfection chrétienne*, Garrigou took St. Thomas as his theological guide and St. John of the Cross as his spiritual companion. From his first encounter with Juan Arintero as a colleague at the Angelicum, Garrigou had been impressed by the recognition that the mysticism of St. John gave further credence to the theological positions of St. Thomas.

From the outset, the reader is introduced to the foundations upon which Garrigou built his spirituality: the life of

étudié surtout dans le livre de la charité car c'est celui qui apprend tout (691). In this same work, Garrigou called attention to St. Dominic under the heading *La perfection est spécialement dans la charité* (159 ff.).

41 Granting, of course, that the distinctions between these branches of theology did not exist in St. Thomas's day.

42 See, for instance, *Perfection chrétienne*, 691: *Il serait facile de montrer par de nombreuses citations que la tradition dont nous venons de parler sur le caractère normal, quoique éminent, de la contemplation infuse, a toujours subsisté dans la spiritualité dominicaine. Le Père Arintero, O.P., a fait ce travail, auquel nous sommes heureux de renvoyer*. Garrigou cites Arintero's *Unidad de la vida y homogeneidad de la vida espiritual en la tradición dominicana*, 1917. [It originally appeared in *Ciencia tomista* (1916).]

43 Benedict M. Ashley, *Spiritual Direction in the Dominican Tradition* (New York: Paulist, 1995), 159.

grace, the virtues, the gifts of the Holy Spirit, and the indwelling of the Holy Trinity. These themes are the quintessence of the Dominican approach to spirituality. We will use the next several sections to explore Garrigou's explication of their significance.

The Life of Grace

The title of the first chapter of *The Three Ages* is revelatory: "The Life of Grace, Eternal Life Begun." Garrigou was drawn to connect grace closely with ultimate human destiny. He underscored that every soul is either turned toward God – its "supernatural last end" – or is turned away from God.[44] "The state of grace" is the way the Catholic tradition speaks of one who is in fact turned toward God; "the state of mortal sin" is the way this tradition speaks of those who are turned away from God. And, "in the present plan of Providence every soul is either in the state of grace or in the state of mortal sin."[45] These two states mirror the two destinies open for men and women: eternal life or eternal damnation.

Catholic teaching holds that all people are "ordered" toward eternal life with God. Such was God's will in creating men and women in the first place, and God's will has not changed. "It is toward this end that we are led by Christ who, after the Fall, offered himself as a victim for the salvation of all men."[46] The life of grace is, therefore, seen as making the individual a new creation; it restores in the individual the original intention of the Creator.

Garrigou made every effort to emphasize two points in his opening discussion. The first is that grace is a supernatural reality; the second is that the life of grace is truly a new life whereby the individual is interiorly changed.

For his first point, Garrigou relied on St. Thomas's reflection that *Bonum gratiae unius majus est quam*

44 Garrigou-Lagrange, *The Three Ages*, I, 29.
45 Ibid.
46 Ibid.

bonum naturae totius universi: "The good of grace in one is greater than the good of nature in the whole universe."[47] Garrigou adds: "If we had a profound knowledge of the state of grace, we would see that it is not only the principle of a true and very holy interior life, but that it is the germ of eternal life."[48] Since humanity is called to a supernatural end – eternal life with God – grace, that which actualizes our movement toward that end, must be distinguished from every earthly reality.

The second point turns upon a fundamental disagreement with the classical Lutheran teaching on justification. Imbued with a nominalist conception of reality, Luther had what Garrigou considered to be a debased understanding of sanctifying grace.

> In Luther's opinion, man is justified not by a new infused life, but by the exterior imputation of the merits of Christ, in such a way that he is not interiorly changed and that it is not necessary for his salvation that he observe the precept of the love of God above all else. . . . This doctrine constituted the negation of the essentially supernatural life; it was a failure to recognize the very essence of grace and of the theological virtues.[49]

Garrigou marshals a host of New Testament passages to ground his position. Jesus's words in St. John's gospel, "Amen, amen, I say to you, whoever believes in the one who sent me has eternal life and will not come to condemnation, but has passed from death to life" (John 5: 24) and the promises of the Beatitudes (Matthew 5:3–12) are particularly helpful in establishing the supernatural destiny of the human person and in highlighting that that destiny begins in the here and now. The teaching of the First Letter of John (3: 2) – "Beloved, we are God's children now;

47 Ibid., I, 29. See: *Summa theologiae*, I-II, q. 113, a. 9, ad 2.
48 Ibid.
49 Ibid., I, 29–30, n. 1.

what we shall be has not yet been revealed. We do know that when it is revealed we shall be like him, for we shall see him as he is" – provides a solid basis for disputing the teaching of an extrinsic imputation of the merits of Christ.[50]

Garrigou further bolsters his argument concerning the supernatural nature of grace with the following theological argument:

> If a created intellect could by its natural powers alone see God immediately, it would have the same formal object as the divine intellect; it would then be of the same nature as God. This would be the pantheistic confusion of a created nature and the divine nature.[51]

Hence, grace, which allows us to see God is a supernatural gift; it is not ours by nature, but by divine gratuity – in light of the Passion, Death, and Resurrection of Jesus Christ.

The Virtues and the Gifts of the Holy Spirit

The life of grace is essentially supernatural; it is a participation in the divine life.[52] According to St. Thomas, reminds Garrigou, "Even now this life of grace develops in us under the form of the infused virtues and of the seven gifts of the Holy Spirit."[53] The infused virtues and the gifts are constitutive of the gratuity of God's salvific work in redeemed humanity. In this section we will highlight Garrigou's reflection on these most important topics.

50 See: Ibid., I, 31–33.
51 Ibid., I, 33–34.
52 See: Ibid., I, 50–51: "Sanctifying grace, which makes us begin to live in this higher, supra-angelic order of the intimate life of God, is like a divine graft received in the very essence of the soul to elevate its vitality and to make it bear no longer merely natural fruits but supernatural ones, meritorious acts that merit eternal life for us. This divine graft of sanctifying grace is, therefore, in us an essentially supernatural life, immensely superior to a sensible miracle and above the natural life of our spiritual and immortal soul."
53 *Summa theologiae*, I-II, q. 63, a. 3; cited in Ibid., I, 51.

In the second part of his *Summa theologiae*, St. Thomas devoted a considerable amount of time to the question of virtue (and vice). Brian Davies explains that for St. Thomas virtues are good dispositions of the human person. "They are abilities, tendencies, or capacities which help us act in ways which contribute to our flourishing, or to our functioning to our best advantage, so that our needs as people are satisfied."[54] St. Thomas organized his reflection around the most fundamental of distinctions – the theological virtues and the moral virtues, infused and acquired virtues – and then proceeded to show how each gift of the Holy Spirit is allied to one of the virtues.[55]

Following St. Thomas, Garrigou taught that the theological virtues – faith, hope, and love – are "infused virtues which have for their object God Himself, our supernatural last end."[56] To faith is allied the gift of understanding; to hope is allied the gift of knowledge; to love is allied the gift of wisdom.[57]

A most significant distinction must be made between the infused and the acquired moral virtues. As the word "infused" indicates, the former are given by God as a gift: "God alone can produce them in us."[58] Acquired virtues, "as their name indicates, are acquired by the repetition of acts under the direction of more or less cultivated natural reason."[59] It is important to note that the actualization of the acquired moral virtues in a person's life does not presuppose the life of sanctifying grace. A person in the state of sin might have acquired, say, the virtue of justice: he or she might readily give to others what is their due. Therefore, witnessing the performance of an act of justice (like an act of prudence, temperance, or courage) does not

54 Davies, *The Thought of Thomas Aquinas*, 239.
55 Garrigou provides a helpful chart of this schema in Ibid., I, 51.
56 Ibid., I, 52.
57 Ibid., I, 51.
58 Ibid., I, 57.
59 Ibid.

properly lead to a judgment that there was a supernatural foundation for the act.

Let us explore further this question. Garrigou notes that St. Thomas held that people in the state of mortal sin – devoid of the life of sanctifying grace – often have "false virtues." For example, the miser practices a certain kind of temperance – not out of love for the good and the true, but out of the love of money. In the same way, if he pays his debts, it is not out of love for justice, but rather to avoid the fines he might have to pay if he were to be caught.[60]

At the same time, there are those who are in the state of mortal sin who have true acquired moral virtues. "Some practice sobriety in order to live reasonably; for the same motive they pay their debts and teach some good principles to their children."[61] None of these things demand the gift of God's grace.[62]

Unlike the acquired moral virtues, the infused moral virtues have for their object "the supernatural means proportioned to our last end."[63] In this conception of things,

> prudence directs our acts to this end; religion makes us render to God the worship that is due Him; justice makes us give to everyone what we owe him; fortitude and temperance regulate the sensible part of our soul to prevent it from going astray and to make it cooperate, according to its manner, in our progress toward God.[64]

60 See: Ibid., I, 58.

61 Ibid.

62 It is important to note that as long as one remains in the state of mortal sin, these true virtues are in a precarious state. In St. Thomas's Latin, they are *in statu dispositionis facile mobilis*. Unlike the virtues of those in the state of grace, they are not *difficile mobilis*. Garrigou explains: "as long as a man is in the state of mortal sin, his will is habitually turned away from God. Instead of loving Him above all else, the sinner loves himself more than God, with the consequent result that he shows great weakness in accomplishing moral good, even of the natural order." (Ibid.)

63 Ibid., I, 52.

64 Ibid. In St. Thomas's system, the gift of counsel corresponds with prudence, the gift of piety corresponds with justice, the gift of fear

This entire discussion is grounded upon the Thomistic position that there is a real distinction between natural morality and supernatural, or Christian, morality.[65] In any number of instances, the outward appearances might be the same, but the inner reality is not. Garrigou cites St. Thomas's discussion on the essential difference between acquired temperance and infused temperance to make his point:

> As St. Thomas remarks, acquired temperance has a rule and formal object different from those of infused temperance. Acquired temperance keeps a just medium in the matter of food in order that we may live reasonably, that we may not injure our health or the exercise of our reason. Infused temperance, on the contrary, keeps a superior happy mean in the use of food in order that we may live in a Christian manner, as children of God, en route to the wholly supernatural life of eternity. Infused temperance thus implies a more severe mortification than is implied by acquired temperance; it requires, as St. Paul says, that man chastise his body and bring it into subjection, that he may become not only a virtuous citizen of society on earth, but one of the "fellow citizens with the saints, and the domestics of God (Ephesians 2: 19)."[66]

Garrigou goes on to note that the acquired virtues are subordinate to the infused virtues[67] and, that according to authoritative Catholic teaching, God gives the infused

of the Lord corresponds with temperance, and the gift of fortitude corresponds with the virtue of fortitude. [See: Ibid., I, 51.]

65 Ibid., I, 57.

66 Ibid., I, 61. This teaching has significant ramifications for Christian ethics. In particular, it offers a Thomistic response to the vexing questions involved in the contemporary debate surrounding the distinctiveness of Christian ethics.

67 Ibid., I, 63. Garrigou writes that "the acquired virtue is subordinated to the infused virtue as a favorable disposition. Thus, in another domain, the agility of a pianist's or a harpist's fingers, which is acquired by a repetition of acts, favors the exercise of the musical art that is in the artist's intellect and not in his fingers." (Ibid.)

virtues with the gift of sanctifying grace.[68] Since the infused virtues are so closely allied with the life of grace and are themselves spiritual realities – not human achievements – it might seem that for the Thomistic tradition the gifts of the Holy Spirit are all but superfluous. How does Garrigou explain the role of the gifts of the Holy Spirit in the spiritual life?

In the first place, Garrigou notes that the Church's teaching on the gifts of the Holy Spirit is grounded in the witness of Sacred Scripture. The classic text is from the prophet Isaiah: "The spirit of the Lord shall rest on him, the spirit of wisdom and understanding, the spirit of counsel and might, the spirit of knowledge and the fear of the Lord" (11: 2).[69] An allied text, says Garrigou, is Wisdom 7: 7–28, the scriptural passage which insists that wisdom is the highest of the gifts of the Holy Spirit. The culmination of the scriptural witness is found in the gospel of St. John. "If you love me, you will keep my commandments. And I will ask the Father, and he will give you another Advocate, to be with you forever . . ." (John 14: 15–16).

The Fathers of the Church commented frequently on these passages of Scripture "and, beginning with the third

68 Following a decision of Pope Clement V at the Council of Vienne (see: *Denz.*, n. 483), the *Catechism of the Council of Trent*, speaking on baptism and its effects, taught that "The grace (sanctifying), which baptism confers, is accompanied by the glorious cortege of all the virtues, which, by a special gift of God, penetrate the soul simultaneously with it." (cited in Ibid., I, 60.) Garrigou adds the following gloss: "God provides for our needs not less in the order of grace than in the order of nature. Therefore, since in the order of nature He has given us the capacity to succeed in practicing the acquired moral virtues, it is highly fitting that in the order of grace He should give us infused moral virtues." (Ibid.)

69 One notes immediately that the text only enumerates six gifts. How is it that the tradition speaks of the *seven* gifts of the Holy Spirit? The editors of *La Bible de Jérusalem* explain: *L'énumération de ces dons par les LXX et la Vulgate (qui ajoutent la 'piété' par dédoublement de la 'crainte de Yahvé') est devenue notre liste des 'sept dons du Saint-Esprit.'* (*La Bible de Jérusalem*, footnote to Isaiah 11: 2.)

century, tradition explicitly affirms that the seven gifts of the Holy Spirit are in all the just."[70] In this regard, the high point of Patristic teaching in the Latin Church is undoubtedly St. Augustine's commentary on the Sermon on the Mount. In this work, St. Augustine "shows the correspondence between the evangelical beatitudes and the seven gifts."[71] According to Servais Pinckaers, this is the most original aspect of the commentary:

> Augustine's idea, original in its form, was actually a development of the thought of St. Paul, frequently commented on by the Greek Fathers, that the Christian life is a life in the Holy Spirit. . . . According to him, the Beatitudes described the stages of the Christian life through which the Holy Spirit guides us progressively.[72]

Garrigou, following the characteristic methodology of the Neo-Thomists, was intent on incorporating the latest instance of authoritative Church teaching into his own work. And so, he quotes a significant section of Pope Leo XIII's encyclical *Divinum illud munus* (published 9 May 1897) on the Holy Spirit. Summarizing Leo's teaching, Garrigou says that his text shows "(1) the necessity of the gifts; (2) their nature: they make us docile to the Holy Spirit; (3) their effects: they can lead us to the summit of sanctity."[73]

70 Garrigou-Lagrange, *The Three Ages*, I, 67. Garrigou calls attention to Ambroise Gardeil's article "Dons du Saint-Esprit," in the *Dictionnaire de théologie catholique* (IV, 1728–81).

71 Ibid., I, 67–68.

72 Pinckaers, *The Sources of Christian Ethics*, 151. See page 153 for St. Augustine's schema showing the relations between the Beatitudes and the gifts of the Holy Spirit.

73 Garrigou-Lagrange, *The Three Ages*, I, 70, n. 16. Bede Jarrett, O.P. wrote an important commentary on *Divinum illud munus* entitled *The Abiding Presence of the Holy Ghost in the Soul* (Westminster, Md.: Newman Bookshop, 1944); Jarrett's original text dates from 1918. Jarrett offers insightful reflections on each of the gifts of the Holy Spirit. The most complete exposition in English on the meaning of the indwelling of the Holy Trinity probably remains Francis L. B. Cunningham, *The Indwelling of the Trinity: A Historico-*

Adducing support from Leo's encyclical, Garrigou emphasizes the necessity of the gifts. Leo had written: "The just man, that is to say, he who lives the life of divine grace and acts by the fitting virtues as by means of faculties, has need of those seven gifts which are properly attributed to the Holy Spirit."[74] What arguments might be marshaled to support this teaching? If one is in the state of sanctifying grace and has been blessed with the gift of the infused virtues (grounded, let us say, upon the acquired moral virtues), what could be the need for the gifts of the Holy Spirit?

Following St. Thomas, Garrigou says that the gifts dispose one "to obey the Holy Spirit promptly, as sails prepare a ship to follow the impulse of a favorable wind."[75] Here, Jesus's words to Nicodemus in the gospel of John guide the reflection: "The wind blows where it chooses, and you hear the sound of it, but you do not know where it comes from or where it goes. So it is with everyone who is born of the Holy Spirit" (3: 8). The gifts of the Holy Spirit, creating docility in their host, "help us to produce those excellent works known as the beatitudes."[76]

In the following passage, Garrigou provides a succinct explanation of the Thomistic rationale for distinguishing the gifts from the infused virtues:

> According to these principles, the great majority of theologians hold with St. Thomas that the gifts are really and specifically distinct from the infused virtues, just as the principles which direct them are distinct: that is, the Holy Spirit and reason illumined

Doctrinal Study of the Theory of St. Thomas Aquinas (Dubuque, Ia.: Priory Press, 1955).

74 Ibid., I, 69. Garrigou is citing the encyclical, as he says, *circa finem*.

75 Ibid., I, 72; cf. *Summa theologiae*, I-II, q. 68, a. 3 ("The gifts of the Holy Spirit are habits whereby man is perfected to obey readily the Holy Spirit") and I-II, q. 70, a. 2 ("The beatitudes are none but perfect works, which, by reason of their perfection, are assigned to the gifts rather than to the virtues").

76 Ibid., I, 72.

> by faith. We have here two regulating motions, two different rules that constitute different formal motives. It is a fundamental principle that habits are specified by their object and their formal motive, as sight by color and light, and hearing by sound. The human mode of acting results from the human rule; the superhuman mode results from the superhuman or divine rule, from the inspiration of the Holy Spirit, *modus a mensura causatur*. Thus even infused prudence proceeds by discursive deliberation, in which it differs from the gift of counsel, which disposes us to receive a special inspiration of a superdiscursive order. Even infused prudence hesitates, for example, about what answers to give to an indiscreet question so as to avoid a lie and keep a secret; while a special inspiration of the Holy Spirit will enable us to find a proper reply, as Christ told His disciples (Matt. 10: 19).[77]

Perhaps the clearest example of this comes from the relationship of faith (infused theological virtue) to the gifts of understanding and wisdom. Garrigou writes: "while faith adheres simply to revealed truths, the gift of understanding makes us scrutinize their depths, and that of wisdom makes us taste them."[78] And, without the gifts, faith remains essentially imperfect for the following three reasons:

> (1) because of the obscurity of its object, which it does not attain immediately, but "through a glass in a dark manner" (1 Cor. 13: 12); (2) it attains its object only by multiple dogmatic formulas, whereas God is supremely simple; (3) it attains its object in an abstract manner, by affirmative and negative propositions, whereas, on the contrary, the living God is the light of life, whom we ought to be able to know, not in an abstract manner but in a quasi-experimental manner.[79]

77 Ibid., I, 73.
78 Ibid.
79 Ibid., I, 74.

The Indwelling of the Holy Trinity

> The God who made the world and everything in it, he who is Lord of heaven and earth, does not live in shrines made by human hands, nor is he served by human hands, as though he needed anything, since he himself gives to all mortals life and breath and all things. . . . For 'In him we live and move and have our being' . . . (Acts of the Apostles 17: 24–25, 28)

The most sublime teaching of Christian spirituality is the doctrine of the indwelling of the Holy Trinity in the souls of the just. This teaching, often little known and under-appreciated, plays a central role in the spirituality of Réginald Garrigou-Lagrange.[80] Put in its simplest terms, Garrigou teaches that the Holy Trinity is "the uncreated Source of our interior life."[81]

Garrigou provides reflections on the biblical witness and the testimony of tradition before moving to a theological explanation of the teaching.[82] This is the same pattern he followed in his discussions on the virtues and the gifts of the Holy Spirit; it was his preferred pattern for doing systematic theology.

From the Bible, Garrigou began by focusing on passages that speak of God's presence in the world – "a general presence, often called the presence of immensity."[83] Psalm 139, for instance, asks of the Lord: "Where can I go from your spirit? Or where can I flee from your presence? If I ascend to heaven, you are there; if I make my bed in Sheol, you are there" (vv. 7–8).

80 See, in particular, *The Three Ages*, I, 97–108 and *Perfection chrétienne*, I, 145–50; II, 111–20.

81 Garrigou-Lagrange, *The Three Ages*, I, 97.

82 For this theological explanation, Garrigou calls his readers' attention to Froget's *De l'habitation du Saint-Esprit dans les âmes justes* (Paris: Lethielleux, 1900), Gardeil's *La structure de l'âme et l'expérience mystique* (Paris: Gabalda, 1927), as well as his own *L'Amour de Dieu et la croix de Jésus*, I, 163–206; II, 657–86.

83 Garrigou-Lagrange, *The Three Ages*, I, 97.

Of course, Christian teaching knows that there is more to God's presence than this presence of immensity: God is present intimately to his creatures, in such a way that their very existence depends upon God's dynamic support.[84] And, Jesus's words in the gospel of John provide the foundation for the Church's doctrine of the indwelling of the Holy Trinity in the souls of the just: "Those who love me will keep my word, and my Father will love them, and we will come to them and make our home with them" (14: 23). Garrigou offers the following gloss on this passage: "We will dwell in him as long as he remains just, or in the state of grace, as long as he preserves charity."[85]

The Letters of St. Paul and the Letters of St. John are replete with references to the indwelling of the Holy Trinity. The passage that readily comes to mind is 1 John 4: 16: "God is love, and those who abide in love abide in God, and God abides in them." Likewise, St. Paul's question in 1 Corinthians 3: 16 is an archetypical example of this theme: "Do you not know that you are God's temple and that God's Spirit dwells in you?" Garrigou is not without good reason when he concludes: "Scripture thus teaches explicitly that the three divine persons dwell in every just soul, in every soul in the state of grace."[86]

The testimony of tradition is equally clear. Garrigou exposes the teaching of Saints Ignatius of Antioch, Athanasius, Basil, Cyril of Alexandria, Ambrose, and Augustine. He also comments on the "Credo of St. Epiphanius" (*Denz.*, n. 13) and the "Decrees of the Council of Trent" (*Denz.*, n. 799).[87] However, he focuses most of his attention on Leo XIII's *Divinum illud munus*.

After having himself called attention to the teaching of the ancient Doctors of the Church, Leo explained:

84 Ibid. Garrigou cites St. Paul's preaching to the Athenians in Acts 17.
85 Ibid., I, 98.
86 Ibid., I, 99.

> . . . God is in man, not only as in inanimate things, but because He is more fully known and loved by him, since even by nature we spontaneously love, desire, and seek after the good. Moreover, God by grace resides in the just soul as in a temple, in a most intimate and peculiar manner. From this proceeds that union of affection by which the soul adheres most closely to God, more so than the friend is united to his most loving and beloved friend, and enjoys God in all fullness and sweetness.[88]

Leo affirmed that the Holy Trinity dwells in the souls of the just, but taught that it is most proper to attribute the indwelling to the person of the Holy Spirit:

> Now this wonderful union, which is properly called "indwelling," differing only in degree or state from that with which God beatifies the saints in heaven, although it is most certainly produced by the presence of the whole Blessed Trinity – "We will come to him and make Our abode with him" (John 14: 23) – nevertheless is attributed in a peculiar manner to the Holy Spirit. For, whilst traces of divine power and wisdom appear even in the wicked man, charity, which, as it were, is the special mark of the Holy Spirit, is shared in only by the just. . . .[89]

Recalling that for Garrigou theology exists primarily to explain the teaching of the Church, we turn now to Garrigou's theological explanation of the indwelling of the Holy Trinity.

The first lines in this regard are quintessentially his own: "Different explanations of this mystery have been proposed. Among these different points of view, that of St. Thomas, preserved by Leo XIII in his encyclical on the Holy Spirit, seems the truest."[90] We have come to expect that Garrigou will do all in his power to bolster the

88 Leo XIII, *Divinum illud munus*, cited in Ibid., I, 101.
89 Ibid.
90 Ibid.
91 One notes that on the topic of the indwelling of the Holy Trinity,

standing of St. Thomas and the current teaching of the magisterium.[91]

Garrigou guides his readers to the heart of the Angelic Doctor's teaching on the indwelling: question 43 of the first part of the *Summa*. St. Thomas writes:

> For God is in all things by his essence, power, and presence, according to His one common mode, as the cause existing in the effects which participate in His goodness. Above and beyond this common mode, however, there is one special mode belonging to the rational nature wherein God is said to be present as the object known is in the knower, and the beloved in the lover. And since the rational creature by its own operation of (supernatural) knowledge and love attains to God Himself, according to this special mode, God is said not only to exist in the rational creature, but also to dwell therein as in His own temple. So no other effect can be put down as the reason why the divine Person is in the rational creature in a new mode, except sanctifying grace.[92]

The indwelling of the Holy Spirit brings with it the knowledge of God offered as a gift. This gift allows one to know the divine persons "in a quasi-experimental and loving manner, based on infused charity, which gives us a connaturality or sympathy with the intimate life of God."[93] Only this teaching can make sense of a passage like the following: "For all who are led by the Spirit of God are children of God. For you did not receive a spirit of slavery to

Garrigou held that St. Thomas's thought and Leo's teaching contain "in the form of a superior synthesis, all that is positive in the other explanations" (Ibid., I, 102). And in classic Dominican style (cf. "Never deny, seldom affirm, always distinguish"), Garrigou remarks that "the systems which do not attain to a superior synthesis, are generally true in what they affirm, and false in what they deny" (Ibid., I, 102, n. 19).

92 *Summa theologiae*, I, q. 43, a. 3; cited in Ibid., I, 103.

93 Garrigou-Lagrange, *The Three Ages*, I, 103; he cites St. Thomas's *Commentary on the Sentences*, I, 14, q. 2, a. 2 and his *Summa theologiae* II-II, q. 45, a. 2.

fall back into fear, but you have received a spirit of adoption. When we cry, 'Abba! Father!' it is that very Spirit bearing witness with our spirit that we are children of God . . ." (Romans 8: 14–16). Only this teaching does justice to the promises of Jesus to his disciples in the High Priestly Prayer of chapters 14 through 16 of St. John's gospel. As Garrigou remarks, St. Thomas's explanation of the indwelling of the Holy Trinity "simply shows us the profound meaning of the words of Christ that we cited previously: 'If anyone loves Me, he will keep my word. And my Father will love him and we will come to him, and will make our abode with him'" (John 14: 23).[94]

What are the consequences of this doctrine for the spiritual life? The first returns us to a theme associated with the early twentieth-century debates on contemplation. In speaking of the quasi-experimental knowledge of God that accompanies the indwelling of the Holy Trinity, Garrigou highlights that it follows that "this knowledge, far from being something essentially extraordinary, like visions, revelations, or the stigmata, is in the normal way of sanctity."[95] It follows that "this knowledge ought normally to grow with the progress of charity, either under a clearly contemplative form, or under a form more directly oriented toward action."[96] The doctrine concerning the indwelling of the Holy Trinity provides support for the Dominican position that infused contemplation is part of the ordinary way of holiness.

Secondly, the doctrine means that not only does the Holy Trinity dwell within the just "as an object of supernatural knowledge and love, but as principles of supernatural operations."[97] At the same time, says Garrigou:

> We should . . . remember in a practical way that ordinarily God communicates Himself to his creature only

94 Ibid., I, 104.
95 Ibid., I, 105.
96 Ibid.
97 Ibid., I, 106.

> in the measure of the creature's dispositions. When these become more pure, the divine persons also become more intimately present and active. Then God belongs to us and we to Him, and we desire above all to make progress in His love.[98]

The doctrine of the indwelling of the Holy Trinity is therefore one of the most powerful motives conceivable for advancement in the spiritual life[99] and, of course, the cause of that very advancement.

The Three Ages

Advancement in the spiritual life is the subtext running through both volumes of Garrigou's *The Three Ages of the Interior Life*. In this regard, we have saved for last the discussion of the most obvious contribution of Garrigou-Lagrange to the field of Catholic spirituality: his synthesis of Thomistic theology and San Juanist mysticism. Following the lead of Juan Arintero, Garrigou's *summa* of spirituality shows the wonderful harmony between the Mystical Doctor and the Angelic Doctor.

The very title of Garrigou's work comes from the elemental starting point of the spirituality of St. John of the Cross. There are three ages of the interior life – three distinct moments through which the believer passes (if he or she is progressing in the spiritual life). These three ages are the purgative, the illuminative, and the unitive.

The purgative way[100] is proper to beginners. This stage of the journey toward union with God is marked by the "removal of obstacles, the struggle against sin and its results and against . . . [one's] predominant fault;" it is the time of "the active purification of the senses, of the memory, the will, and the understanding."[101]

98 Ibid.
99 Ibid.
100 See: Ibid., I, 267–469.
101 Ibid., I, 24.
102 See: Ibid., II, 3–349.

The illuminative way[102] begins with what is called the "second conversion" – that process whereby the person in the state of grace enters more deeply into intimacy with the divine.[103] It is a period of progressive illumination; the proficient, under the guidance of the Holy Spirit, sees all the more profoundly the saving work of Christ in his or her life.[104]

The unitive way[105] "demands a passive purification of the spirit, which is like a third conversion, or rather a transformation of the soul, similar to that experienced by the apostles when, after being painfully deprived of the presence of Christ on Ascension Day, they received the Holy Spirit on Pentecost."[106] The unitive way is the way of the perfect, the way of those who are being prepared for radical union with God; it is known by a heroic degree of the virtues[107] and is marked by apostolic works and contemplation.[108]

Conclusion

In all of Garrigou-Lagrange's spiritual writings, the person of the Blessed Virgin Mary is never absent. "He knew that one cannot explain the eternal design of the Father and its realization in the fullness of time through the mystery of the Savior, without recognizing his Mother and the place that God gave to her."[109] Mary is the ultimate model of

103 The Church's liturgical year is helpful in understanding the need for a second conversion. In Advent and Lent, for example, all are called to conversion: the sinner from his state of sin and the just from his lack of fervor. See: Ibid., II, 21–23.

104 See especially: Ibid., II, 65–70.

105 See: Ibid., II, 353–572.

106 Ibid., II, 353–54.

107 See: Ibid., II, 440–79.

108 Ibid., II, 489–96.

109 M.-Benoît Lavaud, "Garrigou-Lagrange (Réginald)," in *Dictionnaire de spiritualité* (Paris: Beauchesne, 1937–), VI, 133. [. . . *il sait qu'on ne peut exposer, tel qu'il est dans l'éternel dessein du Père et sa réalisation en la plénitude des temps, le mystère du Sauveur sans reconnaître à sa Mère la place que Dieu lui a donnée.*]

what God's grace can do in a person's life; what is more, it is part of God's salvific will that she be Mother of all of humanity – "the universal mediatrix in the service of the one mediator."[110] The Blessed Virgin, herself full of grace, intercedes on behalf of all, that all might grow in grace and come to the fullness of the love of God – through Christ – and in the power of the Holy Spirit. This is manifestly the teaching of the Second Vatican Council:

> The entire body of the faithful pours forth urgent supplications to the Mother of God and of men that she, who aided the beginnings of the Church by her prayers, may now, exalted as she is above all the angels and saints, intercede before her Son in the fellowship of all the saints, until all families of people, whether they are honored with the title of Christian or whether they still do not know the Savior, may be happily gathered together in peace and harmony into one People of God, for the glory of the Most Holy and Undivided Trinity.[111]

In the next chapter our work comes to its end. We will conclude by commenting on various dimensions of Garrigou's philosophy, theology, and spirituality that could be profitably retrieved as the Church journeys further into the twenty-first century.

110 Ibid. Cf. Lavaud's explication of Garrigou's primary theme in his *La Mère du Sauveur et notre vie intérieure*: *Il y considère Marie dans sa maternité divine, raison d'être de toutes ses autres prérogatives, dans la plénitude de grâce: au début, à l'heure de l'incarnation, à la fin de sa vie terrestre, comme mère céleste de tous les hommes, médiatrice universelle auprès du médiateur, Reine de miséricorde.*

111 Second Vatican Council, *Lumen gentium*, n. 69. [These are the last lines of the document.]

9. Conclusion: Retrieving Garrigou-Lagrange

People cannot be genuinely indifferent to the question of whether what they know is true or not. If they discover that it is false, they reject it; but if they can establish its truth, they feel themselves rewarded. It is this that St. Augustine teaches when he writes, 'I have met many who wanted to deceive, but none who wanted to be deceived.' Pope John Paul II, *Fides et ratio,* n. 25

To believe it possible to know a universally valid truth is in no way to encourage intolerance; on the contrary, it is the essential condition for sincere and authentic dialogue between persons. Pope John Paul II, *Fides et ratio,* n. 92

Aidan Nichols, Dominican theologian at Cambridge University, recently published *Christendom Awake: On Reenergizing the Church in Culture.*[1] Nichols's work is a challenge to the Church as it enters the third millennium. It is nothing short of a call to the Church to grapple with the question: "To what degree are we legitimately satisfied with the current basic condition of our culture?"[2] As he

1 (Grand Rapids, Mich.: William B. Eerdmans, 1999).
2 Ibid., 1.

writes: “What I am concerned with is . . . the *basic nature* of . . . contemporary society in the West, which we can sum up as progressive, secular, and pluralistic.”[3] Nichols judges that much of this culture is overtly hostile to Christian faith and many in the Church are unwittingly colluding in Western society’s marginalization of Christianity.

The various chapters of *Christendom Awake* explore dimensions of the Church’s life and practice which need bolstering. The following quotation from Thomas C. Oden is a significant fundament for chapter 4, “Reviving Doctrinal Consciousness:”

> The rediscovery of boundaries in theology will be the preoccupation of the twenty-first century of Christian theology. Some within the Church – a party I call post-modern palaeo-orthodoxy – are increasingly gaining the courage to enquire: Is pantheism heresy? Is reductive naturalism as reliable as any other assumption? Can Christianity make friends with absolute relativism? What would the Church look like if it were apostate?[4]

Oden’s questions – written more than thirty years after Garrigou’s death – are fundamentally the same questions that animated Garrigou’s life project. One way of describing Garrigou’s work in philosophy, theology, and spirituality is in reference to the task of judging the adequacy of contemporary formulations to account for the divinely revealed truths of Christian faith. As we have seen, this project did not necessarily win him friends: more often than not, it caused various epithets to be thrown his way – “rigid,” “intransigent,” “*intégriste*,” “fascist,” etc.

Ralph McInerny, writing the article on Garrigou in the *Routledge Encyclopedia of Philosophy*, has this to say:

> The style and approach of Garrigou-Lagrange have been deplored by some post-conciliar Catholics. This is

3 Ibid.
4 Thomas C. Oden, “Can We Talk About Heresy?,” in Ibid., 48.

> in many ways unjust. He is an engaging writer, a thinker of great power, a Thomist who takes the thought of his master to be the answer to some of the twentieth century's more vexing philosophical divagations. But that, of course was the message of *Aeterni Patris*.[5]

In spite of Oden's prognostication and McInerny's irenic judgment, a sizable number of Christians would prefer to forgo the question of boundaries in theology. This seems to be due to theological indifferentism – "no theology is better than another" – grounded upon the agnostic postulate that "one cannot really know the truth." This stance is in line with a "live and let live" social ethos; it asks the question "What is all the fuss about?" Because of this, it is outraged when the Church's magisterium judges that a particular theological position cannot be reconciled with the apostolic rule of faith. As Aidan Nichols notes: "Of course the identification of *lacunae* in the form or substance of such proceedings is not what is objectionable but the assumption of folly in their happening at all."[6]

Oden's understanding of what will be a feature of twenty-first-century theology, opponents notwithstanding, makes opportune a retrieval of aspects of the thought of Réginald Garrigou-Lagrange. Hugh Bredin provides for the appropriateness of this when he remarks, "Garrigou-Lagrange provided a clear, accessible and well-argued Thomism; . . . he is useful in establishing the orthodoxy against which subsequent developments must be measured."[7]

In this concluding chapter we will discuss both how Garrigou's thought has contributed to developments in

5 Ralph, McInerny, "Garrigou-Lagrange, Réginald," in *Routledge Encyclopedia of Philosophy* (New York: Routledge, 1998), 847.

6 Nichols, *Christendom Awake*, 48.

7 Hugh Bredin, "Garrigou-Lagrange, Réginald," in *Biographical Dictionary of Twentieth-Century Philosophers*, ed. Stuart Brown, Diané Collinson, Robert Wilkinson (New York: Routledge, 1996), 267.

contemporary Catholicism and intimate what more might be fruitfully retrieved as the third millennium unfolds. Our considerations will be bounded by the three areas that have provided a focus for the second half of our discussion of Garrigou-Lagrange: philosophy, theology, and spirituality

Philosophy

Immediately following the Second World War, the young Polish priest, Karol Wojtyla, was sent to the Angelicum for doctoral studies. As we have noted, Garrigou-Lagrange became Wojtyla's dissertation director and guided him in the successful defense of a thesis on the understanding of faith in the works of St. John of the Cross.[8] As we have had occasion to see, the themes underlying this thesis – faith, San Juanist theology, and mysticism – were all near and dear to Garrigou's heart.

No one could have known that this intense, intellectually gifted young Pole would one day be elected Pope. As Pope, John Paul II has shown frequently his indebtedness to Thomism; his having been mentored by Garrigou-Lagrange was one of the more formative experiences of his life.[9]

It was not altogether surprising, then, that John Paul II would publish, in the twentieth year of his pontificate, an encyclical on the relationship between faith and reason – or, more precisely, the relationship between theology and philosophy. His entire intellectual formation, beginning with his studies in Rome and continuing through studies in Lublin and teaching at Kraków, served as a prolegomenon to *Fides et ratio*.

As is the tradition in papal encyclicals, John Paul II pays his respects to his predecessors and their work on the

8 John Paul II's dissertation was published in English as *Faith According to St. John of the Cross* (San Francisco: Ignatius, 1981).

9 Cf. Buttiglione, *Karol Woytyla*.

question. Here, of course, the outstanding figure is Pope Leo XIII and his encyclical *Aeterni Patris*. Referring to Leo's work, John Paul II writes:

> More than a century later, many of the insights of his encyclical letter have lost none of their interest from either a practical or pedagogical point of view – most particularly his insistence upon the incomparable value of the philosophy of St. Thomas. A renewed insistence upon the thought of the Angelic Doctor seemed to Pope Leo XIII the best way to recover the practice of a philosophy consonant with the demands of faith. "Just when St. Thomas distinguishes perfectly between faith and reason," the pope writes, "he unites them in bonds of mutual friendship, conceding to each its specific rights and to each its specific dignity."[10]

Speaking to the continued importance of the Thomistic synthesis, John Paul also cites the Second Vatican Council's *Optatam totius*:

> The philosophical disciplines should be taught in such a way that students acquire in the first place a solid and harmonious knowledge of the human being, of the world and of God, based upon the philosophical heritage which is enduringly valid, yet taking into account currents of modern philosophy.[11]

And, further, he relates a personal frustration in all of this:

> If it has been necessary from time to time to intervene on this question, to reiterate the value of the Angelic Doctor's insights and insist on the study of his thought, this has been because the magisterium's directives have not always been followed with the readiness one would wish. In the years after the Second Vatican Council many Catholic faculties were in some ways impoverished by a diminished sense of

10 John Paul II, *Fides et ratio* (1998), n. 57.
11 Ibid., n. 60.

> the importance of the study not just of Scholastic philosophy, but more generally of the study of philosophy itself. I cannot fail to note with surprise and displeasure that this lack of interest in the study of philosophy is shared by not a few theologians.[12]

It is important to note that the pope sees both St. Pius X's *Pascendi dominici gregis* and Pius XII's *Humani generis* as examples of the magisterium's reiteration of the value of St. Thomas's thought.[13] And he will forcefully validate the teaching of Pius XII on the problem of the enduring value of the conceptual language used in conciliar definitions. This question is the same one that Garrigou-Lagrange entertained with Edouard Le Roy in *Le sens commun* and with the proponents of the *nouvelle théologie* in any number of his publications. John Paul writes:

> This is a complex theme to ponder, since one must reckon seriously with the meaning which words assume in different times and cultures. Nonetheless, the history of thought shows that across the range of cultures and their development certain basic concepts retain their universal epistemological value and thus retain the truth of the propositions in which they are expressed. Were this not the case, philosophy and the sciences could not communicate with each other, nor could they find a place in cultures different from those in which they were conceived and developed. The hermeneutical problem exists, to be sure; but it is not insoluble.[14]

Fides et ratio makes two fundamental points as regards the relationship of faith to reason and of philosophy to theology. First, priority goes to faith. John Paul quotes approvingly from the First Vatican Council:

> There exists a twofold order of knowledge distinct not only as regards their source, but also as regards their

12 Ibid., n. 61.
13 Ibid., n. 54.
14 Ibid., n. 96.

object. With regard to the source, because we know in one by natural reason, in the other by divine faith. With regard to the object, because besides those things which natural reason can attain, there are proposed for our belief mysteries hidden in God which, unless they are divinely revealed, cannot be known.[15]

Reason is imbued with a natural dignity; the Catholic tradition has upheld the fact that philosophical reflection is "one of the noblest of human tasks."[16] At the same time, it is an indispensable tool for understanding the faith.[17] Yet the knowledge that comes through faith is a knowledge that has its origin in God[18] – while not in contradistinction to the knowledge that come through reason, it has, by definition, an existential priority.[19]

The second fundamental point is that not all philosophies are of equal value; they do not all lead as directly to the truth. At the same time, it is wrong to think that the Christian faith can enter into a synthesis equally well with any philosophy. It does not take too much reflection to appreciate the pope's argument in nn. 45–56 that

15 Ibid., n. 9, quoting First Vatican Council, *Dei Filius*, IV, 3015.

16 *Fides et ratio*, n. 3.

17 See, for instance, Ibid., nn. 100–108.

18 John Paul writes that the acceptance of Christian revelation by faith leads one to "the ultimate possibility offered by God for the human being to know in all its fullness the seminal plan of love which began with creation" (Ibid., n. 15).

19 John Paul explains the problematic at the time of the First Vatican Council which helped to bring the Church's teaching into greater focus: "At the First Vatican Council, the fathers had stressed the supernatural character of God's revelation. On the basis of mistaken and very widespread assertions, the rationalist critique of the time attacked faith and denied the possibility of any knowledge which was not the fruit of reason's natural capacities. This obliged the council to reaffirm emphatically that there exists a knowledge which is peculiar to faith, surpassing the knowledge proper to human reason, which nevertheless by its nature can discover the Creator. This knowledge expresses a truth based upon the very fact of God who reveals himself, a truth which is most certain, since God neither deceives nor wishes to deceive" (Ibid., n. 8).

materialism, rationalism, and nihilism do not provide helpful tools for understanding the revelation of the God of Jesus Christ. And the pope is not exaggerating when he writes:

> It is not too much to claim that the development of a good part of modern philosophy has seen it move further and further away from Christian revelation, to the point of setting itself quite explicitly in opposition.[20]

The work of Garrigou-Lagrange provides ample testimony to the importance of these two points. Both the priority of divine revelation and faith and the scrutiny that one must offer modern philosophy find great support in his teaching.

There is one point that the pope reiterates several times in *Fides et ratio* that might lead one to wonder if Garrigou would agree. It is stated most clearly in this way: "The church has no philosophy of her own nor does she canonize any one particular philosophy in preference to others."[21] While it is the Church's duty "to indicate the elements in a philosophical system which are incompatible with her own faith,"[22] a philosophy "which did not proceed in the light of reason according to its own principles would serve little purpose."[23] There are, and there always have been, different schools of thought; John Paul does not judge that this pluralism in philosophy is a bad thing.[24]

Garrigou-Lagrange, as the epitome of Strict-Observance Thomism, was deeply committed to the Aristotelianism of

20 Ibid., n. 46.
21 Ibid., n. 49.
22 Ibid., n. 50.
23 Ibid., n. 49.
24 However, he will say that "this pluralism . . . imposes on the magisterium the responsibility of expressing a judgment as to whether or not the basic tenets of these different schools are compatible with the demands of the word of God and theological inquiry" (Ibid., n. 50).

St. Thomas's works. He was eager to underscore the inadequacies of other philosophical systems. In light of this, one is justified in wondering if Garrigou would have admitted John Paul's point that the Church is not out to "canonize" one particular school of thought over another.

On this question, it is important to note that the very same principle is implicitly in an encyclical as "traditional" as Pope Pius XII's *Humani generis*. Pius XII, while upholding the pride of place that St. Thomas's teaching has in the Church,[25] nonetheless recognizes that "this philosophy deals with much that neither directly nor indirectly touches faith or morals, and which consequently the Church leaves to the free discussion of experts."[26] It is not a question of there being a specifically Catholic response to every conceivable question.

This, it seems safe to say, would have been readily accepted by Garrigou. While it makes good sense to work from within one school of thought – a radical eclecticism would border on the irrational – it is ultimately a question of a search for the truth, not an *a priori* loyalty to a way of doing philosophy or theology. At the same time, Garrigou would have been heartened, and, indeed is in large part vindicated, by John Paul II's teaching that the lion's share of what was once known as "Thomism" ought now simply to be called "right reason." This deserves a full citation:

> Although times change and knowledge increases, it is possible to discern a core of philosophical insight within the history of thought as a whole. Consider, for

25 Cf.: ". . . the method of Aquinas is singularly preeminent both for teaching students and for bringing truth to light; his doctrine is in harmony with divine revelation, and is most effective both for safeguarding the foundation of the faith, and for reaping, safely and usefully, the fruits of sound progress" (*Humani generis*, n. 31). Pius will also say that because of this, future priests should be instructed in philosophy "according to the method, doctrine, and principles of the Angelic Doctor" (*Humani generis*, n. 31; Pius is citing the 1918 *Code of Canon Law*, can. 1366, a. 2).

26 *Humani generis*, n. 30.

> example, the principles of noncontradiction, finality and causality, as well as the concept of the person as a free and intelligent subject with the capacity to know God, truth and goodness. Consider as well certain fundamental moral norms which are shared by all. These are among the indications that beyond different schools of thought there exists a body of knowledge which may be judged a kind of spiritual heritage of humanity. It is as if we had come upon an implicit philosophy . . . shared in some measure by all. . . . Once reason successfully intuits and formulates the first universal principles of being and correctly draws from them conclusions which are coherent both logically and ethically, then it may be called *right reason* or, as the ancients called it, *orthos logos, recta ratio*.[27]

This is of capital importance. The heart of Garrigou-Lagrange's Strict-Observance Thomism has been identified by the pope as "a kind of spiritual heritage of humanity" – as "right reason" itself. This is what allows him to say that the Church has no philosophy of her own, no philosophy that she insists upon. But, if a philosophy were to repudiate "right reason," then, of course, it would have shown itself to be wildly deficient.

Fides et ratio can be read as a vindication of Garrigou-Lagrange's lifework. Because of this, his *opus* ought to be afforded a new currency: it will be of help in grounding the "fourth Thomism" – a Thomism that is called to learn "the lessons of the postmodern assault on modernity."[28]

27 *Fides et ratio*, n. 4.

28 Nichols, *Christendom Awake*, 66. John Paul II diagnoses the problem to which Thomism must respond in the following manner: "Abandoning the investigation of being, modern philosophical research has concentrated instead upon human knowing. Rather than make use of the human capacity to know the truth, modern philosophy has preferred to accentuate the ways in which this capacity is limited and conditioned. This has given rise to different forms of agnosticism and relativism, which have led philosophical research to lose its way in the shifting sands of widespread skepticism" (*Fides et ratio*, n. 5).

Theology

In Chapter 7 we took time to contrast Garrigou's approach to the questions of theology and theological method with those of two representative contemporary theologians, Roger Haight and Monika Hellwig. In this section, we will bring the teaching of Pope John Paul II in *Fides et ratio* to bear upon the discussion. We will see that in this Garrigou-Lagrange's fundamental commitments find added support.

Fides et ratio is at great pains to uphold the supernatural reality of God's revelation. God has revealed himself to humankind in Jesus Christ: "this initiative is utterly gratuitous, moving from God to men and women in order to bring them to salvation."[29] As a result, "underlying all the Church's thinking is the awareness that she is the bearer of a message which has its origin in God himself (cf. 2 Cor. 4: 1–2)."[30] John Paul assesses the significance of this in the following fashion:

> The truth made known to us by revelation is neither the product nor the consummation of an argument devised by human reason. It appears instead as something gratuitous, which itself stirs thought and seeks acceptance as an expression of love. This revealed truth is set within our history as an anticipation of that ultimate and definitive vision of God, which is reserved for those who believe in him and seek him with a sincere heart. The ultimate purpose of personal existence, then, is the theme of philosophy and theology alike. For their difference of method and content, both disciplines point to that "path of life" (Ps. 16: 11) which, as faith tells us, leads in the end to the full and lasting joy of the contemplation of the triune God.[31]

Philosophy must answer to reason; theology is first of all answerable to God's revelation in Jesus Christ. The

29 *Fides et ratio*, n. 7.
30 Ibid.
31 Ibid., n. 15.

relationship between philosophy and theology is, in John Paul's description, best seen in terms of a circle:

> Theology's source and starting point must always be the word of God revealed in history, while its final goal will be an understanding of that word which increases with each passing generation. Yet, since God's word is truth (cf. Jn. 17: 17), the human search for truth – philosophy, pursued in keeping with its own rules – can only help to understand God's word better.[32]

There are numerous references to truth and the human search for truth in *Fides et ratio*. In light of our discussion of the long-standing dispute between Garrigou and Maurice Blondel on the most proper definition of truth – a dispute that has serious ramifications for contemporary theology – it is important to note that *Fides et ratio* stands firmly with Garrigou. Pope John Paul II says that a significant requirement is "that philosophy verify the human capacity to know the truth, to come to a knowledge which can reach objective truth by means of that *adaequatio rei et intellectus* to which the Scholastic doctors referred."[33] Truth is to be defined in reference to the conformity of the mind to reality, not *vice versa* as in Blondel's *adaequatio realis mentis et vitae*.

The pope says that in seeking to understand the truths of the faith – truths revealed by God – theology "needs . . . the contribution of a philosophy which does not disavow the possibility of a knowledge which is objectively true, even if not perfect."[34] The goal, of course, is to support the "givens" of Christian faith, to help God's revelation in Christ to be better known and better understood. To disavow the very possibility of objective truth disqualifies a

32 Ibid., n. 73.

33 Ibid., n. 82. The pope's major reference here is *ST*, I, q. 16, a. 1.

34 Ibid. The encyclical calls attention to the teaching of the Second Vatican Council in *Gaudium et spes* (n. 15): "Intelligence is not confined to observable data alone. It can with genuine certitude attain to reality itself as knowable, though in consequence of sin that certitude is partially obscured and weakened."

philosophy from serving as an *ancilla theologiae*.[35] What is more,

> The word of God refers constantly to things which transcend human experience and even human thought; but this "mystery" could not be revealed nor could theology render it in some way intelligible were human knowledge limited strongly to the world of sense experience. Metaphysics thus plays an essential role of mediation in theological research. A theology without a metaphysical horizon could not move beyond an analysis of religious experience nor would it allow the *intellectus fidei* to give a coherent account of the universal and transcendent value of revealed truth.[36]

A timely example of the problematic to which *Fides et ratio* is addressed can be found in Elizabeth Johnson's "Mary, Friend of God and Prophet: A Critical Reading of the Marian Tradition."[37] Johnson, professor of theology at Fordham University, asks: "What would be a theologically sound, spiritually empowering, and ethically challenging view of Mary, mother of Jesus the Christ, for the 21st century?"[38] Through a methodology "rooted in scripture interpreted through the lens of feminist hermeneutics"[39] Johnson is led to conclude that "interpreting this Jewish woman of faith as friend of God and prophet allows her dangerous memory to inspire our own lives."[40] In her judgment, traditional Mariology has done a disservice to Mary and has had a deleterious effect on the Church because it has been the fruit of patriarchy and has functioned to oppress women.[41]

35 Ibid., n. 77.

36 Ibid., n. 83.

37 *Theology Digest* 47 (2000): 317–25. Johnson's article was first delivered as the seventeenth annual Aquinas Lecture at Aquinas Institute of Theology, St. Louis, on 27 January 2000.

38 Ibid., 317.

39 Ibid.

40 Ibid., 324.

41 For example, putting the worst possible interpretation on the

What is most germane to our present discussion is that Johnson eschews commenting on the great revealed truths of Catholic faith concerning the Virgin Mary: her Immaculate Conception (and subsequent preservation from personal sin), her status as *Theotokos* – the God-bearer, her unique cooperation in the work of human salvation, and her Assumption into heaven.[42] And, contrary to Catholic teaching and practice,[43] she wishes to downplay Mary's singular role in salvation history and view her as simply one member among the throng in the Communion of Saints. For less-than-clear reasons, Johnson's ideological commitments lead her to hold that emphasizing Mary's uniqueness is a bad thing for the cause of justice for contemporary women.[44]

Johnson is strong on what has come to be known as the "hermeneutics of suspicion"; she has, as it were, undertaken

"Marian principle" in Hans Urs von Balthasar's theology, Johnson says: "This Marian principle indicates that women ought to divest themselves of self-will in order to be obedient to the word of God as articulated by male authority figures" (Ibid., 319).

42 Her one mention of the Immaculate Conception serves to insinuate a correlation between Pius IX's definition of the dogma with "his aggrandizement of papal power" (Ibid., 317).

43 A host of sources could be marshaled here. The following suffice to make the point: "Through the gift and role of divine maternity, Mary is united with her Son, the Redeemer, and with His singular graces and offices. By these, the Blessed Virgin is also intimately united with the Church" (*LG*, n. 63); "The Son whom she brought forth is He whom God placed as the first-born among many brethren (cf. Rom. 8: 29), namely the faithful. In *their* birth and development she cooperates with a maternal love" (*LG*, n. 63, emphasis added); "Her role in relation to the Church and to all humanity goes still further. 'In a wholly singular way she cooperated by her obedience, faith, hope, and burning charity in the Savior's work of restoring supernatural life to souls. For this reason she is a mother to us in the order of grace'" (*CCC*, n. 968, citing *LG*, n. 61).

44 Her argument for assigning Mary an indistinct place in the Communion of Saints is grounded on the following *non sequitur*: "Since Mary was a first-century Jewish woman of faith, and since she has obviously also died, she belongs in this company of grace" (Ibid., 320).

"a critical reading of the Marian tradition."[45] In this, she "suspects" that the Church's teaching on Mary is none other than an expression of patriarchy's desire to subjugate women. It is not possible to entertain here all the philosophical underpinnings (conscious or unconscious) of Johnson's approach. Suffice it to say that it cannot be fully accounted for without mention of the hermeneutics of Ludwig Feuerbach, Friedrich Nietzsche, and Karl Marx.[46]

What is most remarkable about "Mary, Friend of God and Prophet" is that it sidesteps the question of the existence of a nonnegotiable set of divinely revealed truths pertaining to the Blessed Virgin Mary, truths which theology – using the tools afforded by philosophical reflection – is called upon to explain for each generation of believers. Johnson's *praxis* insinuates that it is methodologically appropriate to relegate the defined Marian dogmas and doctrines to the periphery of one's theological vision and to

45 Ibid., 324.

46 Jean-Pierre Torrell, *La théologie catholique* (Paris: Presses Universitaires de France, 1994), discusses the philosophical foundations of feminist theology on pages 108–14. He shows, for instance, that the theological project of Mary Daly in *The Church and the Second Sex* (1968) was philosophically inspired by Nietzsche and Whitehead and that Rosemary Radford Ruether *s'est plutôt inspirée de L. Feuerbach, de K. Marx et de la théologie de la libération* . . . (109). Frederick Copleston's *A History of Philosophy*, volume 7: "Modern Philosophy," part II: "Schopenhauer to Nietzsche" (Garden City, N.Y.: Doubleday, 1963) is a most helpful introduction to these thinkers. Fr. Copleston notes that Feuerbach "was principally concerned with clarifying the real significance of religion in the light of human life and thought as a whole. . . . He can be said, therefore, to have substituted anthropology for theology" (60–61). Marx's well-known critique of Christianity and his identification of "vested interests" fuel a great deal of "critical" theologies. Nietzsche, says Copleston, has been particularly important on the question of meaning. His was a campaign against "all beliefs and philosophies . . . which ascribe to the world and to human existence and history a meaning or purpose or goal other than the meaning freely imposed by man himself" (194). It is the human being "who confers intelligibility on the world and creates values" (194).

set out to create something new, something which need not be shown to be in radical continuity with the Tradition. This, of course, she does because she has judged that the Tradition has been devised by "patriarchy" in order to oppress women. It must be underscored that this judgment functions as an *a priori*: it is not the product of deduction from the *fontes theologiae*.

Garrigou-Lagrange spent his theological career warning against the extremes of agnosticism and pantheism and the philosophical errors he found in the work of Bergson and Blondel. In the end, his works call one to a serious reflection on the distinction between the *fides qua* and the *fides quae*. This is a distinction that lies at the heart of Catholic theology: without it one will be forced to submit the Church's dogmas and doctrines to the extraneous judgment of some other "orthodoxy" (Freudian, Marxist, secular feminist, postmodern, etc.) and "to propose [their] reconstitution on that basis."[47] That, says Aidan Nichols, would disqualify one from claiming membership in the "specifically Catholic Christian theological sorority/fraternity."[48] If orthodoxy will be a particular concern for the Church in the twenty-first century, the work of Réginald Garrigou-Lagrange will prove to be a most helpful resource.

Spirituality

We have been arguing that as regards philosophy and theology the Church's authoritative teaching in *Fides et ratio* amounts to a vindication of the major concerns of Garrigou-Lagrange and that, therefore, a renewed study of Garrigou's works would in turn aid the further plumbing of the depths of the Church's teaching. In this last section, we will argue that a study of Garrigou's thought on spirituality would also prove helpful for a fuller appropriation of the

47 Nichols, *Christendom Awake*, 120.
48 Ibid.

Christian tradition. We begin this reflection with a word on the relationship of Garrigou's teaching on holiness with that of the Second Vatican Council.

Chapter 5 of *Lumen gentium* is entitled "The Call of the Whole Church to Holiness." At paragraph 40 we read:

> The followers of Christ are called by God, not according to their accomplishments, but according to His own purpose and grace. They are justified in the Lord Jesus, and through baptism sought in faith they truly become sons of God and sharers in the divine nature. In this way they are really made holy. . . . Thus it is evident to everyone that all the faithful of Christ of whatever rank or status are called to the fullness of the Christian life and to the perfection of charity.[49]

Of course, for centuries this teaching was not so "evident." We have seen how much it was opposed by a figure like Albert Farges and how a two-tiered approach to the question was standard in preconciliar Catholicism. It is clear that Garrigou-Lagrange, with his fifty years of lecturing on spirituality at the Angelicum, played a significant role in the Council's formulation of its teaching on the universal call to holiness. The disputes concerning contemplation which now sound utterly arcane have moved the Church to be able to proclaim: "In the various types and duties of life, one and the same holiness is cultivated by all who are moved by the Spirit of God, and who obey the voice of the Father, worshiping God the Father in spirit and in truth."[50]

In this vein, one finds in the *Catechism of the Catholic Church* the following paragraph that reads as if it could have been written by Garrigou-Lagrange:

> Spiritual progress tends toward ever more intimate union with Christ. This union is called "mystical" because it participates in the mystery of Christ

49 *LG*, n. 40.
50 *LG*, n. 41.

> through the sacraments – "the holy mysteries" – and, in him, in the mystery of the Holy Trinity. God calls us all to this intimate union with him, even if the special graces or extraordinary signs of this mystical life are granted only to some for the sake of manifesting the gratuitous gift given to all.[51]

It is a commonplace to assert that much of what is published in spirituality is grossly deficient or outright defective.[52] One must search through a lot of dross before finding a nugget of gold. In this regard, many voices have judged that Ronald Rohlheiser's *The Holy Longing: The Search for a Christian Spirituality*[53] has succeeded in accounting for the fullness of the Christian tradition.[54]

Rohlheiser, intent on reflecting on an incarnational spirituality, claims that there are four pillars common to any healthy Christian spirituality. These pillars are "universally prescribed spiritual challenges and are revealed by Christ as being the nonnegotiable elements within Christian discipleship."[55] He explains:

51 *CCC*, n. 2014. It is evident that Garrigou's choice of the three-fold purgative, illuminative, and unitive ways signifies a progressively more intimate union with God. See *The Three Ages*, II, 575 ff. for Garrigou's discussion of the graces *gratis datae*.

52 This is not exactly a new phenomenon; Garrigou himself had this to say in his *The Three Ages*: ". . . many books on religious subjects that are written in a popular style, and many pious books lack a solid doctrinal foundation. Popularization, because the kind of simplification imposed upon it is material rather than formal, often avoids the examination of certain fundamental and difficult problems from which, nevertheless, light would come, and at times the light of life" (I, 9).

53 (New York: Doubleday, 1999).

54 Alan Jones, Sister Helen Préjean, C.S.J., Michael Downey, Basil Pennington, O.C.S.O., and Archbishop Rembert Weakland, O.S.B. offered words of praise for its publication. Archbishop Weakland had this to say: "Without doubt, Ronald Rohlheiser's *The Holy Longing* is one of the best books about Christian spirituality that has been published in many a year. Its insights are just what all of us need at this moment of history. It blends the old and new in ways that few other authors can do" (from the dust jacket).

55 Rohlheiser, *The Holy Longing*, 53.

> we see that Jesus was prescribing four things as an essential praxis for a healthy spiritual life: a) private prayer and private morality; b) social justice; c) mellowness of heart and spirit; and d) community as a constitutive element of true worship.[56]

Rohlheiser does an admirable job explaining his distillation of Jesus's message to these four points; his examples of the spiritual problems that exist in the lives of people who do not hold all four of these in a healthy tension is highly instructive. It will come as no surprise, however, that our contention is that this good book on Christian spirituality would have been made much better had some of the major themes found in the work of Garrigou-Lagrange been reflected upon.

Three such themes immediately come to mind: the ultimate priority of God's grace in the Christian life; the necessity of the gifts of the Holy Spirit; and the foundational doctrine of the indwelling of the Holy Trinity in the souls of the just. Rohlheiser fails to offer an explicit theology of grace; he does not speak of the significance of the gifts of the Holy Spirit for Christian discipleship; nor does he mention the indwelling of the Holy Trinity. As a result of these *lacunae*, his last chapter, "Sustaining Ourselves in the Spiritual Life," seems, to one formed in the Dominican tradition, to veer perilously close to Pelagianism.[57]

56 Ibid.

57 Rohlheiser frames the discussion along the following lines (lines which focus on *us* rather than *divine gratuity*): "How do we develop the heart to sustain ourselves on the long road? How do we move beyond our fatigue, loneliness, laziness, bitterness, and bad habits so as to become gracious, happy, self-sacrificing, generative, adult Christians? . . . What practices and exercises (analogous to keeping our bodies physically healthy) are helpful for us as we struggle as Christians to live healthy spiritual lives?" (214–15) Writing on a related topic, Servais Pinckaers says: "The Christian cannot follow the way of the Beatitudes and virtues without the help of the Holy Spirit, and we cannot obtain this help without continual prayer, the model for which is the Lord's prayer" (*Sources of Christian Ethics*, 155).

Conclusion

Garrigou-Lagrange was the leading Neo-Thomist of his generation. His life – formed and nurtured in the Order of Preachers – was a life offered for the advancement of the Church's intellectual mission. His many works – books, articles, conferences, and homilies – remain signs of his fervent commitment to Christ and his Church. As this Church begins its journey through the third millennium of Christian faith, it would be well served by taking another look at Garrigou-Lagrange. His works in philosophy, theology, and spirituality, while written in the early years of the twentieth century, are far from being outdated; they possess the effervescence associated with the recognized classics in all fields of inquiry. Jacques Maritain's affirmation of the place of Thomism, for instance, speaks eloquently of Garrigou's vision:

> [Thomism] remains the royal way for attaining not a new ideology nor a new hermeneutic for the present time but a 'wisdom' which extends in our day the biblical and Christian wisdom, to bring together harmoniously contemplation, reason and love, and to reconcile in a sound way transcendence and immanence."[58]

Jean-Hervé Nicolas, O.P., long-time professor of theology at the University of Fribourg, captured both the strength and weakness of Garrigou-Lagrange in a memorial article in the *Freiburger Zeitschrift für Philosophie und Theologie*.[59] Nicolas says that Garrigou was at times overly severe in his criticism of new developments in theology

58 Jacques Maritain, *Sagesse* (1951), cited in Fouilloux, *Une Eglise en quête*, 118. [*Elle demeure donc la voie royale pour atteindre non pas une nouvelle idéologie ni une nouvelle herméneutique pour le temps présent, mais une 'sagesse' qui prolonge aujourd'hui la sagesse biblique et chrétienne, la seule à conjuguer harmonieusement contemplation, raison et amour, à réconcilier de façon juste transcendance et immanence.*]

59 Jean-Hervé Nicolas, "*In Memoriam*: Le Père Garrigou-Lagrange," *FZPT* 11 (1964): 390–95.

– failing to recognize that almost by definition "valid developments" come through initial research that is one-sided or exaggerated. Yet, at the same time, a strong criticism of a theologian's work does often function "to help him assure his footing and even at times to see more clearly the well-founded nature of the renewal for which he is calling."[60] In other words, Garrigou's critiques had an objectively good end, even if one judges that they were at times *outré*.

By temperament, Garrigou was not disposed to take kindly to what he held to be philosophical or theological error. "He loved truth too passionately; error appeared to him as the most serious of evils."[61] There was, however, an important distinction in Garrigou's praxis. When it came to doctrinal errors in a book or an article, Garrigou could become vehement in his denunciations; when it came to being face-to-face with a person who held erroneous positions, a different Garrigou came to the surface. In that setting, "the profound goodness of his heart" informed his intelligence and kept him from any such vehemence.[62]

Nicolas highlights that at the Second Vatican Council open dialogue between the magisterium and the Church's theologians was the clarion call. *Gaudium et spes* and its openness to the world and its questions, moreover, contrasts rather sharply with the stances of St. Pius X, Pius XI, and Pius XII. The context and the ethos of Catholic theology had shifted significantly; within a few short years, Garrigou's approach appeared out of sync with that espoused by the Council.

However, this was almost exclusively a matter of style – not content. Does anyone need to be convinced that the

60 Ibid., 395. [. . . *soit à mieux assurer son pas, soit même à voir plus clairement le bien-fondé du renouvellement qu'il propose*.]

61 Ibid., 394. [*Mais il aimait trop passionnément la vérité pour que l'erreur ne lui paraisse pas le plus grave des maux* . . .]

62 Ibid. [Cf.: *En réalité, quand il était en présence des personnes, la profonde bonté de son cœur lui donnait cette compréhension à laquelle ne le disposait pas le mouvement propre de son intelligence*.]

Second Vatican Council upheld the distinction between the *fides qua* and the *fides quae* and that the Apostolic rule of faith remains *the* standard for theological reflection? Whether one appeals to the "letter" or the "spirit" of Vatican II, it is clear that these concerns are perennial for the Church. And because of this, Réginald Garrigou-Lagrange commends himself to us. In him, we see

> the greatness of an admirable life completely consecrated to research and the teaching of the truth which saves, and the importance of an *opus*, the defects of which do not conceal its value: a lasting value that history will certainly hallow.[63]

63 Ibid., 395. [. . . *la grandeur d'une admirable vie tout consacrée à la recherche et à l'enseignement de la vérité qui sauve, et l'importance d'une oeuvre dont les défauts ne doivent pas dissimuler la valeur. Valeur durable que l'histoire certainement consacrera*.]

10. Select Bibliography

Major Works of Réginald Garrigou-Lagrange, O.P.

Le sens commun: La philosophie de l'être et les formules dogmatiques. Paris: Beauchesne, 1909.

Dieu: Son existence et sa nature. Solution thomiste des antinomies agnostiques. Paris: Beauchesne, 1914. [English translation: *God, His Existence and His Nature: A Thomistic Solution of Certain Agnostic Antinomies*. 2 vols. Trans. Bede Rose. St. Louis: B. Herder, 1934 and 1936.]

De Revelatione per Ecclesiam catholicam proposita. Rome: Ferrari-Gabalda, 1918.

Perfection chrétienne et contemplation selon S. Thomas d'Aquin et S. Jean de la Croix. Var: Saint-Maximin, 1923.

L'Amour de Dieu et la Croix de Jésus. Juvisy: Cerf, 1929. [English translation: *The Love of God and the Cross of Jesus*. 2 vols. Trans. Sister Marie, M.M. St. Louis: B. Herder, 1948 and 1951.]

La Providence et la confiance en Dieu. Fidelité et abandon. Paris: Desclée de Brouwer, 1932. [English translation: *Providence*. Trans. Bede Rose. St. Louis: B. Herder, 1937.]

Le réalisme du principe de finalité. Paris: Desclée de Brouwer, 1932.

Les trois conversions et les trois voies. Juvisy: Cerf, 1933.

Le Sauveur et son amour pour nous. Juvisy: Cerf, 1933. [New edition—Paris: Editions du Cèdre, 1952; English translation: *Our Savior and His Love for Us*. Trans. A. Bouchard. St. Louis: B. Herder, 1951.]

Le sens du mystère et le clair-obscur intellectuel. Nature et surnaturel. Paris: Desclée de Brouwer, 1934.

La prédestination des saints et la grâce. Doctrine de S. Thomas comparée aux autres systèmes théologiques. Paris: Desclée de Brouwer, 1936.[English translation: *Predestination*. Trans. Bede Rose. St. Louis: B. Herder, 1939.]

De Deo Uno. Commentarium in primam partem S. Thomae. Paris: Desclée de Brouwer, 1938. [English translation: *The One God: A Commentary on the First Part of St. Thomas' Theological Summa*. Trans. Bede Rose. St. Louis: Herder, 1943.]

Les trois âges de la vie intérieure prélude de celle du ciel. Traité de théologie ascétique et mystique. Paris: Cerf, 1938. [English translation: *The Ages of the Interior Life*. 2 vols. Trans. M. Timothea Doyle. St. Louis: Herder, 1947 and 1948.]

La Mère du Sauveur et notre vie intérieure. Paris: Cerf, 1948. [English translation: *The Mother of the Savior and Our Interior Life*. Trans. Bernard J. Kelly. Dublin: Golden Eagle Books, 1948.]

De Deo Trino et Creatore. Commentarium in Summam Theologicam S. Thomae. Paris: Desclée de Brouwer, 1943. [English translation: *The Trinity and God the Creator. Commentary on St. Thomas' Theological Summa*. Trans. Frederic C. Eckhoff. St. Louis: Herder, 1952.]

De Christo Salvatore. Commentarius in IIIam partem

Summae Theologicae S. Thomae. Paris: Desclée de Brouwer, 1945. [English translation: *Christ the Savior: A Commentary on the Third Part of the Theological Summa of St. Thomas*. Trans. Bede Rose. St. Louis: Herder, 1950.]

De Gratia. Commentarius in Summam Theologiae S. Thomae. Torino: Berrutti, 1946. [English translation: *Grace: A Commentary on the Summa Theologica of St. Thomas*. Trans. by the Dominican Nuns, Menlo Park, Calif. St. Louis: Herder, 1952.]

La synthèse thomiste. Paris: Desclée de Brouwer, 1946. [English translation: *Reality: A Synthesis of Thomistic Thought*. Trans. Patrick Cummins. St. Louis: Herder, 1950.]

L'éternelle vie et la profondeur de l'âme. Paris: Desclée de Brouwer, 1950. [English translation: *Life Everlasting*. Trans. Patrick Cummins. St. Louis: Herder, 1952.]

De unione sacerdotis cum Christo Sacerdote et victima. Cursus theologiae spiritualis pro sacerdotibus. Rome: Marietti, 1948. [English translation: *The Priest in Union with Christ*. Trans. G. W. Shelton. Westminster, Md.: Newman Press, 1952.]

De virtutibus theologicis. Commentarius in Summam theologicam S. Thomae. Torino: Berrutti, 1949.

De Beatitudine, de actibus humanis et habitibus. Commentarius in Summam theolgicam S. Thomae. Torino: Berrutti, 1951. [English translation: *Beatitude*. Trans. Patrick Cummins. St. Louis: Herder, 1956.]

La seconde conversion et les trois voies. Paris: Cerf, 1951.

The Last Writings of Réginald Garrigou-Lagrange. Trans. Raymond Smith and Rod Gorton. New York: New City Press, 1969.

References Cited

Alberigo, Guiseppe. "Christianisme en tant qu'histoire et

'théologie confessante.'" In *Une école de théologie: Le Saulchoir*. Paris: Cerf, 1985.

Arintero, Juan Gonzalez. *The Mystical Evolution in the Development and Vitality of the Church*. Trans. and ed. Jordan Aumann. St. Louis: B. Herder, 1950.

Ashley, Benedict M. *The Dominicans*. Collegeville, Minn.: Liturgical Press, 1990.

———. *Spiritual Direction in the Dominican Tradition*. New York: Paulist, 1995.

Bedouelle, Guy. *Saint Dominic: The Grace of the Word*. Trans. Mary Thomas Noble. San Francisco: Ignatius, 1987.

Bergson, Henri. *Oeuvres*. Paris: Presses Universitaires de France, 1970.

———. *Matter and Memory*. Trans. Nancy Margaret Paul and W. Scott Palmer. New York: Macmillan, 1911.

———. *The Two Sources of Morality and Religion*. Trans. R. Ashley Audra and Cloudesley Brereton. New York: Macmillan, 1935.

———. *Creative Evolution*. Trans. Arthur Mitchell. New York: Modern Library, 1944.

Bettenson, Henry, ed. *Documents of the Christian Church*. New York: Oxford University Press, 1963.

Blondel, Maurice. *L'Action: essai d'une critique de la vie d'une science de la pratique* [1893]. Paris: Presses Universitaires de France, 1950. [English translation: *Action: Essay on a Critique of Life and a Science of Practice*. Trans. Oliva Blanchette. Notre Dame, Ind.: University of Notre Dame Press, 1984.]

———. Letter to the Editor. *Angelicum* 24 (1947): 211–12.

Bochenski, I. M. *Contemporary European Philosophy*. Trans. Donald Nicholl and Karl Aschenbrenner.

Berkeley and Los Angeles: University of California Press, 1957.

Bonino, Serge-Thomas. "Le thomisme du P. Labourdette." *RT* 92 (1992): 88–122.

Book of Constitutions and Ordinations of the Order of Friars Preachers. Rome: General Curia of the Order of Friars Preachers, 1984.

Bouillard, Henri. *Conversion et grâce chez saint Thomas d'Aquin*. Paris: Aubier (Editions Montaigne), 1944.

———. *Blondel et le christianisme*. Paris: Editions du Seuil, 1961. [English translation: *Blondel and Christianity*. Trans. James M. Somerville. Washington, D.C.: Corpus Books, 1969.]

Bredin, Hugh. "Garrigou-Lagrange, Réginald." In *Biographical Dictionary of Twentieth Century Philosophers*. Ed. Stuart Brown, Diané Collinson, Robert Wilkinson. New York: Routledge, 1996.

Buttiglione, Rocco. *Karol Wojtyla: The Thought of the Man Who Became Pope John Paul II*. Trans. Paolo Guietti. Grand Rapids, Mich.: William Eerdmans, 1997.

Chadwick, Owen. *The Secularization of the European Mind in the 19th Century*. New York: Cambridge University Press, 1990.

Charlier, Louis. *Essai sur le problème théologique*. Thuillies: Ramgal, 1938.

Chenaux, Philippe. *Entre Maurras et Maritain: Une génération intellectuelle catholique (1920–1930)*. Paris: Cerf, 1999.

Chenu, M.-Dominique. *Introduction à l'étude de saint Thomas d'Aquin*. Paris: J. Vrin, 1950. [English translation: *Toward Understanding St. Thomas*. Trans. A.-M. Landry and D. Hughes. Chicago: Henry Regnery, 1964.]

———. *La théologie comme science au XIIIe siècle*. Third revised edition. Paris: J. Vrin, 1957.

———. *La théologie au XIIe* siècle. Paris: J. Vrin, 1957.

———. *Une école de théologie: Le Saulchoir*. With studies by Guiseppe Alberigo, Etienne Fouilloux, Jean Ladrière, and Jean-Pierre Jossua. Paris: Cerf, 1985.

———. "Regard sur cinquante ans de vie religieuse." In *L'hommage différé au Père Chenu*. Ed. Claude Geffré. Paris: Cerf, 1990. 257–68.

Congar, Yves. "Profile of Father Lacordaire," in *Faith and Spiritual Life*. New York: Herder and Herder, 1968.

———. *Journal d'un théologien, 1946–1956*. Ed. Etienne Fouilloux. Paris: Cerf, 2000.

Connolly, James M. *The Voices of France: A Survey of Contemporary Theology in France*. New York: Macmillan, 1961.

Copleston, Frederick. *A History of Philosophy*. Volume 7: "Modern Philosophy," Part II: "Schopenhauer to Nietzsche." Garden City, N.Y.: Doubleday, 1963.

———. *A History of Philosophy*. Volume 9: "Maine de Biran to Sartre," Part II: "Bergson to Sartre." Garden City, N.Y.: Doubleday, 1974.

Cunningham, Francis L. B. *The Indwelling of the Trinity: A Historico-Doctrinal Study of the Theory of St. Thomas Aquinas*. Dubuque, Ia.: Priory Press, 1955.

Daniélou, Jean. "Les présentes orientations de la pensée religieuse." *Etudes* no. 249 (April-May-June 1946): 5–21.

———. *Et qui est mon prochain?: mémoires*. Paris: Stock, 1974.

Dansette, Adrien. *Religious History of Modern France*. 2 Vols. Trans. John Dingle. New York: Herder and Herder, 1961.

Davies, Brian. *The Thought of Thomas Aquinas*. New York: Oxford University Press, 1992.

de Lubac, Henri. *L'Eglise dans la crise actuelle*. Paris: Cerf, 1969.

————. *At the Service of the Church*. Trans. Anne Elizabeth Englund. San Francisco: Ignatius, 1993.

Devaux, André. "Bergson, Henri." In *Dictionnaire des philosophes*. Paris: Presses Universitaires de France, 1984.

Doering, Bernard E. *Jacques Maritain and the French Catholic Intellectuals* Notre Dame, Ind.: University of Notre Dame Press, 1983.

Dorcy, Mary Jean. *St. Dominic's Family: Lives and Legends*. Dubuque, Ia.:Priory Press, 1964.

Emonet, Pierre-M. "Un maître prestigieux." *Angelicum* 42 (1965): 195–99.

Evans, Joseph W. *Jacques Maritain: The Man and His Achievement*. New York: Sheed & Ward, 1963.

Farges, Albert. *Les phénomènes mystiques distingués de leur contrefaçons humaines et diaboliques*. Paris: Librairie Saint-Paul, 1923. [English translation: *Mystical Phenomena Compared with their Human and Diabolical Counterfeits*. Trans. S. P. Jacques. London: Burns, Oates & Washbourne, 1926.]

————. *Les voies ordinaires de la vie spirituelle, traité de théologie ascétique*. Paris: Librairie Saint-Paul, 1924. [English translation: *The Ordinary Ways of the Spiritual Life*. Trans. not given. New York: Benzinger, 1927.]

Fouilloux, Etienne. *Une Eglise en quête de liberté: la pensée catholique française entre modernisme et Vatican II (1914–1962)*. Paris: Desclée de Brouwer, 1998.

————. "Le Saulchoir en procès (1937–1942)." In *Une école de théologie: Le Saulchoir*. Paris: Cerf, 1985. 37–60.

Froget, Barthélemy. *De l'inhabitation du Saint-Esprit dans les âmes justes*. Paris: Lethielleux, 1900.

Gagnebet, M.-Rosaire. "L'oeuvre du P. Garrigou-Lagrange: itineraire intellectuel et spirituel vers Dieu." *Angelicum* 42 (1965): 7–31.

Gardeil, Ambroise. *Le donné révélé et la théologie*. Paris: Victor Lecoffre, 1910.

————. "Dons du Saint-Esprit." In *DT*.

————. *La structure de l'âme et l'expérience mystique*. Paris: Gabalda, 1927.

Gardeil, Henri-Dominique. *L'oeuvre théologique du Père Ambroise Gardeil*. Etiolles: Le Saulchoir, 1954.

Garrigou-Lagrange, Réginald. "La vie scientifique. Note sur la preuve de Dieu par les degrès des êtres chez saint Thomas." *RT* 12 (1904): 363–81.

————. "Bulletin d'histoire de la philosophie." *RSPT* 1 (1907): 732–40.

————. "Le Dieu fini du pragmatisme." *RSPT* 1 (1907): 252–65.

————. "Intellectualisme et liberté chez saint Thomas." *RSPT* 1 (1907): 649–73, and *RSPT* 2 (1908): 5–32.

————. "Dieu," in *Dictionnaire apologétique de la foi catholique* (1911).

————. "La théologie ascétique et mystique ou la doctrine spirituelle." *VS* 1 (1919): 7–19.

————. "L'ascétique et la mystique. Leur distinction et l'unité de la doctrine spirituelle." *VS* 1 (1919): 145–65.

————. "La mystique et les doctrines fondamentales de saint Thomas." *VS* 1 (1919): 216–28.

————. Review of Juan Arintero *Cuestiones misticas o sea las alturas de la contemplacion accesibles a todos*. *VS* 3 (1920): 158–60.

————. "Le caractère et les principes de la spiritualité dominicaine." *VS* 4 (1921): 365–84.

————. "Thomisme." In *DT*.

————. "La théologie nouvelle: où va-t-elle?" In *La synthèse thomiste*. Paris: Desclée de Brouwer, 1946. 699–725.

————. Letter to Maurice Blondel. *Angelicum* 24 (1947): 212–13.

Geffré, Claude, ed. *L'hommage différé au Père Chenu*. Paris: Cerf, 1990.

Gillon, Louis-Bertrand. *Christ and Moral Theology*. Trans. Cornelius Williams. Staten Island, N.Y.: Alba House, 1967.

Gorce, M.-M. "Arintero (Juan Gonzalez)." In *DS*.

Goyau, Georges. "Auch." In *CE*.

Granfield, Patrick. *Theologians at Work*. New York: Macmillan, 1967.

Guillet, Jacques. *La théologie catholique en France de 1914 à 1960*. Paris: Médiasèvres, 1988.

Haight, Roger. *The Dynamics of Theology*. New York: Paulist, 1990.

Heany, J. J. "Modernism." In *NCE*.

Hellwig, Monika. "Theology as a Fine Art." In *Interpreting the Tradition: The Art of Theological Reflection*. Ed. Jane Kopas. New York: Scholars Press, 1983. 3–10.

————. *The Role of the Theologian*. Kansas City, Mo.: Sheed & Ward, 1987.

Hinnebusch, William A. *The History of the Order of Preachers*. 2 vols. Staten Island, N.Y.: Alba House, 1966 and 1973.

————. *The Dominicans: A Short History*. Staten Island, N.Y.: Alba House, 1975.

Hoehn, Matthew. *Catholic Authors: Contemporary Biographical Sketches, 1930–1947*. Newark, N.J.: St. Mary's Abbey, 1948.

Hugon, Edouard. *Les vingt-quatre thèses thomistes*. Paris: Téqui, 1926.

Jarrett, Bede. *Life of St. Dominic*. Washington, D.C.: Dominicana Publications, n.d.

————. *The Abiding Presence of the Holy Ghost in the Soul*. Westminster, Md.: Newman Press, 1944.

Jedin, Hubert and John Dolan, eds. *History of the Church*. Vol. 8, *The Church in the Age of Liberalism*, by Roger Aubert, et al., trans. Peter Becker. New York: Crossroad, 1981.

John, Helen James. *The Thomist Spectrum*. New York: Fordham University Press, 1966.

John Paul II. Encyclical Letter *Fides et ratio* (1995).

Johnson, Elizabeth. "Mary, Friend of God and Prophet: A Critical Reading of the Marian Tradition." *Theology Digest* 47 (2000): 317–25.

Kerr, Fergus. "Chenu, M.-Dominique." In *NCE* (Supplement, 1989).

Kolakowski, Leszek. *Bergson*. New York: Oxford University Press, 1985; South Bend, Ind.: St. Augustine's Press, 2001.

Komonchak, Joseph. "The Ecclesial and Cultural Roles of Theology." *CTSA Proceedings* 40 (1985): 15–32.

Kwitny, Jonathan. *Man of the Century: The Life and Times of Pope John Paul II*. New York: Henry Holt, 1997.

Labourdette, M.-Michel, M.-J. Nicolas, R.-L. Bruckberger, eds. *Dialogue théologique*. Var: St-Maximin, 1947.

La Brosse, Olivier, ed. *Le Père Chenu: La liberté dans la foi*. Paris: Cerf, 1969.

Lacroix, Jean. "Blondel, Maurice." In *Dictionnaire des philosophes*.

Ladouze, André. *Dominicains français et Action Française (1899–1940): Maurras au couvent*. Paris: Editions Ouvrières, 1989.

Lasserre, Henri. *Notre-Dame de Lourdes*. Montréal: J. B. Rolland & Fils, 1871.

Latourelle, René. *Théologie de la révélation*. Paris: Desclée de Brouwer, 1963.

Lavaud, M.-Benoît. "Garrigou-Lagrange (Réginald)." In *DS*.

———. "Le Père Garrigou-Lagrange: *In memoriam*." *RT* 64 (1964): 181–99.

Leo XIII. Encyclical Letter *Aeterni Patris* (1879).

———. Encyclical Letter *Divinum illud munus* (1897).

Leprieur, François. *Quand Rome condamne: Dominicains et prêtres-ouvriers*. Paris: Cerf, 1989.

Macquarrie, John. "Blondel, Maurice." In *EP*.

———. *Principles of Christian Theology*. New York: Charles Scribner's Sons, 1977.

Maritain, Jacques. *Bergsonian Philosophy and Thomism*. Trans. Mabelle L. Andison. New York: Philosophical Library, 1955.

———. *Notebooks*. Trans. Joseph W. Evans. Albany, N.Y.: Magi Books, 1984.

McBrien, Richard P. *Catholicism*. Minneapolis: Winston, 1981.

McCool, Gerald. *The Neo-Thomists*. Milwaukee: Marquette University Press, 1994.

McInerny, Ralph. "Garrigou-Lagrange, Réginald (1887 [*sic*]–1964)." In *Routledge Encyclopedia of Philosophy* (1998 ed.).

Milbank, John. *Theology and Social Theory: Beyond Secular Reason*. Cambridge, Mass.: Blackwell, 1991.

Mortier, Daniel-Antonin. *Histoire abrégée de l'Ordre de Saint-Dominique en France*. Tours: Alfred Mame & fils, 1920.

Mowat, C. L., ed. *The New Cambridge Modern History*. Volume 12: "The Shifting Balance of World Forces, 1898–1945." New York: Cambridge University Press, 1968.

Nichols, Aidan. *The Shape of Catholic Theology*. Collegeville, Minn.: Liturgical Press, 1991.

————. *Christendom Awake: On Reenergizing the Church in Culture*. Grand Rapids, Mich.: William B. Eerdmans, 1999.

————. "Thomism and the *Nouvelle Théologie*." *The Thomist* 64 (2000): 1–19.

Nicolas, Jean-Hervé. "*In memoriam*: Le Père Garrigou-Lagrange." *FZPT* 11 (1964): 390–95.

Noye, Irénée. "Farges (Albert)." In *DS*.

————. "Saudreau (Auguste)." In *DS*.

O'Collins, Gerald and Edward Farrugia. *A Concise Dictionary of Theology*. New York: Paulist, 1991.

O'Meara, Thomas F. *Thomas Aquinas, Theologian*. Notre Dame, Ind.: University of Notre Dame Press, 1997.

Osgood, Samuel M. *French Royalism since 1870*. The Hague: Martinus Nijhoff, 1970.

Palmer, Alan. *The Penguin Dictionary of Twentieth Century History, 1900–1978*. New York: Penguin Books, 1979.

Pinckaers, Servais. *The Sources of Christian Ethics*. Trans. Mary Thomas Noble. Washington, D.C.: Catholic University of America Press, 1995.

Pius X. Encyclical Letter *Pascendi dominici gregis* (1907).

Pius XI. Encyclical Letter *Studiorum ducem* (1923).

Pius XII. Encyclical Letter *Humani generis* (1950).

Pizzorini, R. M. "Garrigou-Lagrange, Réginald." In *NCE*.

Radcliffe, Timothy. *Sing a New Song: The Christian Vocation*. Springfield, Ill.: Templegate, 1999.

Rahner, Karl and Herbert Vorgrimler. *Dictionary of Theology*. Trans. Richard Strachan, David Smith, Robert Nowell, and Sarah O'Brien Twohig. New York: Crossroad, 1985.

Reardon, Bernard M. G., ed. *Roman Catholic Modernism*. Stanford, Calif.: Stanford University Press, 1970.

Rohlheiser, Ronald. *The Holy Longing: The Search for a Christian Spirituality*. New York: Doubleday, 1999.

Sacred Congregation for Studies, "Decree of Approval of Some Theses Contained in the Doctrine of St. Thomas Aquinas and Proposed to the Teachers of Philosophy" (27 July 1914).

Schwalm, M.-Benoît. "Les illusions de l'idéalisme et leurs dangers pour la foi." *RT* 4 (1896): 413–41.

Simon, Yves. "Jacques Maritain: The Growth of a Christian Philosopher." In *Jacques Maritain: The Man and His Achievement*. Ed. Joseph W. Evans. New York: Sheed & Ward, 1963. 3–24.

Torrell, Jean-Pierre. *La théologie catholique*. Paris: Presses Universitaires de France, 1994.

————. *Saint Thomas Aquinas*, volume 1: "The Person and His Work." Trans. Robert Royal. Washington, D.C.: Catholic University of America Press, 1996.

Tribout de Morembert, H. "Maurice-Marie-Mathieu Garrigou." In *DBF*.

————. "Réginald Garrigou-Lagrange." In *DBF*.

Tugwell, Simon. *The Way of the Preacher*. Springfield, Ill.: Templegate, 1979.

———, ed. *Early Dominicans: Selected Writings*. New York: Paulist, 1982.

Vicaire, M.-Humbert. *Saint Dominic and His Times*. Trans. Kathleen Pond. Green Bay, Wisc.: Alt Publishing Co., n.d. [First published under the title *Histoire de saint Dominique* by Les Editions du Cerf, 1957.]

Vidler, Alec R. *The Church in an Age of Revolution: 1789 to the Present Day*. New York: Penguin Books, 1990.

Walshe, T. J. *The Principles of Catholic Apologetics*. St. Louis: B. Herder, 1926.

Weber, Eugen. *Action Française: Royalism and Reaction in Twentieth-Century France*. Stanford, Calif.: Stanford University Press, 1962.

Weigel, George. *Witness to Hope: The Biography of Pope John Paul II*. New York: HarperCollins, 1999.

Zorcolo, B. "Bibliografia del P. Garrigou-Lagrange." *Angelicum* 42 (1965): 200–250.

Index